CW01263010

ONCE UPON A TRIBE

by

Ian Snowball and Pete McKenna

First Edition published July 2012 by Heavy Soul Records
www.heavysoul45s.co.uk

Text copyright 2012 Ian Snowball and Pete McKenna.
ISBN 978-0-9570559-2-6
All rights reserved.
Contents layout, front and rear sleeve design by Adam Cooper.

All song titles quoted in this book are for the purposes review, study or criticism.
No part of this book may be reproduced or transmitted in any form or by any means, electronic or mechanical, including photocopying or any information storage and retrieval system, without permission in writing from the publisher.
This book is sold subject to the condition it shall not, by way of trade or otherwise, be lent, resold, hired out or otherwise circulated without the publishers prior consent in any form of binding or cover other than that in which it is published and without a similar condition being imposed on the subsequent purchase.
All characters testaments within the book are factual and their accounts are created by themselves and not of the author and are used with total permission.

Contents
Page 6 Contributors
Pages 8 – 15 Introductions by the authors
Pages 18 – 23 Once Upon A Tribe
Pages 26 – 196 Once Upon A Tribe (Their Memories In Their Words)
Pages 197 – 198 Outro: If The Kids Are United

ONCE UPON A TRIBE CONTRIBUTORS

DEDICATIONS (Snowy) - TO ALL THE TRIBAL WARRIORS.

ACKNOWLEDGEMENTS (Snowy); Stu Deabill, Pete McKenna, Adam Cooper, all the memoirs and photo contributors, to my mum and dad for never getting in the way and to the people and friends from the early days that helped shape me, those of the Howard De Walden, Trinity, Sunset Club, Ditton Disco's, Ringlestone Hut, Sittingbourne Road and Penenden Heath car parks, South Ockenden Service Station, days out at Chelsea, Brighton and Clecky, Yorks, Gabriels, The Bull, The Rose and Banks.

ACKNOWLEDGEMENTS (Pete) - a massive thanks to John King, Paolo Hewitt, Mark 'Sarge' Sargent, and Stewart Home - to Karmen Del, to Ged and the family - to my partner in crime Ian Snowball - to Walshy, Scotch Billy and Millwall Terry and to everyone who was there then and now who took the time and effort in contributing to this book about the wonderful inventive phenomena that is British street culture and the way it's consistently managed to turn high fashion upside down and adopt it to its own needs. It just wouldn't be the same without you.

PHOTO ACKNOWLEDGMENTS
Lorraine Dent, Mick Habshaw Robinson, Paul Crittenden, Michael Denton, Aaron Perks, Nick Robins and Bar Italia scooter club, Bill and Jackie Newberry.

Rear cover design Adam and Paul 'Chang' Martin of Jigsaw Print

CONTRIBUTORS
Carlos Sesto, Neil Sheasby, John Hellier, Lee Barden, Bob Manton, Steve Sparkes, Chris Harris, Richard Llewellyn, Nigel Harris, Edu, Paolo Hewitt, Garry Bushell, Jane Harrison, Jennie Baillie, Spencer Vinten, Matty Morris, Iain McCartney, Perry Neech, Mark 'Sarge' Sargent, Rob Parker, Will Vincent Hunt, Mark Smith, Val Weedon, Eddie Piller, Simon Stevenson, Nicky Porter, Stu Deabill, Dan Derlin, Geoff Blythe, Paul Crittenden, Russ Baxter, Jason Yeandle, Jay Toby Hall, Paul Hallam, Tom Edwards, Michelle Collins, Richard Lambert, Adam Cooper, Irish Jack.

INTRODUCTIONS BY THE AUTHORS

Living in the United Kingdom eh! What other nation can boast such a rich and impressive youth culture?
We have a youth culture linked together by music, passion and fashion. Nowhere else can boast the same! This book is a celebration and dedication to some of the most diverse, passionate and individual street culture tribes to have sprung up in the UK since the 60's. A frank colourful recollection that should never be forgotten about and written by those who were there and many who still are from a variety of people who know what it's like to be a part of a scene and who continue to live their lives by it. Visually the difference could not be more opposite but deep down where it matters they all share a common generic DNA; Obsessive attention to detail when it comes down to clothes and style, a passion for their particular music and an attitude that sticks an irreverent two fingers up to world in general and a special closed camaraderie for everyone in their scene.
This book only exists because of two major cultural shifts in British social history that helped to change the attitudes and landscape of this once green and pleasant land forever, for better or worse. I'm talking about the abolition of conscription and the turn on – tune in – drop out – sex drugs rock and roll revolution that was the 60's. Ever since Boadicea fought the Roman invaders, the UK has been a warrior island race and up until fairly recent times has fought a war every thirty years or so in the name of King, Queen and country.
Battlefields the world over are strewn with the corpses of young English youth who were offered no choice but to sign up, rally to the flag and march off to foreign lands to do their bit. The abolition of conscription changed all that overnight. It offered the new generation an option previously denied to generations past. Those wanting to join up and fight could willingly pack up their troubles in their old kit bag, kiss goodbye to family, friends and loved ones and march off to glory. Those who didn't could remain at home being labelled unpatriotic cowards afraid to show their faces down the local just in case one of their school chums was reported to have paid the ultimate price.
The Second World War had cost Britain dearly, almost bringing her down to the knees of bankruptcy. Years of hardship and poverty were the way of life long after the last bullet had been fired in anger, continuing into the 50's as the country finally managed to claw itself back to its feet in order to offer the new generation a glimmer of hope, of better financially secure times ahead.

The arrival of the 60's heralded an unprecedented wave of social change, much to the disgust of the old school, dyed in the wool establishment who'd controlled the country and the lives of the people in it for centuries. Unlike America, who continued to recruit and send its young men off to fight and die in the swamp, snake infested jungles of Vietnam, British kids were having a ball of a time enjoying a sense of freedom attitude and individuality their predecessors were denied.
 They had education, secure jobs, apprenticeship, cash in their pockets, dreams and ambitions and mobility as they stuck a firm two fingers up to the old order while searching for their own identities and values and a fair number of kicks to match. Admittedly the 50's spawned the Teddy Boys, Rockers and Beatniks, each of them with their own distinctive music and look, much of it heavily influenced (if not in total) by the good old USA. Live and let live, each to their own and all that but for me, the emergence of the Mod scene epitomised the definition of cool youthful attitude and style that set the benchmark for future tribes to follow.
 Thank God the Mods looked to European Italian and French influences instead of following the time honoured prescription of the stars and stripes to show them the way forward. Sharp expensive tailor made suits in the finest materials with footwear and haircuts to match. Instead of souped up gas guzzlers and ape hanger choppers, they opted for Italian scooters; Vespa's and Lambretta's, adopting a way of thinking that its not how fast you get there, its how you arrive and that was everything. Nights spent down sweaty clubs dropping speed and dancing to the home grown and imported R and B and Soul music that set another fresh new benchmark for a different generation to follow. Brighton, May bank holiday 1964 and the mass battles on the beaches between the Mods, Rockers and police. By then the original Mod scene had died a death, many of them moving on to the new acid dope free sex and love scene sweeping all corners of the UK but we must never ever forget the attitudes and style of those pre '64 Mods who continue to live on today and hopefully forever more.
 Linked in so many ways to the early Mod scene, the next big street cred tribe to hit the streets were the Skinheads. 'Hard Mods' some of the early skins preferred to be called who stuck true to the old Mod ethics doing it in a different way. Bethnal Green 1966 was the place where the first mob of skins were seen on the streets. Grandad shirts, Ben Sherman's, Fred Perry's, braces, hobnail boots and Levis. How fiercesome to the general public must they have looked, swaggering, barging their way through everyone and everything without a care in the world on their way to the dancehall for a piss up on the

Ska and Reggae, long before the skinhead army grew in numbers across the nation, every city, town and village boasting its own skin army, fuelled up on the stylish cult series of Skinhead – Bootboy – Skingirl – Suedehead books featuring the skin Joe Hawkins and his bunch of mates.

The skins were effectively Mods without scooters, sharing so many similarities to their predecessors. A love of black music, booze and speed to help them dance the night away, sharp clothes and attention to detail and seaside weekends battling with the bikers and other rival skinhead gangs. Setting the seeds that grew into the mass hooligan football riots that were a big part of 70's youth culture and also, the more streamlined undercover football hooligan battles of the 80's, courtesy of the good old Nokia mobile phone. The 70's skins received bad press when many of them turned to the National Front who used them as Nazi style SS style bodyguards protecting the NF hierarchy John Tyndall and Martin Brown whenever they organised demonstrations through many West Indian and Asian communities. On a plus note, skins were responsible for saving a little known Northampton footwear manufacture from certain disaster, the firms name Doctor Marten who produced the iconic eight and ten hole black and cherry red stitch up Air Ware sole bovver boot, now worn by rich and famous celebrities the world over who are clueless to what they meant to a certain faction of UK youth at the time who spent countless hours in their bedrooms softening and polishing them to get them looking the business only to go out on another Saturday afternoon terrace war to get them scuffed up again.

There was nothing more scary seeing a bunch of skins marching down the road for a night out and from that classic shaven headed, denim wearing Doc Marten bovver boot image, the skins spawned several new tribes similar in attitude and fashion who did things a little different. The boneheads who went one step further in their quest to be different. The Suedeheads, skinheads with longer hair imbued with the same arrogance and meticulous attention to detail when it came down to fashion. Even the designer hungry casuals and hoolies of the 80's – the decade dubbed the golden age of soccer violence by the media - who proved themselves to be a constant and embarrassing thorn in Maggie Thatcher's side every time England played away owed their existence to the early skins. Same attitude with a different uniform as expensive prized designer names came to the forefront of the new culture. Fila, Lacoste, Sergio Tachinni, Nike, Adidas, Kappa (oh God those scousers at it again), Burberry, Aquascutum, John Smedley, Ralph Lauren and Stone Island. High fashion brands that will forever be linked to the casual and hooligan culture who turned them into something a tad more sinister and made them their own.

What more can be written that hasn't already about the Northern Soul scene, the longest existing underground dance scene this country has spawned, stretching back to the early 60's when sharp suited Mods danced the night away to the new imported soul sounds in West End clubs like The Flamingo and The Scene. Unlike most scenes that started out with a word and a whisper where to go, the Northern Soul scene has shunned the limelight and still remains a scene where you have to know where to look for it. The music gradually drifted to the north of England, finding a welcome home in cities and towns steeped in the faded heritage of the Industrial Revolution. The Golden Torch in Tunstall Stoke – the Catacombs in Birmingham – Samantha/s in Sheffield – the VaVa's in Bolton – the Highland Room in Blackpool and inevitably so, the legendary Casino Soul club in Wigan where it remained the headquarters of the scene from 1973 to December 1981 when a mysterious fire destroyed the heart and soul of the Northern Soul world.

It was largely a working class dance scene populated by guys and girls who took themselves and the music they loved very seriously indeed, creating an image and attitude all of their own. There was a stereotypical image of a northern soulie – long leather coat, baggy trousers, berets, tee shirts – and the girls long flared skirts, low cut tight tops and white socks – but fashion didn't mean a thing on the Northern Soul scene but being there did. Poor guys and girls mixed with those more fortunate, wearing what they could just be a part of the scene and everyone came together under the ghostly glow of the ultra violet strip light to dance the night away soaked in amphetamine soul sweat. Words can only come close to describing what the feeling was like when the Casino was running on all engines, packed to the rafters and everyone on the dance-floor dancing like demons from dusk till dawn. End of!

Pete McKenna

Mods are a British phenomenon, so are Skinheads, Suedeheads, Teddy Boys, the Northern Soulies, Ravers of the second Summer of love (Hippies of the first) and the football casuals, to mention just a few. They are the lost tribes of a mis-spent youth. Did they crop up in France, Germany, America?...there's no evidence to say so is there? So being a young person in Britain throughout the 1950's up until the early or mid- 1990's meant you would be exposed to the tribes. This did not mean you had to be British either or working class, middle class or white. You just needed to be exposed to it and two examples in this book from Edu (Spain) and Carlo (Italy) demonstrate this. So we do not hold an opinion that someone has to be British to be a mod, skin, casual, but we do not believe these things could have been born anywhere else other than in the United Kingdom. But, like we say, this is only an opinion.

And so to quote from Mark Smith's contribution, *'Some of us chose to pick the pocket of the past'*. That's what the bands of the 1978/79 Mod era did. That's what many of us still do today and frequently seek out vintage clobber or records on eBay and the charity shops. For many a young person in the late seventies and early eighties the bands like The Purple Hearts, Secret Affair and of course The Jam were the gateway back towards the sixties bands of The Small Faces, The Creation and The Action. Not very forward looking eh...or Modernist thinking for that matter but it worked because of the attitude, passion and angst of the British youth of those grey days. *'Pick those pockets'* we did eagerly and still do.

We think Bob Manton's contribution sums so much up in his words *'It is impossible to over-state how important music was to us compared with the situation for today's kids'*. Several contributions in this book refer to the importance of Top Of The Pops, The Tube, Ready Steady Go, Old Grey Whistle test, the Top 100 charts on Thursday's and Sunday's. Teenagers lived their lives and made their choices according to what they heard, what they liked, what they could buy. What do the kids have today?

Now don't get us wrong we also take advantage of YouTube and Facebook and MySpace or use the brilliant online sites like Soul Source but our foundations are firmly in place. They should be after years of listening, discovering, and contributing to the 'scenes'. When we see the crap on the music channels today we get angry and frustrated. It's the poor quality of it all. In our opinion the youth of today is missing out on something so special because they do not have Top Of The Pops, The Tube and the like. *'Dance, dance, dance to the radio'* sang Ian Curtis, and for decades the kids did.

We recently caught a few minutes of one of the Glastonbury festivals. It fucking disgusted us. When did Glastonbury STOP being a music festival? Clearly a fucking lot of people who go to the festival do not go and support live music any other time of the year. That is why the British music scene is dying. We suppose the youth of today do not need to go and see bands. We don't think they have the hunger for it. They can get their 'fill' with a press of a button. Mind you, in some ways we cannot blame them. In our opinion, there has not been much quality bursting out of the music biz in recent years. Of course there are exceptions like The Arctic Monkeys or The Libertines to name just two from recent years...but we could probably only add a handful more to the list. But our question is will there ever be any iconic albums again?

'Searching For The Young Soul Rebels' comes to mind. We just cannot see it, *'Where have you hidden them?'*

Going to a gig does not offer the raw power and energy that it used to. What with a million security guards and Health and Safety rules it's hard to fart without someone taking offence. We have never complained when some drunken nutter has spilt beer down our backs or dropped a hot rock onto our shirt. I never complained when one of the members of the band Fishbone jumped into the audience at a gig in Bristol that we drove to with a bunch of mates on a Wednesday evening (we lived in Kent so it was not just around the corner) and broke his nose as he landed on me (Snowy) - I still has the scar and bent nose to prove it. For us these were the type of experiences that raw gigs had to offer and made us hungry for more.

It appears to us that it has all gone a bit too TAME. The live music of any decade or generation reflects its youth groups. When we hear The Jam, Clash or Joy Division...and this list can go on much further we are transported back to the feel of the times and the type of youths that lived in those days. We are not saying it was all perfect and we do not intend for this to appear like we are looking through rose tinted glasses and dribbling nostalgia, we all know the real truth. And like Eddie Piller says in his contribution *'London was a violent place to be'*, as was every other town and city in the U.K really. And, so back to Glastonbury again...move with the times eh! Leave your fag lighter in your pocket and wave your mobile phone around instead. Fuck right off!

And whilst the venting of our spleen continues what else can be blamed for the demise of the tribes. Well the casuals would scream....all seating stadiums. And it is true. Any football fan who went to a game before the Premiership burst onto the scene knows the atmosphere at a game was different. Today really is not as exciting, vibrant, energetic, violent or atmospheric. Many casuals will say they miss the sensation of piss and beer running down the back of their jeans, or slipping on burgers, beer, piss and fag butts. The new football spectator will not know the sensation of being squeezed, pushed and swayed from side to side from one end of the terrace to the other. Nowadays to the larger extent it is sedate and pleasant to sit all comfortable on a plastic seat and sip coffee instead of beer.

And it goes on. Where have the record shops gone? The traditional corner pubs and the menswear shops? These examples were places that young people went to so they could keep up to speed with what was 'in'. They were meeting places to check one another out. We all know the sound and feel of a 33rpm is better, warmer than any CD or any other such format. Putting a record on the deck was like a ritual. It was a process. A journey! What happens now has less charm. Just press the button or push the disc in the hole! No crackles, no anticipation, no effort.

And effort was a large part of being a Mod or Casual or so on. To be a member of a tribe meant you had to devote time, money and energy to getting the 'look' right. But we enjoyed doing it. We had pride. We looked forward to the weekend gig, disco or match to sport our new shirt, coat or trainers. We recently saw a young man wearing a pair of Ugg boots, the ones the girls wear. What the fuck! The chap then spoke with that white boy trying to sound like a black boy talk. Please! No style. No pride. If he was part of the tribes he would have something to belong to, feel proud about, represent.

So what else helped kill off the tribes? Was it something in the water? Not exactly, but it was as if something was in the air. Rave. The second summer of love. 1988 or 1989 (depends who you talk to). Many of us were apart of it and therefore contributed to it. It all happened very fast. There were pockets of the old tribes in corners of discos and cafes and then the raves arrived. Within months it appeared that the the whole nation was scooped up by its energy and momentum and then a year later it had run out of steam, in the same way that people say Punk only really lasted six months. This left a generation waiting for the next thing...we do not believe there has been a 'next thing' yet, and suspect that these times, society and young people have changed so much that there will never be another 'next thing'...a TRIBE.

But on a more positive note to help any lost soul there have been brilliant books like the 'Soul Stylist' and 'Sharper Word' from Paolo Hewitt (one of the contributors in this book), 'The Fashion Of Football' by Paolo and Mark 'Bax' Baxter, 'Hoolifan' by Martin King/Martin Knight and 'A Boys Story' by Martin King, 'Football factory' John King and 'Casuals' by Phil Thornton, 'Nightshift' by Pete McKenna, the list goes on. All brilliant and incredibly informative about the things that they write about. We have enjoyed reading their books and have learnt a lot. This book is intended to just tickle the toes of the tribes and invite the general public to take a peek.

We are all fortunate that these days all the tribes live side by side and generally 'get along' okay. Of course it was not always like that. Like Eddie Piller points out *'London was a violent place for young Mods and we were extremely tribal by necessity.'* We are sure that many people who read this book can relate to what Eddie is saying.

It appears to me that the current tribes that hang around the decaying multi-cultural estates of the nation's cities are bound together by violence and crime of an order and immorality that far exceeds the decades of before. These tribes know nothing or care nothing about music, fashion and style. They are a lazy and apathetic youth culture that are content in their Reebock classics, 'snide' togs and baggy track bottoms that hang around the arse. And they have returned to looking and dressing just like their dad's. Nowadays the whole family can be dressed from top to toe in moody Burberry and Nike. And to think this was one of the major motivators of the Teddy boys. They wanted to get away from looking like their dads and uncles. But there is hope and to quote Perry Neech (who is one of this books youngest contributors), *'We are in it for the love of the music and the dancing'*. This love of the powerful and emotive music and dancing leads the way for those that want it. It did for generations before.

Will there ever be a return to youth cultures stylish tribes? We think doubtful, certainly not on the mass scale that the previous four decades have witnessed. We cannot see how, with all the time that youth has, there is no real passion for music and the clothes they wear that will set them apart from the boring masses. Our society today has become infiltrated by too many cultures that care not for style. It's not their fault, it's just not important to them like it was to the British youth of the 50's, 60's, 70's and 80's. They do of course bring over other 'goodies' to the table, but this book is concerned with youth culture and music and not a spicy fish dinner.

The two favourite things that we enjoy reading about are music and biographies. And when these two incorporate fashions we are in our element. So, thankfully, this 'Once Upon A Tribe' book ticked all those boxes for us and we hope it will for others, who can relate to the content and spirit of the book.

And so as the memoirs and interviews arrived over a nine month period (we announced three deadline dates in total that were all ignored) a common thread and feel revealed itself. It was obvious that everybody was writing about the same thing. It was their personal relationship and love of music, clothes and the part that these had in their own personal mis-spent youths. The book was taking on a presence full of richness because the honest words being written came from deep down in the hearts of the contributors. What happened was that the book turned into the participants of youth culture writing about youth culture from within looking out and not from the outside looking in. We didn't write this book, we only steered in a direction and then compiled the contributions. To quote from Gary Bushells contribution *'A casual observer would be hard pressed to tell the two tribes apart on the clothes front'*. There are so many similarities in the contributions and it's true, would a casual observer correctly label the Mohair suit wearing Mod from the Mohair wearing suit of the Skinhead?

Snowy (Ian Snowball)

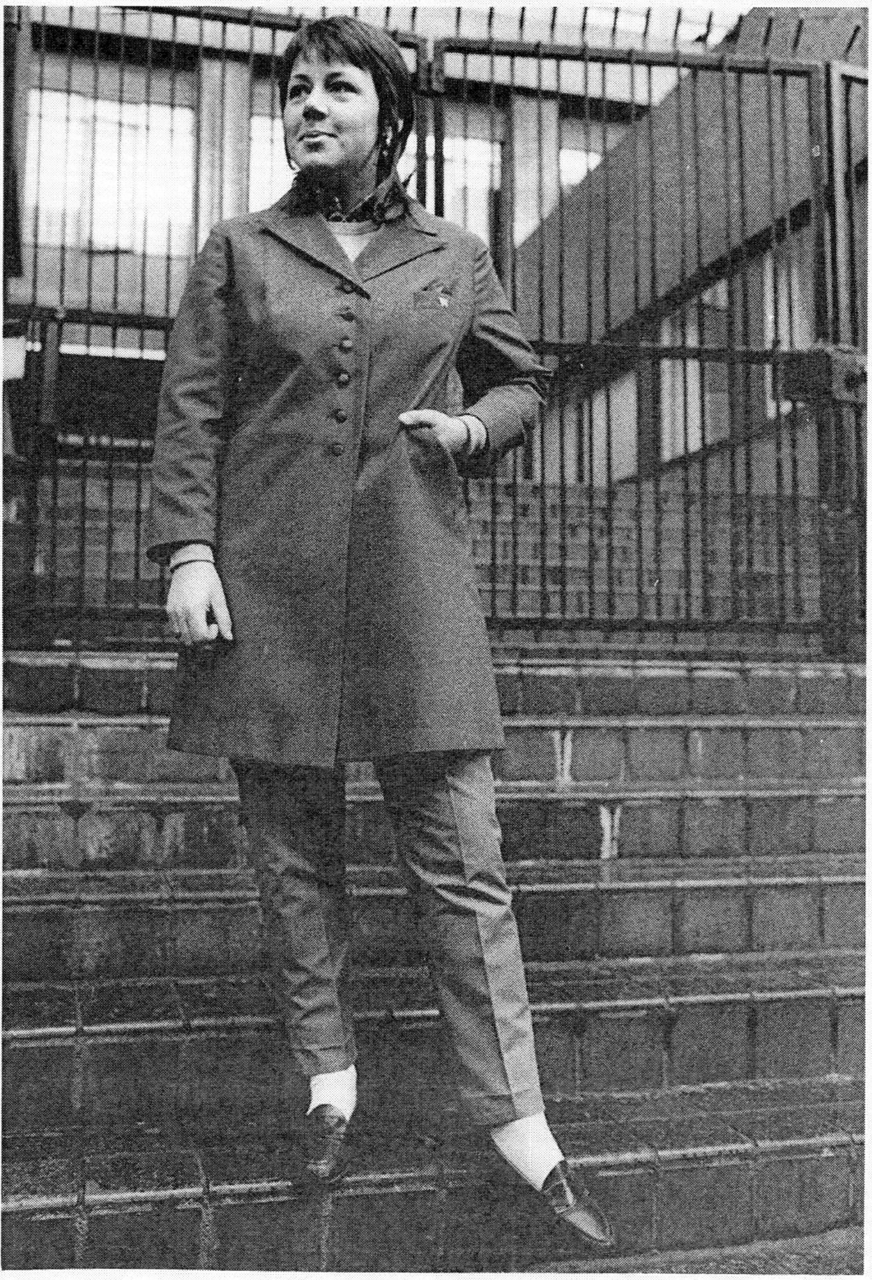

You Have Been
Nominated and
Dealt With By
The
CHELSEA
HEADHUNTERS

ONCE UPON A TRIBE

I remember when I quizzed Pete McKenna over the use of talcum powder at the Wigan Casino. He said in all the years from 1974 to 1981 that he attended The Casino not once did he see any talc on the floor. This is Pete's experience where as someone else may say they did see talc at the club. Both are right because both had their experience. Even when inviting people to contribute to the book a couple of people wanted to, but backed out. When they were asked why they said they didn't want to put their 'heads on the block' and have others judge them by saying things like who do they think they are? The response they got was *"just write about what you know, what you did, because those experiences are unique to you and nobody can take that away from you"*.

Each contribution is also a personal celebration of the individual's youth. It is also an admission to their passion for the music, fashion and era that they grew up with and participated in. Who knows, perhaps a thousand years from now historians will read 'Once Upon A Tribe' and understand the truth about Mods, Casuals, Soulies and so on. In the compiling of the book I learnt a lot from the people I spoke with. Eddie Phillips of the Creation once told me that when he played with The Creation he didn't think of the music as Mod music, he simply considered it to be Rock and Roll. The labels attached are more often than not attached by those (like the media) looking from the outside inwards. It's common knowledge now that many Mods in the sixties did not refer to themselves as Mods at all. So perception is everything and the tribes were not built on labels but on passion, attitude and wanting something different than just a nine to five, a week's holiday in Spain every year and a new fire place for their two up two down. The tribes belong to something different. It's hard to communicate in words alone but those involved will know what is being referred to because of a special feeling.

It is accepted that the Teddy boys, the Mods, the Skinheads and so on were all squeezed out of the working classes. The fifties put money into the pockets of young people that their war ridden fathers had not had. It's reactionary in the same way that when the Mods went all psychedelic a new breed known as the hard Mods stepped away and gave birth to the Skinheads and then the Suedeheads. Many of these would have been the younger brothers and sisters of the original Mods.

The tribes wanted to be noticed. Most of us know that feeling that we get when we enter a club in a new shirt or pair of trainers. We want others to notice us. Casuals know it, Mods know it, all of the tribes know it. Perhaps it stemmed from the working classes wanting to get noticed and because they couldn't do it with a flash motor they decided on style and attitude instead.

This book is in no way meant to be a comprehensive account of every British youth sub culture that ever roamed Albion. It is only a crude account of the lives of thousands of young people. Young people that use to hang around in cafes (the teams that meet in cafes comes to mind), disco's, youth clubs and street corners. The last couple of decades have provided a generation with inspirational and informative accounts of the 'Tribes'. Brilliant films for example like Bronco Bullfrog, Quadrophenia, Away Days, Football Factory, This is England and more recently NEDS (Scottish Boot boys) really help too.

And some people in this book like Geoff Blythe for example certainly played their part in shaping something in many young lives and hearts and definetley enriching it because of his contribution on the '*Searching For The Young Soul Rebels*' album. And then there is Eddie Pillar of the wonderful Acid Jazz Records. It's fair to say that without Eddie and Acid Jazz we may not have even been blessed with Mother Earth, Corduroy, Brand New Heavies and so forth. Yes, the bands would have existed but the fact that Acid Jazz existed as a vehicle for them makes the whole thing just that little bit more special.

Acid Jazz is another example of an anchor/pillar that something great builds itself on and around. During a conversation I had with Paolo Hewitt once I was struck when Paolo referred to Acid Jazz Records as a Mod label. I asked Paolo what he meant and he replied by saying that Eddie Pillar simply responds to what is on the streets and in that sense is Modernist. I had to agree. The other labels that come to mind are Tamla Motown, Two Tone and Trojan.

Contained in the book is also Val Weedon's account of being a teenage girl in the 60's. Whilst sitting around Val's house one night with her fella Phil she skipped away and disappeared upstairs for a few minutes. When she returned she was clutching a 40 year old scrap book. It was her personal scrap book from a 16 year girl old on her favourite band at the time The Small Faces. As I carefully turned the pages and looked at the newspaper cuttings of the band members I noticed that every other page had autographs of The Small Faces. Amazing! So for you Small faces fans reading this you will enjoy reading Val's memoirs. If you are a female reading this you will be insanely jealous of her.

So for those who were not paying attention as a teenager or lived on the Isle of Sheppey what is a Mod, Skin, Casual or some of the other youth tribes? So much has been written before on the subject and really the contributions in this book explain what Mod or Skin is in great accurate detail. But in a brief and crude way we can add a few things to help put things into some kind of context and we will only mention some of the tribes to give a flavour and set the tone. When you read the actual contributions in the book you will be hopefully be left with a more informed understanding of what a Mod is or a Skinhead was/is.

It is generally accepted that Mod evolved from the term Modernist and had its roots in the modern Jazz music and clubs of the late fifties. So Modernist and Modernism suggest the direction. These young people were attending clubs that played modern, hip Jazz and within a couple of year's American R&B and then Soul music was introduced. The original Mods gathered in the city of London's coffee bars at first. Then London clubs like The Flamingo, The Scene, La Discoteque and The Roaring Twenties turned to cater for the young Mods needs. Many Jazz musicians evolved into playing their version of the American R&B and Soul and bands like The Rolling Stones and The Yardbirds were formed. Of course as Mod became more popular and commercial it spread throughout the nation and to other clubs like The Twisted Wheel in Manchester or The Cavern in Liverpool who adjusted to satisfy their young people's needs. A useful book that was written at the time 1959's 'Absolute Beginners' by Colin Mcinnes provides a detailed and accurate flavour of a young Modernist in London.

This Modernist group originated out of the working classes from the East End of London. The Mods were young people with a few quid in their pockets to burn and wanted to burn it on clothes and generally having a good time. They would have been the younger siblings of the Teddy boys and girls and so owe the Teds recognition because it was the Teds that gave the male Mods the go-ahead to take an interest in themselves where fashion was concerned.

London retailers responded and boutiques like John Stephen or Mary Quant opened to supply the Mods with the clothes they wanted. The American Ivy League was popular alongside tailor made suits and shirts and other garments that took their inspiration from Italian and French styles. The shirt makers Ben Sherman and Brutus also sprung up and Fred Perry was worn. Desert boots and Loafers were also popular. The overall look intending to be sharp, clean and stylish. *'Clean living under difficult circumstances'* said The Who manager Pete Meaden in describing the Mods. The look would also reflect the elegance of a Vespa or Lambretta which was the Mods preferred choice of transport.

The look would also evolve and develop with speed and this need to 'move on' constantly and quickly would then re-appear within the Football Casuals several years later. For example the length of a shirt collar would be hip one month and out of favour the next. With the Casuals they adhered to a similar template and attitude. Any aspiring Mod or Casual had to keep their wits about them. That's if they wanted to be part of the 'In crowd'.

In the late 70's there was another surge of Mods. A newer crop of bands born out of the 1976/77 punk explosion like The Jam, Purple Hearts, Merton Parkas and The Chords turned many young people's attention back onto the clothes that their much older Brothers and Uncles wore like Parkas, Button down shirts and desert boots. Fred Perry and Ben Sherman were extremely popular within this generation. Carnaby Street was revamped and new shops opened to cater for the new young mods needs of Jam shoes and Boating blazers. This was a much shorter lived period and really only lasted three or four years before the casuals appeared. This second generation of Mods were however turned on to a whole new world of music from bands like The Creation, The Action and Northern soul.

Many consider the original Mod years to be between 1958 and 1964. After this the media had commercialised the Mods to the extent that many moved away from it. Also the introduction of Psychedelia turned some off. One reaction to the Hippy scene was the formation of the Hard Mods. A friend of mine recounted a story that he was told by a Bristol City fan. The fan said that he remembers Arsenal fans turning up in Sheepskin coats and Army boots and the year was 1966.

The Hard Mods eventually morphed into the Skinheads on account that they chose to wear they hair in a short crop similar to the Black Afro cut that the musicians had of the music they were listening to called Reggae and Ska. The Hard Mod look was stream line and cool. They kept the button collar style shirt from Brutus and Ben Sherman and added Braces and they introduced Harrington and Crombie overcoats. They wore Sta-prest trousers and returned to wearing Brogues, Loafers alongside their Army boots.

By 1968 the media was calling the Hard Mods Skinheads on account of their short hair. Richard Allen helped to commercialise the look in his book *'Skinheads'* and by 1969 the look was totally commercial and then by '70 it was over and pushed aside making room for the Suedeheads. The 70's introduced further trends known as Boot Boys, Smoothies, Glam and then Punk. To ease the 70's along came Slade, Bowie, Bolan and of course The Sex Pistols.

Again it is generally accepted that both Mods and Skinheads originated out of the working classes of London. However, when it comes to the Casuals this is an area for some debate. As the years have rolled by the Northerners have claimed the Casual look for their own and the Southerners have done the same. A close friend of mine from Leeds said he was calling himself a 'Dresser' in 1983 and only started to use the term Casual when he moved down South. In other areas up North the lads called themselves 'Perry Boys' on account of their wearing Fred Perry's. What is certain about Casuals, Dressers and so on is that the look grew from out of the football terraces of Great Britain.

Sportswear was without doubt a common denominator whether you were from up North or down South. For the first time youths really got stuck into designer sportswear from the likes of Sergio Tachinni, Fila and Ellesse. A multitude of trainers were worn with names like Trim Trab, Gazelle, Forest Hills and Samba. Then there were new jean manufacturers being introduced like Lois and Firorucci. And the ever popular Golf style Argyle patterned jumpers from Pringle and Lyle and Scot. It really was the boy next door look adopted to evade the Police on the streets surrounding football stadiums. A whole new style of haircut swept through the nation and had names like the Mullet, Perm and Wedge. These cuts replaced the skinhead and French line cut almost over-night.

There was something fresh and inviting about the Casual look and within a few months it seemed that every young male had turned into a casual. In my novel 'Long Hot Summer' I used this idea and based the story around a six week school holiday period where the main character experiences a transition from being a school boy to working boy and mod boy to Casual boy.

Some Casuals got involved just because of the football hooliganism element and others simply because of the look. Trip's to a shop called 'Stuarts' in Shepherds Bush in London was a requirement. The other new addition about the Casuals was that they were not responding to any certain kind of music. If you were a Casual you could listen to whatever music you wanted to listen to. Casuals were governed by the clothes they wore and not the music they listened to.

Many agree that Casual peeked in '85 before fading and then was overtaken in 1987 as the first drum beats of Acid house entered onto the scene. Then as if from out of nowhere a new style of music from Chicago entered the British blood stream. It was called House music. Within two years of its arrival thousands of kids would find themselves dropping LSD and dancing to the hypnotic music in disused warehouses. The second summer of love had begun and the party people were called Ravers because they were Raving to the music. This scene most certainly originated out of the depths of London in clubs like Shoom and Clinks. And of course Ibiza played its part. But this was not enough for a hungry nation of kids. Pirate radio stations like Centre Force and Sunrise sprung up and supplied thousands of kids with new House tunes and even better where to go and dance to the music. The venues would be either fields or warehouses within spitting distance of the M25. The Raves adopted wonderful names like 'Biology' or 'Back to The Future' and catered for the needs for ten or twenty thousand wide eyed up kids.

The look of the average Raver was a pair of Timberland boots or Kickers, baggy track suits bottoms or denim dungarees. Long hair often pulled back into pony tails or with centre partings. In the earlier Acid House days it had been yellow tee shirts with Smiley faces on them or Tie dyed garments. Some youths even wore White gloves and hung whistles around their necks. The look of the Raver did not differ much whether you were from London or Manchester.

The Rave scene was also a response to a new drug called Ecstasy. The Acid House parties had been dominated by LSD with names like 'Strawberry Fields' or 'Micro Dots', but the Rave scene was most certainly fuelled by the E's. The drug assisted the Raver on their journey through a night of partying on some field or in some warehouse in Essex. With an E inside, the Raver had no choice but to dance.

By 1990 the authorities were clamping down and preventing Raves by issuing mighty fines to promoters. The kids responded with the 'Freedom To Party' rally in Hyde Park but it was to no avail. By '91 the Rave scene was all but dead and pushed back into the night clubs. The North continued to party in the Hacienda and support their bands like The Happy Mondays and The Stone Roses and from here on the slow decline and erasure of the great spirit of British youth Tribes faded. Of course there were some that persisted with their choice of fashion and groupings of Mods, Scooter boys and Skinheads continued and within a few more years it had all merged into one scene which is pretty much where it is today. Any one of us can attend a Northern Soul all-nighter and dance next to a Skinhead, a Mod, a Scooter boy or a Suedehead.

Nowadays people are more tolerant of each other and this is because it is generally accepted that all tribes need to stick together so that at least some kind of a night can be achieved. After all if you came through the Rave scene and were used to dancing beside 10,000 other kids you hardly want to be dancing in a small room at the back of an old boozer with only 10 other like-minded people do you?

But it appears to me that there are no Tribes anymore because the young people of this nation are not hungry anymore and that is a great loss and a great shame. I feel privileged to of been part of the last generation of the now Lost tribes of British youth cultures.

This was our England.
This is 'Once upon a tribe'

NORTHERN SOUL
KEEP THE FAITH
ABERDEEN
19
80
SOCCER CA ALS
mod
TR
FREEDOM TO PARTY
CAMPAIGN
RALLY, SATURDAY, MARCH 3, 1990, 2.00pm, HYDE PARK, LONDON
ARE YOU GOING TO LET THEM TAKE AWAY YOUR RIGHT TO PARTY ?
CAMPAIGN INFORMATION
Freedom to Party Campaign, 27 Old Gloucester Street, London, WC1N 3XX.
Soul Club

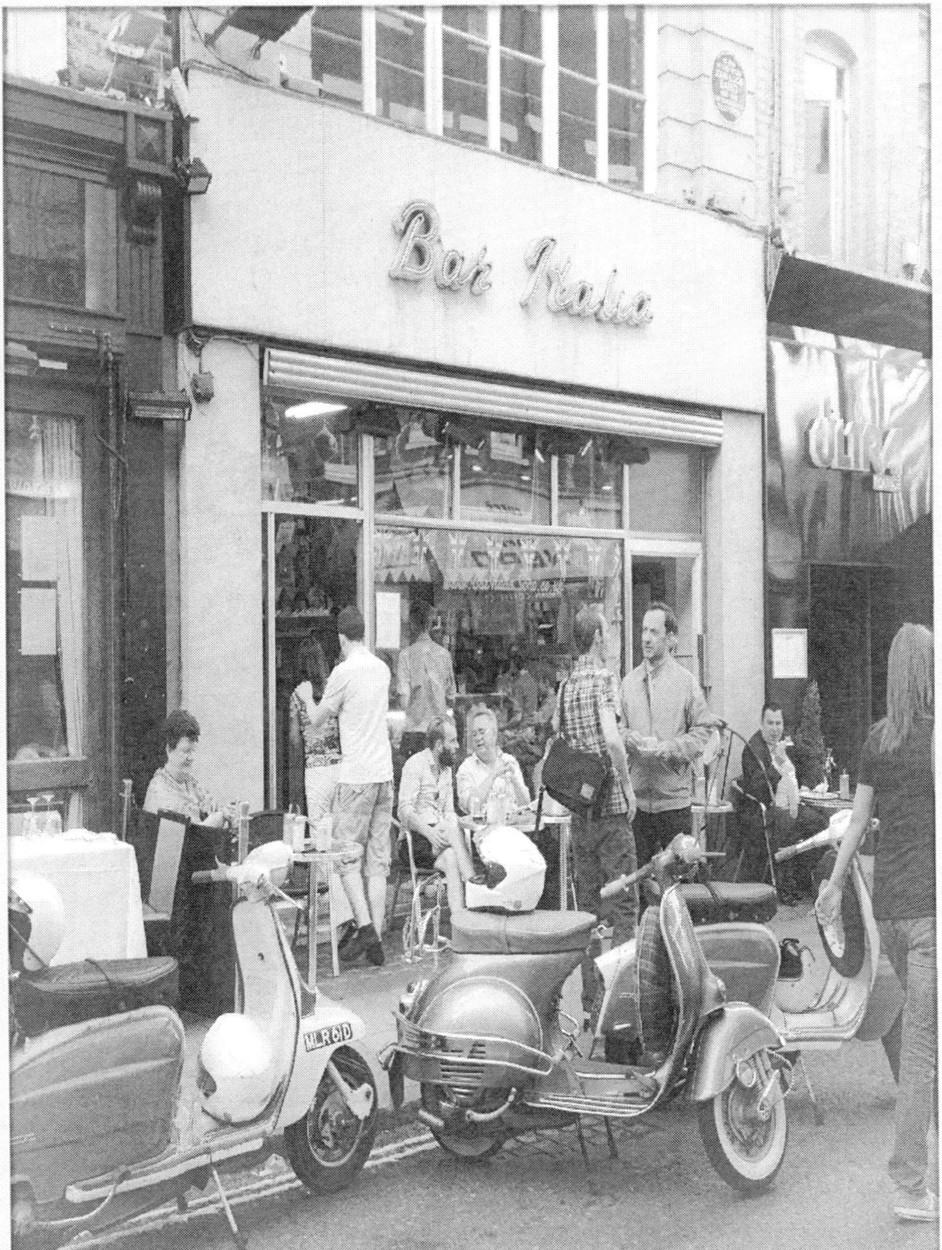
Bar Italia
MLR 61D

ONCE UPON A TRIBE
(Their memories in their words)

This first contribution comes from **Adam Cooper**, a Mod from the '80s who writes the fanzine 'Heavy Soul' and the Mod friendly record label of the same name. Adam has written his piece in his words and like all the other contributions we have decided that is important to keep the contributions unedited so they retain the feel and tongue of the authors. After all, these are the tribal members and this is what they have to say.

1. 'FOR A SUSSED GENERATION'

I don't think my introduction to Mod is any different to anyone else of my generation. I was born in 1972, thus missing the original revival of 1979, only latching on in around '83 as an eleven year old at school. The 'big lads' at the time had moved on from Mods to scooter boys and that meant they didn't want their suits, button down shirts and most importantly, their records anymore. It only took one enterprising younger brother to bring his siblings clothes to school along with a few cassettes of The Kinks and the first Who LP and that was it – I was hooked. I remember buying an old Ben Sherman and I think a few cassettes with my pocket money.....but that wasn't enough. Around that time after The Jam had split, Paul Weller was in The Style Council, a more poppy band and that meant I could read about them in 'Smash Hits' and 'Record Mirror' and I could also see what Weller was wearing then (remember this was '83/'84 when Weller was at his smartest). This led me to backtrack and buy the customary Parka and hunt around millets for a boating blazer. I was quite happy progressing to being the only Mod in the school (what had started as about 10-15 dwindled down to me). I was also the only mod within a 10 mile radius of where I lived (a small town in Buckinghamshire). I began to research more as I hit 14/15 years old and Mum and Dad often went to London sightseeing, which meant I could have a wander down Carnaby Street and the first time I wandered into The Cavern, it literally blew me away. Racks and racks of suits just like I had seen in pictures, jumpers, button downs, sta-prest and scarfs. A walk upstairs and a poky little room had all the latest releases on vinyl, along with badges, posters and video's. A few yards down from Ganton Street was The Merc which had even more vinyl etc. Over the next year or so I must have spent all my paper round and first job wages on LPs and singles by The Times, Makin' Time, The Kick, The Moment, The Scene etc. along with those lovely Kent compilations.

The next logical step was a scooter. My under-15 football manager, Colin, had been a revival mod and still had a couple of scooters in a garage. Now remember again this is around 1987, so I gladly parted with around £100 for a Vespa 50 Special and a Vespa 90 – both of which were pushed home and the restoration began. The 50 Special had 'Nine Below Zero' on the side, which was then covered in white spray and a hastily made template of the first Specials LP was made and sprayed on in black. Tassels for the handlebars, fly screen, back rack, and chrome wheel covers, and of course crash bars laden with mirrors were purchased. My perfect mod scooter!

It was late '87 that I caught my first glimpse of Mods en masse. The Great Yarmouth CCI rally was taking place where I was on holiday at the time and the sights were amazing – hundreds of scooters, well dressed kids and for me as a 15 year old it was my idea of heaven. Luckily I had packed my Cavern Dogtooth suit and my Dad kindly took me to Gorleston-On-Sea for my first taste of a Mod do. The James Taylor Quartet was the live band. I had no idea at the time of any of the songs being spun by the DJs but knew I had to be a part of this. I met a chap from Luton during the day and we kept in touch during 1988 and by 1989 I was ready to travel to my first rally on a scooter. How the hell I managed to get from near Aylesbury all the way to Lowestoft without a spare tyre, AA cover or even the basic tools I still don't know, but when I arrived on the Friday to be greeted by hundreds of like-minded people it didn't matter that I couldn't feel my backside or my thumbs. That year I managed I think six or seven rallies (we used to haggle over spending more than £10 on a nights B&B - £7 - £8 was the norm!). I was also now in The Moreton Parkas A.M.S. (you had to be affiliated back then) and the group of us spent 1990 the same as we had the year before – travelling all over the UK without a care on 125 scooters. The bands I saw were also amazing; The Clique, The Babysnakes, The Boys (pre Ocean Colour Scene), The Moment, Small World.

I was also a tailored Mod by now; hours were spent in 'Textile King' on Wardour Street looking at material, then once the correct mohair was sifted, it was the five minute walk to 'Charlie' to get measured up. Really nice guy, always pleasant, with his wife in the corner beavering away on the sowing machine. Charlie used to give a discount to the Mods and his tiny office was always packed on Saturdays – standing room only! I must have had a dozen suits made; I had jeans and cords made too. Katy Stevens was the shirt maker to go to as well, again a nice lady who always had ideas for shirts – contrasts, extra buttons etc – real attention to detail.

The Mod scene in 1990 / '91 was different then from five years previous – it had become more elitist, smarter and basically tightened up. The CCI rallies had become a bit passé – Dee-Lite and The Charlatans were being played and that put a lot of people off. The Untouchables started their own rallies along with The Rhythm & Soul Set. I attended all three variants during '90 and '91; to me The Rhythm & Soul Set rallies were the best – loads of quality jazz and R&B, club soul and British Beat – just what I wanted to hear. Numbers were poor though and The Untouchables were now in the driving seat. The rallies then were great times – I was 18/19 and loving it! Tailored, scooter, growing record collection, nearly perfected Marriott hair, good group of friends and a proper Mod. Work and the week got in the way – I just wanted to get out and dance and be part of a scene. Friday night was spent in either Euston station for the club there, or maybe Circles. Saturday was The Mildmay Tavern and then, later, Drummonds on Euston Road and Sunday was the best – The Kings Tavern in Reading. The closest I think anyone could have got to replicating The Scene (as we hoped it would have been) or Tiles. The music was blinding – just R&B, both British and American, hardly ever any northern soul, just Motown now and again, the odd ska record and then loads of jazz. Tracks like *'Crawdaddy Simone'*, *'Bring it to Jerome'*, *'Think twice before you go'* *'Walkin''* even Van Morrison's *'Moon dance'*. Everyone was suited, both boys and girls and it didn't matter it finished at eleven as it was a relief after the whole weekend spent scooting everywhere!

I attended the rallies and various clubs regularly all over the country (including the infamous 'Blankenberge') up until the late '90s, but it went a bit too psychedelic for me and also most others, but my interest didn't dwindle – I still collected records, got more scooters, dressed the same. My interest was rekindled in the early 2000s by clubs like 'Shotgun' and the 'Mousetrap' R&B all-nighters; I also started to attend more Northern Soul clubs around the Peterborough area as I had moved up that way. Lincolnshire may be a horrible place to live (sorry PHK) but they like their soul up there which proved an okay contrast.

Around the mid-2000s there was also a growing interest in late '50s / early '60s RnB or 'popcorn', a scene started in Belgium in the '70s. New DJs were emerging and bringing with them their influences from other genres. Personally I'm not a fan of this style of music, Mod RnB to me will always be Sonny Boy Williamson, John Lee Hooker and Slim Harpo et al, but I can recognise a need for progression and if it makes the scene attract newer, younger faces who will bring with them a regenerative attitude then so be it. The scene had turned into an almost 'Saga' night with most attendees in their late 30s / early 40s or older – the same as I has noticed on the northern soul circuit – moving forward to 2010 and the mod scene in the UK is back on its feet thanks to a handful of young, enthusiastic Mods prepared to put on nights/clubs. Good luck to them, may they carry the torch onwards, it was after all, supposed to be a 'youth cult'!

In 2006 I decided to start my own record label as I had always been jealous of Dizzy's success at Detour Records and thought I would have a stab at that! I approached the first band 'The Shake' (now The Screenbeats) and pressed up 300 7" singles, this was followed by a CD compilation and another couple of EPs. In 2009 I really went for it – not for any ego reasons (I find it hard to do sales face to face), just because there are some great bands out there. I loved The Shake; The Patterns from Manchester are just like The Prisoners, The Lost 45s from Leeds also. The scene musically is now very healthy, but without it being strictly mod in the sense of the word I grew up with. The sound is the same, but the dress sense is different – no 60s or suits, still smart though.

It's now 2012, I've still got my scooter (as has Abby, my wife), still got the records, still collecting 45s (as, again, is my wife), still getting clothes tailor-made – now at George Lilley in Leeds, rather than Charlie and still very much into a scene that has seen me go from young lad to father of two (my old clothes are still under my bed in the vain hope that either Sam or Ben will want to follow my path! I can hope!!!!).

So on reflection, Mod has been to me, a way of life – clichéd, but ultimately true – it occupied my teens, twenties and now thirties. I still dress the same, always smart, always mod or my interpretation of it, still crave that GS 160, still have a big wants list for 45s and still look down on other fashions as inferior. That has been my life as a mod, I was lucky to be around, as a teenager, a big mod scene and those memories will stay with me forever, wherever Mod may go in the future I will follow as I believe it to be the only cult worth following, always evolving, always exciting.......
Adam from Rowed Out / Heavy Soul Records

2. Next up is an article donated to this book from **John Hellier**. John has written books on his beloved Small Faces and also publishes the 'Darlings of Wapping Wharf' magazine. John is an original Mod from the 60's with much to say on the matter. After all, he was there!

DRESSED TO KILL (life as a Mod in the 1960's)
INTERVIEW BY BRENT YEOMANS
BRENT: WHAT TYPE OF MUSIC WERE YOU AND MODS GENERALLY LISTENING TO?
JOHN: Mods in the 60s listened and danced to mainly Black American artistes. At the time that was seen as the real thing, it was fairly snobbish really. British bands in the main got their material from this source and even the early Beatles and Stones records are peppered with covers of American R&B classics. Very early Motown (pre- Supremes, Four Tops) records were particularly desirable to Mods, things like "*Money*" by Barrett Strong, "*Shop Around*" by the Miracles, "*Please Mr. Postman*" by the Marvellettes and the Contours original "*Do You Love Me*". James Brown records (pre-funk) were always popular particularly "*Night Train*" and "*Please Please Please*". Also American blues artists like Jimmy Reed and John Lee Hooker would regularly be played in Soho mod clubs. Very few British artistes were held in high esteem. There were many excellent British Mod bands playing the clubs at that time. Most of them never had hit records and disappeared into oblivion but as I said before their sets were largely made up of US Soul/R&B classics. This included the so called biggies such as the Who and Small Faces, whose stage acts back then didn't include the hit 45's... They saved that material for

pop package tours but doing the clubs was so very different. Mod bands that spring to mind include The Action, The Eyes, The Chasers, Scrooge And The Misers, who went on to become The Attraction (no, nothing to do with Elvis Costello) and the great Johns Children with whom I played, albeit very briefly. Their drummer Chris Townson walked out after a European tour, I got to replace him for about 3 weeks! Unfortunately for me he decided to come back and they took him. Chris had depped for Keith Moon on a Who European tour that tells you how good he was. I had no chance! Chris is still a friend of mine today as is Andy Ellison, the lead singer. (Chris sadly died on 10th February 2008).

By 1967 Mod turned into psychedelic Mod. The bands were no longer playing the R&B classics and the style was now very firmly influenced by what was going on in San Francisco. Incidentally one of the very best live acts on the London scene at this time was Winston's Fumbs led by ex Small Face Jimmy Winston. Don't let anybody fool you that he couldn't play, this band really cooked!

What a lot of people don't realize is that many of the 70's superstars had roots in 60's mod. Rod the Mod we all know about but David Bowie, Marc Bolan, David Essex (yeah, David Essex was the drummer in a very cool mod outfit called Mood Indigo) and even Status Quo were strutting the stages in their peacock suits! Check out pictures of Quo from 1968 with Rossi sporting a Marriott haircut!

As for songs about the London mod scene well you've got the fairly obvious Kinks "*Dedicated Follower of Fashion*" and The Small Faces "*Here Come the Nice*"

but much more importantly check out the REAL mod anthem which has to be "London Boys" by David Bowie from 1966. This tells the tale perfectly of pill-popping Soho in the mid sixties.

BRENT: WHICH BANDS/ARTISTS DID YOU SEE PERFORM LIVE IN THE 60'S?

JOHN: Recently I was telling somebody that I got to see all the major players from the 60's and 70's live but thinking back on it now I overlooked the fact that I never got to see The Kinks play. Of course, I rated them very highly and still do in fact I don't think I know anybody that doesn't like them. Ray Davies was a real wordsmith and just about all the self penned singles and most of the albums were real classics. The Kinks were very much part of that whole Carnaby Street set of the mid sixties. Particular favourite numbers of mine are *"Waterloo Sunset"*, *"Set Me Free"*, a wonderful b side called *"Where Have All the Good Times Gone"* but most all the truly wonderful *"Lola"*. A song about a guy who picks up what he thinks is a gorgeous looking woman in a Soho bar only to find out that "she's" a transvestite! Ray Davies writing is certainly right up there with, not only the best from that era but, the all-time greats. Other than the Kinks I saw all the leading British bands and lots of American ones. I even got to see Blues legend Howlin Wolf in a pub in Dagenham!!

BRENT: WHICH WERE YOUR FAVOURITE MOD VENUES?

JOHN: Favourite venues eh! I loved the Wardour Street Marquee. Very intimate atmosphere where the only drink on sale was Coca Cola (well it was back in 65/66). I saw many bands there that went on to superstardom including the Who, Small Faces, Cream and Jimi Hendrix Experience. Also saw the first gigs from Humble Pie and The Faces in there. I loved the Scene club just off Great Windmill Street in Soho. That was pretty elitist and very snobby and owned by the guy that ran Radio Caroline. You'd only ever hear original American artists in there, with the possible exception of Georgie Fame, Chris Farlowe or Zoot Money. That was where I first met Pete Meadon, a fast talking, over the top sort of guy who managed The Who in the early days as well as working with Andrew Loog Oldham and the Rolling Stones. Pete was a mate but he was a bit of a pain and the type of guy you went out of your way to avoid if you could. He died young and has now achieved legendary status amongst Mods. Dying before your time is certainly the way to achieve that! Other groovy clubs of that era include Tiles in Oxford Street, Billy Walkers Uppercut Club (he was a famous boxer) in the East End and the fantastic Lotus Club in Forest Gate. There were also some great venues near to my home in Romford such as the Wykeham Hall and Willow Rooms, tiny places but very atmospheric.

BRENT: WHAT IS YOUR OPINION ON TODAYS LIVE SCENE?

JOHN: I'm not really clued up enough on today's bands to answer this one really. I hear a lot of 60's influence in some of the new guitar bands i.e. Arctic Monkeys, White Stripes etc. etc. but a lot of the mod bands that I've been associated with over the past ten years or so including a lot of the bands that play Conventions for me are probably more influenced by The Jam than say The Small Faces or Who but there again The Jam got their influence, well a lot of it anyway, from the 60s. So I suppose it goes around in circles really. Going back to the original question though, in my mind none of the current crop make the hairs on the back of my neck stand up as say, the Small Faces and Who did (and still do), they're now part of my DNA! NICE, I think so.......
John Hellier

3. Next up is a 1989 Ravers account of a typical night trying to get to a Rave.

The Police Officer went on to describe the carnage left behind by the ravers and the invasion of peoples good night's sleep. He also mentioned the impact on wildlife; the new drug E's sweeping through every town, hamlet and city in the United Kingdom called Ecstasy. More footage of raves showed wide eyed young people bopping to the trance like music in dry iced filled venues whilst impressive visuals splashed their lights across them. Everything about the images felt familiar to me and I congratulated myself on being a successful raver who also contributed to the second 'summer of love'.

Typically for the summer of 1989 I would put my favourite baseball cap onto my head and pull the pony tail through it. And then put on my Timberlands boots.....the best boots ever made and perfect for dancing in fields and warehouses, then grab some money (twenty for entrance to a rave and twenty for something else) and raced down stairs, through the front room and out of the front door yelling back 'See you later'. Then I would be on my way to meet my mates.

Craig's white Vauxhall would be parked alongside Steve's red Metro and more cars would be parked beside Steve. The doors on Craig's car would be wide open and would be playing something like '*Ride on time*' or '*Rhythm is rhythm*'. Craig would be wearing his new Mash clobber and purple desert boots. Steve was also wearing desert boots in a pastel green. He would also wear his Bright Red long sleeve shirt with Golden shapes and patterns on it.

We would probably discuss Pete's crazy leg dancing at the Red Lion in Gravesend and take the piss out of him for a bit before moving on to somebody else. Craig would turn the volume up further on his car stereo so we could listen to the announcements on Centre Force 88.4. The Dee jays would be suggesting a rave was going to happen somewhere in the Essex country side. That was the place to be on this Saturday night. What we would wait for was the addresses of meeting points. Rumours would have been circulating all week about a rave somewhere but even an hour or so before we would sometimes not know.

There was more laughter and sorting out arrangements and then the Dee jay would reveal that the first meeting point of the night was going to be on Blackheath. Craig would announce it was time to be heading off and the crowd of boys (Chang, Noddy, Colin, Pete, Justin, Tim, Steve S and Steve M to name just a few) would disperse into various cars. Craig would lead the convoy of adventurers out of the car park up the hill and onto the M20. Seven car loads of ravers in all charging down the motorway in the direction of the meeting point on Blackheath common. The buzz and adrenalin kicking in.

Each of the seven cars would be tuned into Centre Force radio. The night would promise something special and all would be totally on board. The Centre Force Dee jay would inform its listeners that Guru Josh or Adamski or list a load of dee jays that are going to be at the rave.

The word is there's a meeting point on Blackheath common so we head there. About three miles before we reached Blackheath the Centre Force Dee jay announced that there was going to be another meeting point at the Black Prince hotel on the A2. Craig changes direction and the six cars behind him followed. Within five minutes of driving at eighty miles an hour Craig steers his car into the Black Prince car park.

There's a few more cars already there that appear to have ravers in them. Everybody eyes one another up suspiciously. The other six cars soon follow and park awkwardly around the car park. Steve pulls up beside Craig's car and winds down his window. Steve is about to yell something when I notice the smile on his face suddenly disappear. Three Police cars screeched into the car park and one stops in the entrance way therefore blocking the cars exits. The Police cars surrounded the cars full of ravers and coppers jump out of their cars and instructed all the drivers to switch off their engines. Craig twists the tuner on the radio to disguise that he had been listening to Centre Force.

There are complaints from the drivers but they were ignored as the Police assumed control of the situation.

'Bollocks' say's Craig 'They must have intercepted the info about the meeting points'.

'Yes, this could mean an early night for us all' I reply.

'Yea trust us to be the first ones here. If we had not of driven so fast we could of spotted the old Bill from the A2' adds Chang.

'Can you all step out of the car please lads' say's the booming voice of an older Police Officer.

Everyone then gets slowly out of the car. The Police Officer asked them to step a few feet away from the car. Police Officers dive into the cars giving them a thorough search for drugs. One Officer pushed and heaved the back seat in Craig's car until he hands out the entire seat. Craig looks like he is going to cry.

'So where are you lads off to tonight?' asked the Copper.

'Just driving around' Craig mumbles.

'Just driving around eh! I don't believe you. I think you have your sights set on going to one of those illegal raves'.

'Not us' say's Pete gurning.

'You look like ravers to me' says the Copper.

The copper then nods towards the other cars in the car park and added.

'Your mates look like ravers too'.

There's some more banging and clattering as the Police Officer inside Craig's car does his best to dismantle the interior. We all keep quiet and try to look innocent. Another much younger police man worked his way around each raver and asked them to remove all the items in their pockets. I grin at the sight of Lighters, Rizlas, Tissues, Hanky chiefs and chewing gum wrappers. The whole debacle last's about thirty minutes and then the old police officer in charge of the operation announces that everything was ok but advised that we all turn around and drive back down the M20. We have no intention of doing so but agreed just so that we can shake of the plod and make a quick get-away to Blackheath before everyone else moves on to the next meeting point.

The Coppers jump back into their cars with disappointed faces and drive off. Craig suggests that we wait five minutes before we set off again for Blackheath. We all laugh and joked about their encounter with the rave busters. In the meantime Craig tunes in again to Centre Force and the Dee jay is still instructing everybody to go to Blackheath. The Dee jay even announced that he had heard that a bust had recently occurred at the Black Prince. We feel like heroes.

Once Craig is satisfied that the coast is clear he leads the charge again out of the car park and down the A2 towards Blackheath. As soon as we have exited the A2 the traffic slows due to the volume of cars heading in the direction of the common. It too a further ten minutes to reach Blackheath. Everyone in the car is astounded by the sheer volume of cars parked all over the common. I estimated that there must have been five hundred cars scattered on the grassy heath. This is one fucking big meeting point.

Craig's mounted the curb and skidded towards a space not far from a small roundabout. The rest of our convoy followed suit and we park in a circle. I've jumped out of the car first and the site of the hundreds of ravers eager to get raving excites me. We have been at meeting points before but we have never witnessed anything like this before. It feels great to be a part of it. Police cars are parked on the fringes of the heath and the coppers roam in amongst the raver's cars wearing their fluorescent over coats. They glow in the parked cars headlights. Car after car has its doors wide open and belt out music from the various pirate radio stations. We even spot a few kids dancing on the roofs of their cars. The site is spectacular.

Craig, Chang and I snake our way in and out of the cars occasionally chatting to other ravers. The atmosphere is one of anticipation, friendliness and nervous excitement. There are several older males holding brick size mobile phones to their ears. They are part of the organisers of the rave. They are surrounded by ravers asking questions and waiting for information regards the location of the next meeting point or the pot of the Gold itself.

'*E's, E's*' whispers the voice of a young man dressed in yellow dungarees and wearing a red beret on his head. The man weaves his way in and around the waiting ravers. A few seconds later I hear another voice advertising purple ohms and black microdots. I look up into the black star lit London sky. It looks still and distant and a universe away from the chaos below on the heath. I knew that this is going to be one of the best nights of my life.

'*Alright man*' booms a gruff voice and I look left to see a familiar face but cannot recall from where. I shake the man's hand desperately trying to place where I recognise him from.

'*Clinks*' the man revealed, '*You don't remember me do you?*'

'*Ah yea, Clink's, of course*' I reply smiling.

'*That was one of the best nights there. Did you have a good one?*'

I cast my memory back to the last time I went to the Clinks club down Clink Street in Southwark. That night had been memorable for two reasons. The first was that on the way into the club the bouncer searched Colin and found a small amount of Hash. Instead of confiscating it all the bouncer tore the hash in half and gave the smaller half back to Colin before allowing him inside. The second salient memory was that the club blew Amyl-nitrate through the club. The effects were horrid and I hated the smell of it.

'Do you remember the Amyl?' asked the man and I nod pretending that I found the whole experience awesome. The man then jogs on the spot for a while, screws his face up and pouts his lips. I understand that the man is coming up on an E. The man then mumbles some more things before being called over by his mates.

There appears to be some instructions about another meeting point from the men with their mobile phones. Ravers started to jump into the cars and dart this way and that attempting to find and follow the leader. Craig and I race back to our vehicle and jump inside. Like a well drilled military operation all the ravers returned to the cars with haste and joined the massive convoy. The Police do their best to ascertain was happening and keep up but they cannot.

'What's the word?' I ask.

'The word is there is another meeting point at the South Ockendon service station'.

'Where the fuck is that?' moans Pete.

'It's off the M25 in Essex' Craig informs before skidding off the grassy common and hitting the tarmac at speed. There's a whoosh of excitement in the car as we follow a Green Golf GTE in front. Craig turns up the volume on the radio and 808 State rocks the inside of the car.

We drive back down the A20 alongside other cars evidently full of ravers. We merged with the M25 and hurtled down it towards the Dartford tunnel. As we approach the tunnel we notice that the Police have closed several of the gates in an attempt to prevent the cars full of ravers crossing the Thames and entering Essex and finding their way to the rave. Fortunately Craig swung the car away from the closed gates and they managed to sneak through undetected. We bolt through the tunnel along with other successful cars of ravers. As we exit the tunnel we feel confident that we are going to reach the rave intact. I'm not familiar with the area of Essex but trust that Craig would find the service station.

On our arrival at the South Ockendon service station we could already see that several cars were leaving. Craig pulls into the service station because he also needed to refuel. It was apparent that we have lost three of our convoy. Craig fills his car with petrol and chats with the ravers in the car behind who were also filling up with fuel. They told him that they were from Hertfordshire and that the rave was nearby. Craig relays the information about the location of the rave to us.

Craig has arranged to follow the ravers from Hertfordshire and we set off down the A13. As we left the service station more and more cars of ravers pulled into it. We get the sense that this rave is going to be a massive affair.

Craig follows the car in front and Steve follows close on the heels of his bumper behind. We drive through Thurrock and North Stifford until we reach a small village called Orsett. There is a stunned silence inside the car. The adrenalin inside us is buzzing. We sense the rave is nearby. The hypnotic sounds of '*Sueno Latino*' on Centre Force reflect our mood and expectations.

We drive through country lanes which were filled with parked cars. Police officers in the fluorescent coats glowed as they lined up along a stretch of lane that led to the rave. They remind me of the lights on the run ways in airports. The police had given up trying to deter the cars full of ravers. They had no choice as twenty thousand excited and determined youths caused havoc.

The car in front finds a spot big enough to park in and as our car passes them they shouted out '*Have a good one'*. We can hear the thumbing deep bass of the house music in the distance. We can see Steve in his Metro behind us bouncing around inside as he responds to the music coming from the rave.

Craig finds the car space and chooses a spot. We gather our coats and jackets and jumped excitedly out of the car. There's a group of men twenty yards in front of them clutching their mobile phones and waving to us to hurry up.

'*Well then'* I say '*Nice one for getting us here Craig'*

'*Piece of piss mate'* he replies.

'*So what do think twenty quid to get it?'*

'*May be twenty five but look at the size of the rave. It's massive, our biggest yet'.*

I soak in the sights and sounds of the rave as we walk nearer to it. We can spot a Ferris wheel and other fairground rides. There are flashing laser lights and psychedelic images being projected all over the site of the rave. We prepare ourselves for the next seven hours of dancing and look forward to the sun coming up at five and the Dee jays responding to it by playing the Beloved's '*The sun rising'.*

Eze E

4. Next one comes from **Bob Manton** who is better known for his time with the late 70's Mod outfit The Purple Hearts. Here Bob tells us what it was like in the years leading up to the formation of the band and the scene it became apart of.

I turned 13 in August of 1974. In those days teenagers only really had two options - Music and Football. It is impossible to over-state how important music was to us compared with the situation for today's kids. Remember

there was no internet, no multi - channel TV, no video games etc. The whole family would watch Top Of The Pops on a Thursday evening and the new chart on a Sunday was a really big deal.
 I didn't have a record player but I did have a radio/cassette and like a lot of people would just tape the stuff I liked. As far as i can remember I liked Glam Rock especially Slade and Sweet. I also liked soul outfits like The Detroit Emeralds and The Stylistics.
 The Record industry then was a multi-million dollar entity, for instance in the mid-seventies in the US it had a higher turnover than the NBL and NFL combined. Clothes wise I would have been wearing flared jeans or cords with big collar shirts and tank tops. I had a bad pudding bowl haircut and sensible shoes.
 In '75 I started to get into Rock music that today would be called `Classic Rock'. Capital Radio in London was very important for me as Nicky Horne had a show every evening called `Your Mother Wouldn't Like It` where all the big rock bands of the day like Deep Purple, The Eagles, Fleetwood Mac etc. could be heard. I got into Ted Nugent and Nils Lofgren. I had a couple of pre-recorded cassette albums including *Space Oddity* by Bowie and *Cry Tough* by Nils Lofgren. I knew Jeff and Simon (later of The Purple Hearts) at school by this time. They were into David Bowie.
 By '76 things were changing a bit. I had a record player and me and Simon were hanging out a lot playing air guitar Tennis Rackets along to *Blue For You* by Status Quo. We had become a lot more aware of Rock`s back catalogue through reading The NME and Sounds who at this time were running very educational articles about sixties music `Happenings Ten Years Ago ` in the NME which reviewed the top Rock Albums of 1966. In the record shops there were no box sets or really anything older than a few months unless it was a band like The Beatles or The Stones but three DJ`s opened my mind and ears to sixties music. Firstly the aforementioned Nicky Horne would devote his Friday night show to the sixties so for the first time I heard The Kinks/Stones/Who/Beatles/Animals/Yardbirds back to back. Then Roger Scott (RIP) had a show earlier on a Friday night called `Crusin` which catered to the American Car enthusiasts who drove down the Chelsea embankment every Friday. So he played a lot of Rock`n`Roll but sometimes a lot of Beach boys and Jan and Dean. Lastly on Radio One John Peel (also RIP) did a series of specials on The Who/Stones/Yardbirds/Hendrix. So anyway I and Simon really got into this stuff which we could relate to much better than the current rock scene. We used to call it 60`s Depression Music as a lot of the songs like

'Heart Full Of Soul' and 'We Gotta Get Out Of This Place' sounded really angst ridden.

In the summer of '76 Queen put on a free concert in Hyde Park supported by Supercharge, Steve Hillage and Kiki Dee. Me and Simon went along in our flared jeans-shirts and baseball boots. We had just become aware of The Ramones but probably hadn't heard much of their stuff. It was a fantastic concert. Supercharge were hilarious. Steve Hillage complained about a fight that had broken out at the front saying - "*stop fighting, this music is about peace*". Kiki Dee was a very soulful and bluesy singer with a great backing band. As 'Don't Go Breaking My Heart ' was number one she performed it with a life size cardboard cut out of Elton John! Queen were at this stage still very much a heavy band and took to the stage dressed all in white a la Mick Jagger at the stones concert in 69. Anyway they put on a great show with plenty of dry ice. That was my first proper exposure to rock outside of seeing a school band in 74 and a Romford band called Baby Grumpling at a youth club.

By the end of the year I had got into Dr Feelgood who provided me (via the 'Stupidity' live LP) with a great R & B starter kit. Then The Sex Pistols went on Bill Grundy's show and the nation woke up to the Punk Rock phenomenon. I saw the promo video for 'Anarchy in the UK' and really dug it although I was a bit freaked out by the bands appearance. The important thing about punk for me was the idea that any kid could form a band; you didn't have to be a great musician, just learn three chords and do it!

In March '77 Simon and I went to see The Jam supporting Meal Ticket and The Troggs at The Royal College of Art in Kensington. I had on a crappy millets Parker and i think a multi coloured stripy jumper with flared cords (I think) and 1970's trainers. As we walked in the band were already playing, I think it was 'I've Changed My Address'. Anyway the adrenalin rush I got seeing them was rather like getting a cattle prod straight to the chest. Here was a young loud band playing fast punky yet melodic music that I could relate to. In those days they still did a lot of covers including 'Much Too Much' and 'So Sad about Us' by The Who. The Troggs were also great, they would only have been in there thirties then I guess and it would have been the original line up. So Anyway me Jeff and Simon started going to Jam gigs at places like the Nashville Rooms and the Red Cow. We would come out of school and get a 25p Red Bus Rover and head into the west end still in our school uniforms and drink half's of Carling Black Label. By the summer I'd gone punk with a jacket full of safety pins, straight or drainpipe trousers and baseball boots, I had a crop at this time, a number 3 I think. I saw most of the big league Punk bands including The Buzzcocks, 999, The Adverts, The

Dammed and Generation X. It was a very exciting time when you really felt part of something. One time I was queuing outside The Vortex and the crowd was getting all these dirty looks from the suits driving by and we all started singing 'Pretty Vacant'.

The punk fashion for the ordinary street kids was very stripped down. I went to see 999 in Chelmsford and on the train back their firm The Southwark Boys were there. They had cropped or short spikey hair, DM's, straight charity shop trousers or jeans, Harrington's or old sixties suit jackets and plain t-shirts. So in a way they looked a bit like the hard mod forerunners of the original skinheads from 1967.

I was still into sixties music at this time not really being able to see too much difference between the energy and stance of groups like The Who and The Kinks and the punk groups. I mainly bought back catalogue sixties singles from Harlequin Records in Romford. It was quite easy to get stuff that had come out on Decca or Deram for instance. By the end of the year I had a couple of Decca single compilations by The Zombies and The Small Faces. These collected all the A and B sides together in one place. I also managed to get hold of a Yardbirds compilation which was a double LP.

The most important re-issue for me however was *Making Time* ' by The Creation on RAW records. This totally changed the way I thought about what a song could be about and the crunching riff and violin bowed guitar really did out Who The Who.

1978 - In the spring The Purple Hearts played their first gig in Harold Hill as a Mod band. Clothes were still hard to come by. We all got these white painters trousers and black Harrington's and used to go around Romford with Jeff's Ghetto blaster playing The Small Faces first L P and 'A Quick One' by The Who. However we did find a shop in Brick Lane that sold every kind of suede boot and shoe you could imagine. About this time the skinhead revival was very big in Romford and the surrounding areas like Dagenham and Barking. This led to a shop in Romford called Mintz and Davis suddenly selling Sta-prest, tonic trousers in various colours, Harrington's in various colours, Brouges, Monkey boots, loafers etc. I had a well paid job for the time so I got loads of this stuff including a couple of Brutus slash neck 'Dennis The Menace' jumpers in red and black. Also a load of Trojan stuff got re-issued as E P's which I really liked. Via the Richard Allen book Jeff and I had a little suede head period at this time with us both wearing Crombie's, brogues and fluorescent socks. I was fascinated by the idea of suede heads as i had never heard of them. In Elm Park there was a gang of very sharp looking skins who all seemed to wear Slazenger v-neck jumpers with Slazenger tennis shirts underneath and loafers/brogues rather than boots. Some of them had a band called Shocks Almighty. In a way 1978 round my way looked a bit like a re-run of 69 - 71.

1979 - By this time the hearts were copying their clothes from all those photos of The High Numbers. We used to play gigs to pretty mixed audiences of straights, skins and punks until the mod revival got going in London. Charity shops were still an important place for clothes. I got a two tone blue mohair suit for 3 quid for instance. The point I would like to make about the mod revival is that to me it was much more of a swinging sixties thing as well with us kids looking back to this mythical age which seemed to be thirty years in the past rather than about twelve. Life in the mid-seventies was pretty grey and repressive and it was natural to want to re-create what seemed like a more exciting and freer time.

The Hearts early sets were mostly covers at first. We used to do a lot of Stones stuff like `Empty Heart` and `Get Off My Cloud'`. They were a massive influence. The Small Faces first LP was also very important. It had so much energy and is a better record musically than The Who`s first one (IMO).We did `Watcha Gonna Do About It` and in 79 `Sorry She`s Mine'`. Sometimes we would learn a cover, do it at a couple of gigs and then try something else. `Come on Children` was an influence on me as a singer as it taught about that sort of gospel style vocal improvisation. Jeff`s parents had an antiques stall on Romford Market and they used to get a lot of old sixties records so we did `Louise` by Paul Revere and The Raiders from a greatest hits LP of theirs. The soul covers we usually nicked from The Stones, `If You Need Me` and `Everybody Needs Somebody To Love` from the 5X5 and Got Live If You Want It EPs. From seeing The Jam I had checked out artists like Lee Dorsey and Wilson Pickett to hear the originals of some of the covers they were doing and got into soul music proper from that. *Otis Blue* by Otis Redding became my favourite. I had been aware of Motown since the mid-seventies but this stuff was obviously much bluesier.

The early Hearts originals were `Frustration'`, `I've Been Away'`, `Jimmy` and `What Am I Gonna Do` which was our first original. Later on we sometimes took a song by someone else and used it as a starting point for one of our own. For example `But She`s Mine` a John`s Children B-Side was ripped off to

make `*Extraordinary Sensations*`(the title being a quote from Oscar Wilde that was a chapter heading in a book about The Who). Other covers included `*I'm Not Like Everybody Else*` by The Kinks and earlier on `*Let's Dance*` by Chris Montez. Other influences were groups like The Yardbirds, Animals and Them. The original version of `*Beat That*` for example has the same sort of stop/start idea as `*Evil Hearted You*`.
Bob Manton (Purple Hearts)

5. A Rude Boy account from the late 70's from **Lee Barden**.

Rude Boy tales. The summer of 1979 and the newly formed 2 Tone records released *Gangster's* by The Specials. Madness appeared on the scene with *The Prince*, this heralded my obsession with Two Tone and Ska music. The music was based on the 60s Jamaican Ska music which in England had a big skinhead following. My Uncle Herbie was into Ska in the 60s and gave me a bit of a history lesson on Ska, so armed with a few facts I set about finding some original recordings. My Uncles mate Kevin Russell had still kept all his old Ska records which were kept in a big old suitcase, there must have been about 300 records, as I started listening to them the original Ska bug set in, as Two Tone took off more re-releases come out, Club Ska 67, Prince Busters Greatest Hits, Intensified volumes 1 and 2, Tighten Up, Catch This Beat, The Trojan Story all joined my collection. To start with I classed myself as a skinhead, wearing Doc Marten boots, braces, Ben Sherman and Fred Perry shirts, tonic trousers and the Harrington jacket, my uncle give me his Crombie from the 60s and I remember having a Silvery Grey tonic suit.

Around 1980 I went and saw The Selecter at the Hammersmith Palais, there was about 50 skinheads standing in a big group Sieg Heiling the whole gig and fighting any one who challenged them. The skinhead movement had always had an element of racism and after I witnessed it I wanted to get well away from it so the move to the Rude Boy culture seemed the best thing to do. The word Rude Boy originated from Jamaica and meant juvenile delinquent, in this country it was adopted by Two Tone as a name for the followers. At the time in Maidstone most skinheads come from the Shepway Estate and trouble always seemed to follow them, I remember going to a party in loose,me,Paul, Leroy, Mark, Cheryl and a few people from Shepway, we all got the bus and was going up the Loose road when the inspector got on and asked for our tickets, Leroy a punk from Bearsted had been chewing his and took it out of his mouth and give it to the inspector who promptly chucked him off the bus, we all followed him, got off the bus ,then there was an almighty smash, one of the Shepway Skins had picked up a rock and threw it through the bus window, we all ran off but didn't get far before a couple of cop cars pulled up and out jumped the Coppers and arrested us all, after a few hours in the cells we was charged and let out although most of us had done nothing we still had to go to court, we all got 'not guilty' because when the inspector got asked to point out who through the rock he more or less said they all looked the same to me, the judge had no evidence and coudn't proceed any further, the first and last time I got in trouble with the police.

The Vinter's Girls School disco was the highlight of the month and was full of different fashion groups, you had Skinheads, Mods, Heavies, Hippies, Punks and Rude Boys and a couple of Adam Ant impersonators. Friday night would consist of going to the 'offy', usually opposite Maidstone prison, to buy some cheap cider, get hammered, go to the disco and loon around. On one occasion me and a mate was dancing to *Concrete Jungle* by the Specials ,when I saw one of our other mates come in, or so I thought ,we both jumped on him and threw him about a bit, when the record finished we realised to our horror it weren't our mate but the local lunatic, thankfully one of our mates knew him and saved us from a beating. The last disco was memorable ,the disco was called Cupids Inspiration and run by a mate's brother and another guy who looked like Herman Munster, I used to take in some original Ska tunes and they would play them. I asked them to play *Madness* by Prince Buster, they said something about you and your mates smashed some of the lights while dancing, the next thing I knew they both started punching me and my mate Paul about the head, with this other people bundled in and chaos ensued. The headmistress stopped the discos, so me and few others got the blame. Discos at other places like the Howard De Walden youth club were good but trouble always seemed to be not far around the corner and in the end most of these discos faded out.

The Specials and Madness were having quite a bit of success in the charts, new groups were appearing like The Beat, The Body Snatchers, Bad Manners, reggae sounding UB40, Dexys Midnight Runners, but as all good things it had

to come to an end. Jerry Dammers steered well clear of the Ska influence for The Specials 2nd album, although a good LP, the raw sound of The Specials LP had gone. Madness had gone for a more poppy sound, The Selecter steered away from Ska and before you new it everything seemed different. The Specials hit no1 with *Ghost Town* and split not long after, Jerry Damners carried on for one more album with a new singer but it was never the same and before you knew it the whole thing was finished. Thirty years down the line The Specials reformed without Jerry Dammers and went on a sell out tour. Madness split and reformed for Madstock and still sound as good today as ever, looking back I'm glad I was around to witness the rebirth of Ska and meet people I wouldn't have otherwise, good times.
Lee Barden

6. Next up is a story of how one young man got some Soul into his life by member of UK soul act Stone Foundation; **Neil Sheasby**.

I suppose I started to draw together the strands and collect some clues at a very early age, little did I realise in those formative moments that I would soon immerse myself straight into the deep end and be forever swimming, usually against the tide, in the very deep but beautiful sea of music and its related cultures and styling's, I was in search of the knowledge, the history, the kick, the now, the next, the thrills. I became an obsessive.

I first became fascinated in the most unlikely of places. The old Southern Division home of 1970's Non - League football, Sheepy Road, Atherstone to be more precise. My Father was involved in Atherstone Town FC at the time, he was on the board of directors and one of the more laborious tasks that came with the territory was to provide Match Day announcements and entertainment which came in the form of just a handful of 45 Rpm 7" Vinyl singles that my Dad would put on repeat at every home game, before the match kicked off, at half time and at the end of the game. When I say a handful, I mean just 6 records.

They were *Telegram Sam* by T-Rex, *Indian Reservation* by Don Farndon, *Woodstock* by Matthews Southern Comfort, *The Witch* by The Rattles, *Patches* by Clarence Carter and *Under my Thumb* by Wayne Gibson.

Now, the first observation you would rightly make upon imagining that unlikely mix of audio ambience crackling out of the tannoy's on a Saturday afternoon at your Town's local football stadium is that it was more than a little odd. 22 players trotting out to the sound of German beat combo The Rattles screaming out "*Can't you see the Witch*" or Don Farndon musing over "*Cherokee tribes*" was at best faintly bizarre.

For reasons best known only to himself, My Father used to take these records home with us at the end of every match and they would reside at our house until the Adders (Atherstone Town FC) next had a fixture at Sheepy Road. This would be around 1974, I was 7 years old and already I had a red plastic toy guitar that I used to mime along to Elvis and Beatles records with and entertain relatives at family gatherings.

I made friends with the stereo early on in life, I was fascinated by the stacking of the singles, the drop down arm, the clicking and whirring and of course that sound that bleared out of the tiny speaker made by just the slightest needle dropping onto rotating plastic wax.

Soon enough I was allowed to operate the Dansette and I'd play those colourful 45's that nestled in a rack by the gram. Those 6 singles must have belonged to an elder, semi-hip cousin. No way had my Dad been out and bought them, he was more a Ted Heath / Big Band sort of fella. I played them over and over. Two stood out and I returned to them much more often than the others, they had a different sound to them - Clarence Carter's story of Patches; a sad tale of father & son, Clarence the narrator, a pleading, commanding vocal, horns complimenting, reaching out, captivating and then Wayne Gibson - *Under my Thumb*. Direct, stomping, shuffling groove, cool, and crisp. I was flabbergasted when years later I found out the Rolling Stones had hi-jacked it, I was even more outraged when I discovered that they actually wrote it and had the cheek to record it before I was even born.

I was captivated by the sound of these songs, I didn't know it then but I do now, this was my first introduction to Soul Music. 1980 was a pivotal year in my life, like a watershed. Everything became clear. The year before, 1979, I noticed change begin to take hold of the School playground. A very small pocket of older kids started to dress differently. It was a stark contrast to the part time punk uniforms all scruffy and cartoon like or the tired denim and leather clad youths that stank of petunia oil. This look opposed all that. It was neat, sharp, tidy almost conformist.

Lads replaced swapping Panini sticker cards and started swapping records, ah, those magical works of plastic art again, this time around coloured vinyl, picture discs. Lists went around certain circles. For sale lists, wants lists. This was more exciting than owning Mario Kempes from Argentina World Cup '78 sticker book, this was for keeps, to have and to hold. This was the soundtrack of our lives.

1980 arrived and the whole Mod revival was in full swing. Quadrophenia was the cult movie doing the rounds, the 2-Tone Movement was also unfolding on our doorstep in Coventry and the biggest band in the country were The Jam.

I loved The Jam, they felt like my band, like they represented kids like me, I found a place to belong, an identity, a voice. It swamped my life, took over me, I felt illuminated. 1980 also tied in with me becoming a teenager and finding my true kindred spirit, a fellow soul brother and young face, Paul Hanlon known locally as Hammy. I now had a sparring partner to plot, learn, dream and obsess with, conviction to my addiction.

We were practically the same age, he a few months my elder, we were incurables completely immersed in music and clothes, almost immediately we started a band (but that's another story) and became fascinated with the whole Modernist look and lifestyle.

But whereas most of our peers were happy enough to don a parka and a pair of Sta-prest or watch Quad over and over again. We wanted to discover more, to dig deeper, go back to the source, the roots of this movement that had just come from leftfield and swept us off our feet.

We sourced books, newspaper cuttings, films, and of course records. Traced it all backwards to move forwards. Paul Weller would name drop Curtis Mayfield, Otis Redding or The Action in that week's NME interview. That weekend we'd catch the bus into one of the big Towns or Cities and find Impressions records, Stax Records, 60's beat groups.

Dexys Midnight Runners, who we absolutely adored with their distinctive, powerful sound and imagery, covered *Seven Days Are Too Long*, *Breaking Down The Walls Of Heartache* and *The Horse* in turn we became acquainted with Chuck Woods, Jimmy Johnson and Cliff Nobles and Co. Soul Music. It became our thing.

A few Summer's later whilst conversing and plotting our next adventure to buy whatever threads or platters that held our attention at the time, we would meet and hang out in Cafes and drink copious amounts of Tea, we had a few hang outs to frequent. Winnie's café, The Corner Caff, Sen's Café, upstairs at the Roe Boat and even the Swimming bath's.

Now it was here at Atherstone Swimming baths, one fateful afternoon that our eyes would be well and truly opened to the weird and wonderful world of Northern Soul. Hammy knew one of the pool attendants reasonably well, Paul "Mitch" Mitchell.

Mitch was several years older than us but grew up on the same estate, he was on a break from his poolside duties this day and saddled over to our table in the reception area where we were sat with two plastic cups of fortnightly (too weak) brew.

After an initial bit of banter, teasing and ribbing us for our impeccable appearance, he seemed impressed at the lengths we'd go to obtain knowledge of records and the attention to detail on display for two young lads. Mitch then dropped it on us.

How did we fancy going to a real Soul do? An all-nighter.

Non-Stop dancing. A twilight world of rare Soul music. Stompers, Floaters, Baggies, talc, Towels, holdalls, backdrops, acrobatics, amphetamines, hand-claps, Keep the faith and a new religion. A way of Life.

"*Where?*"

"*Hinckley*".

"*Hinckley? Fucking Hinckley?*" I think we both spilt our brew.

Hinckley was where my Auntie Pam lived, just up the A5. A sleepy market, two horse town like ours and Mitch is telling us that hundreds of like-minded folk travel the length and breadth of the country to attend.

Furthermore to add to our astonishment he tells us they've just had Jr.Walker on and the next one that's planned will feature none other than Curtis Mayfield.

If we fancy it give him a shout and we may be able to get a lift over, he's sure we'll get in as long as we keep our heads down and cause no fuss.

We're buzzing, this is the real deal, a Northern Soul All-nighter and on our doorstep.

Then reality hits. This is 1982, Hammy's barely 15, I'm 14, still at school and we're planning on fucking off to Hinckley with grown blokes we only loosely know to a dance that doesn't begin until Midnight and doesn't finish until 8am on Sunday morning. This is going to take some planning.

To our surprise, it was fairly straightforward. I would tell my parents that I'm staying at Hammy's for the night and he'd tell his parents that he'd be staying over at mine. Simple. As long as neither parent phoned for any reason we'd be fine.

Before we knew it we were in the back of a car travelling the short journey down the A5 to Hinckley. Mitch's mate and fellow poolside life guard Steve drove. I vividly recall being overcome with excitement, anticipation but also intoxicated with nerves made all the more apparent by the fact that driver Steve, Mitch's mate, only had one arm and he was currently travelling at 100mph like James Hunt at the Monaco Grand Prix, this was probably more to do with the amphetamines that he'd just swallowed rather than any desire to become the first one armed Formula 1 champion.

The venue was also an unlikely location, It was at the Leisure Centre usually used for public swimming and sporting activities. We arrived slightly early just before the doors were due to open and already Queue's had formed to gain entrance. An odd looking bunch gathered, an unlikely mix although I'm not sure what I expected. Sharp threads was a secondary consideration, these types had their own codes in place. Oxford bags, Spencer's, Brogues, embroidered Patches both on holdalls and jackets, Club patches sometimes attached to Blazers, shirts and vests. The music and dancing was king here.

As I approached the hall's entrance doors I was certain that we or at least I would be refused entrance. We'd never really been served at a bar before but that didn't matter here, no Alcohol was on sale, purely soft drinks anyway as I'd later come to find most were too speeded out of their minds on uppers to get bogged down with ale. We just kept our heads down, carried on moving paid our fiver in and walked through the doors into the main hall.

As History now tells us this was probably the third wave of the Northern Soul scene, the original golden era of The Torch and Manchester's Twisted Wheel was just a distant memory and the legendary Wigan Casino closed it's doors for the last time in 1981. But we'd been far too young for any of that, hell, we were still too young now really but for us this was year Zero, our introduction, our beginnings into that spellbinding kingdom of Soul.

That night the dance floor was heaving, this is where the magic happened. We gazed on in wonder at this packed, pulsating floor. Watching some of the Dancers perform, and that's what it's like a performance, a show, it was like observing a work of art. Again codes, routines and a certain etiquette were involved, they would casually warm up, even that looked effortlessly cool, gliding, sliding, spinning then as the music found its way through the gears, drum breaks , choruses and vocal shouts would be met with a series of acrobatic moves, backdrops, flips, drops, handclaps. I was mesmerized by it and had seen nothing quite like it before.

It took a few more visits until I participated fully and had practiced my moves trying them out in the privacy of my bedroom, you had to respect that dance floor not just clumsily barge straight onto it. There was so much for us to take in on that first visit, from the dancing to the attire to the extraordinary music pumping across the hall, that Curtis Mayfield's performance that night was almost a sideshow. Right there and then I'd immediately fell in love with this secret, underground world of Northern Soul, it was obsessive, passionate, consuming, forever changing, totally in step with my young Modernist attitudes.

Daylight was soon seeping through and Dean Parrish's anthem *I'm On My Way* signalled the culmination of my first experience of an All-nighter, as we stepped out to the harsh, bright morning sunlight I felt delirious with excitement, informed and enlightened by the 8 hours that I'd just been witness to. I couldn't wait to return. To learn more. To belong.

Over the next few years I hardly missed an event that Chris King put on in Hinckley and we even spread our wings and ventured further afield to venues like Stafford and Stoke, by now our parents had rumbled us, we'd come clean about our all night escapades and they had begrudgingly given us the nod to continue our adventures knowing we would more than likely find a way out anyway.

I came to meet many good friends from this period all regular attendees to nighters and soul devotees whom I remain close to up to this day. I was lucky enough to see many legendary artists perform, the Leisure Centre was a real draw for putting the live acts on, Major Lance, Martha Reeves, Edwin Starr and the wonderful Ric -Tic revue which also included JJ Barnes, Al Kent, Pat Lewis and Lou Ragland, that particular night I remember the venue being absolutely rammed.

On one occasion I recall queuing in the freezing cold, nervously waiting to gain entry to the Leisure Centre when Eddie Holman was due to perform, I say nervously because I was still fairly young at this point and didn't want to draw any unnecessary attention to myself but word had got out amongst some of our Town associates and a couple of others had tagged along on this occasion, one I knew I could trust not to play up the other, Tommy, a wildcard who was already fairly inebriated with alcohol, not cool.

As we passed the doorman, my intoxicated friend enquired in somewhat slurred tones "*Ay up mate busy tonight init? Who is on?*"

"*The Holman*" came the reply.

Tommy sounded horrified " *Fuckin' hell, not fucking Marc Almond* !?"

I cringed and hastily made my way in trying to shake off any association with Tommy. Even for his naïve ignorance and drunken swagger he was allowed entry and proceeded to fall asleep in the nearest corner until turning out time.

As time passed the scene started to change again, Hinckley also switched venue to the nearby Regent Club, I think the growth of sporting commitments at the Leisure centre made it difficult to book regular nights and the all-nighters became more sporadic.

Some odd, more current names at the time, popped up to Guest as DJ's at the Regent club like Stephen *"Tin Tin"* Duffy and Jo Boxer / Subway Sect drummer Sean McLusky and around 1985 there was a shift towards the tasteless psychobilly scene spearheaded by bands like King Kurt and The Meteors, some of these undesirables filtered into the Northern soul scene more via Scooter rallies than All-nighters at first but soon enough there was divides and the scene cooled off a little for a while.

By 86' I was managing an independent record store and had amassed a sizable record collection of my own and had started DJ-ing at early Rare Groove clubs, once again Black American Soul & R n' B music reinvented, rediscovered, forever changing. This spirit will always live on.

There has always been an extraordinary bond between the music of Black America and the lifestyle of the Working Class British incurable, it's part of that traditional searing Modernist aesthetic.

In very recent times due to my involvement with playing and writing music I have been fortunate enough to work and record with a couple of renowned and respected American soul artists Steve Calloway of 60's Detroit vocal harmony group The Professionals, and the wonderful Nolan Porter. On their visits to the UK both men were enthralled by the knowledge, passion, devotion and appreciation that they encountered from the underground soul fraternity.

They were more excited, inspired, spirited and jubilant to be singing now than they have ever been. As different generations continue to discover the fascinating world of Northern soul, untarnished by commercial pressure, it's legacy will continue for many more years and that flame will indeed keep on burning.

Neil Sheasby

7. Italian Mod **Carlo Sesto** is next with his 90's Mod account.

First image that comes to my mind recollecting my mod days and nights is a picture of a small bunch of youngsters in their parkas going to an all-nighter by bus, all with their bestest three buttons outfit...nothing really appalling or noticeable at first glance...but look well after the detail...none of them, despite most being tired for long hours trips to get to the party, is sitting...and by the time of the night the bus is riding quite empty....

None of them wants to ruin the crease on their trousers and the perfectly neat shape of the suit. It all started, like for many others, with Quadrophenia, some Ska revival tunes, mainly Madness and the Italian Casino Royale, and a tape of *Tommy* by The Who that I was used to play to death in the car with my dad.

It was the end of the 80s and at the time I must confess that when I heard the first compilation on CD (sic!) of The Small Faces I found their sound quite hard and nearly progressive (sic! again). In Pisa there was a small bunch of skinheads and that helped to congregate a small community....being a mod wasn't certainly an easy thing....when you risk to be squeezed between mainstream fashionists and more popular underground trendies.

I made my choice coz Modism had a subtle fashion of rebellion and coolness that nothing else has. It was at the same time belonging to an underground secret society and growing up having yourself as your own trendsetter. I hadn't to modify or change in anything...the freedom of expressing totally my personality. Also it fitted a lot for believing in something that would make you proud to not falling when it was highly predictable given certain hard circumstances and the pressure of just going on with the mass. But, at any cost, I wanted to make my own choices.

On the last year at school we went to Paris. I remember the teacher allowing us for a free walking on our own...after the first few hours I had already finished all my money on records, posters and t shirts (I still got the "Man from U.N.C.L.E." one!) and the teacher had to finance me for the rest of the days. Yes coz collecting records was already something obsessive..I think I started it from the days of my childhood but that's another story. Was quite well chuffed when I could find some picked up choices amongst the singles of my dad...Stones, Kinks, Yardbirds, Ray Charles...and eventually even the Italian only Primitives LP...quite odd if not esoteric choices for the average Italian teen of the 60s more used to cheesy pop trivialities.

My dad and uncle's wardrobe were at the time the first source for clothing too...this at least till 1992 when, high school finished, I went for the first time to London. It was just after one of my very first rallies, hold in Viareggio where I met Mauro Berini from Rome who, between the shades of warm reflections of a September sundown on the chrome plating's of the scooters, wrote a small guide for this young mod enthusiast.

A couple of weeks later I was wearing my very own first (and only) parka...Carnaby street, Merc and Sherry's were obliged destinations and less obviously a friend of mine, Rocco, was working at the Face...that meant that the shop worked as a gathering place for an Italian crew of skinheads and mods to wander around aimless through the Big Smoke nights....it was in those circumstances that I first caught up with Micky aka Lupin....probably one of the most all round talented persons both in cool outfits and dancing steps as well as in falling in the most outrageous troubles...(which to me was quite part of a game I could dig).

Whilst moving my first steps into modernism, a constant thought was aimed to music as obvious...I was used often to save money of my Saturday pizza with my classroom mates to buy some vinyl more delicious plates. At the time my main music provider was a shop in Florence where I could find Rubbles, Pebbles and Kent Northern compilations.

By 1993 I was starting to attend more mod rallies all round Italy, that actually meant in the north side of the peninsula. The Easter mod rally in Rimini, later to be called "The Italian Job", was the main appointment for all the mods of the sunny peninsula.

Sleepless nights were always preceding the event.

Going to Rimini was a kind of initiation. I waited for months, I was already receiving the DTK bulletin, through which mods could get in touch and be updated on last news and events. In times when internet was only a trick for sci-fi films that was the only way that got you linked to the fellas. You couldn't say you were a proper mod though if you haven't been to Rimini.

As for all things, my straightened circumstances were allowing quite restricted means but, as for many of us, that was nicely balanced by a never ending enthusiasm and our young vital batteries. I managed to go to Rimini and come back just after the all-nighter, without any sleep to save on accommodation.

My journeys by train to go to mod do's were always an agony lasting a few hours and some train changes.

I was dressed with my smartest out gear when I entered the Cheers pub that afternoon of many moons ago. Shivers down my spine already when out of the station I started to see scooters buzzing around.

I was literally devouring any image, any sound, looking at clothes, buying modzines and the un-missable rally patch like a campaign ribbon for your army coat. There was a big trade of tapes at the time...after all it was not certainly easy to find that obscure music we were attracted like by a devious magical pied piper.

The music was mainly northern soul based though, being the Rimini gathering quite an international event, with loads of people coming from Germany, Austria and England...some seeds of more acid rhythm and blues were started to be planted amongst the youngest of us. I was honestly disappointed at the beginning by the lack of ska tunes and especially 2 tone...but that was one of the little things to be thrown in to keep boneheads away. Probably the floor-fillers at that time were still *Groovin With Mr Bloe*, Maximillian T*he Snake* and Chubby Checker *At The Discothèque* with the DJ lowering the volume to make the crowd sing along the chorus and clapping in rhythm.

By late 1993 and the following year I immerged myself as intensely as I could in the scene and it was in that September that I met my mod bro Andrea "Mez" Mezzini...it was at the Bibione Mod rally and we shared a dumpy room for a fistful of quids. Another Andrea, Mattioni, was probably the most popular DJ spinning northern but also cool latin jazzy stuff and his sets were quite well balanced by Trisha's (an Irish mod girl living in Italy) ones...whose hits were none else but The Castaways *"Liar, Liar"* and Strawberry Alarm Clock *Incense And Peppermints* frantically danced by the young dandies over watched by the frowns of the "white socks".

These were the years when Untouchables were starting to be our pole star in terms of outlook and coolness and their music was represented by The Clique and The Aardvarks. Hipsters, Chelsea boots and cufflinks were making their way in my mind, The Creation, The Smoke, The Eyes provided the soundtrack for our nights.

Summer 1994 will always be kept in my memory for the Modstock event in Saarbrucken at the German border with France. Travelling abroad was definitely a big experience. The Untouchables started to make a yearly appointment in the continent and the thing lasted for four years. It was The International Mods a Go-Go in Barcelona in 1995 and Groovin' Gourmands in La Rochelle in 1996 and eventually the Italian Job in Cattolica in 1997.

All the most influential faces were present...all the top gunners djs from any nation represented and all the bestest bands were there. The locations were lovely holidays resorts...so you could make some tourism and enlarge your horizons and spread your views...and believe me...WE DID! especially the latter if you know what I mean.

Meeting so many like-minded people or maybe so many like fucked up minded people allowed cultural exchanges of any sort. Again I'm pretty sure you know what I mean. In the summer of 1995 I received a postcard from London from a German buddy called Stephan Golowka (to be known later as a top DJ)...after the greetings there was a PS note advising me of a Art Wood gig in Lyon some days later and no further notice.

It took some tricks to find the means for the trip but since Modstock, like a Nouvelle Verne character I started to get to places, events and meet people - more weird and adventurous. It was by asking through record shops after quite an odyssey night journey that I finally reached Le Voxx bar where the scenesters were sipping their drinks in the sunny afternoon. I was the only Italian.

Making friends and travelling I guess was a great thing. Like an underground jet set we moved and you always found somebody keen to help you with accommodation and stuff. Like in Paris, where, at the first mod rally hold in La Ville Lumiere, I had the chance of a scooter ride to Versailles, where just in front of the palace there was a super cool 60s/mod bar.

By mid 90s the white socks were replaced by the white of loafers and belts...the tide was turning and while I was still in my early 20s some older generation mods were starting not to accept the changes and the evolutions of the scene. Some were stuck to the 80s or whatever 79 revival...some had problems of a more personal kind.

We mostly didn't give a shit about Paul Weller and co., neither about moans and politics and we just wanted to have our well deserved dose of 60s coolness and fun, either by exercising our Northern Soul steps or by just swinging our hips drawing pictures in the air when Mickey Finn's *Garden Of My Mind* or The Who's *Circles* were spun.

I was buying original singles through Record Collector and searching through any shop for deadstock vintage clothes. In 1997 I was already set up a small business with records, the natural evolution of my past trades...and helping with the artwork of the Italian version of the Modstock flyer let the Untouchables allowing me of a free pass for the rally nights, this, helped by my sales let me attend another huge event crowned by the Herbie Goins gig. Just a couple of months later, I felt my London calling and moved to the UK.

Everything was exciting and while the scene both in the UK and Italy but possibly anywhere was splitting, I was rampaging towards the zenith of suave.

Most of the hipsters in the Big Smoke didn't care about politics and were attending like me any event organized by the Untouchables and the New Untouchables. The acid jazz scene first and the Brit pop scene later gave their contribution to revitalize the scene of fresh 60s enthusiasts.

The main club night was the Mousetrap, a terrific night on two floors, definitely the place to be for the gotha of the movement, both a theatre of experimentation and together the epitome of modernism. On top floor northern, R&B and latin jazz spinned by the likes of Catford Chris, Lee Miller, Gavin Evans, Pid and Nick Hudson were setting the pace. In the basement mini skirted chicks were raving to the hippest psychedelic sounds played by Rob Bailey, Speed, Nigel Lees and Mark Ellis to mention just a few well known suspects.

Life was hard for me for the rest of the week, but God...on the weekend i felt like God to quote Townshend. I made lots of friends there and in particular with the Streatham lot...Jack White, Jayne Pountain, Franny, Ian Olsen, Rob, Mandy, Paul Owers, Trevor, JP, Anja and god knows how many others.

We were 100% dedicated. It was an obsession, it was lifestyle, it was our religion, it was our fun, it was our youth. And fuck...I would challenge any bloody Pete Meaden or Weller to say we were not the hippest ever and I would humbly add that we still are! New Years Eves at Ruby's in Carnaby St, Gods *Hey Bulldog*, Lordy Lord in Chinatown, Bulldog Breed *Halo In My Hair*, walking steps in Regent St eyeing some other fellas, dressed to kill, reaching the Purple Pussycat, Herbie Goins *Cruisin'*, the soul nighters at 100 Club, features at ITV studio off Carnaby to record a special about mods and rockers, Don Fardon *I'm Alive*, the first New Untouchables event at London Bridge with Art Wood and the Downliners Sect, Etta James *Seven Day Fool*, the girls at Babzotica...extraordinary sensations that I shared with many of you.

To make it all more real, by the end of the 90s even more 60s bands were making reunions. In some cases they were just all right, in others definitely good but most important for us was just being in front of our myths just like our 60s cousins did at their time. I remember seeing Georgie Fame at the Jazz Cafe' in January 1998 and some months later The John's Children exploding their pop art punk set just off Leicester Square at the Notre Dame Ballroom. The pinnacle was probably the IOW rally of 1998 when on stage there were The Yardbirds and the legendary Action with their complete line up but I must mention also the amazing gig of the reformed Rupert's People at the Hastings Easter rally of 1999 surrounded by a crowd holding sparkles and Brian Auger for the London mod run in 2001.

Some moments are just indelible and the motion of sensations is still sharp in the memory as the goose bumps on our skins I assume were often shared by the performers themselves once again in front of their own audience they thought they left back in the 60s.

In 1999 I started djing myself. My baptism of fire was at Mousetrap. My hands were slightly shaking while putting the stylus on the first record but it went ok and, I had the luck of getting more thrills by playing again and again at scene rallies and clubs all over the continent and once even in the US in the first decade of the new century.

Djing is cool stuff, music is important for anybody but especially for the sophisticated mod collector and having the chance to communicate through it by spinning, give sense to the maniac never ending records archaeology.

The 2000s saw me back in Italy, back to an up and downs life, still with mod at heart. I founded the Impossibles organization and with the help of Frantz and Soulful Jules I attempted to involve all the Italian mods and make a move on, after seeing my scene disintegrating for silly music moans, politics or even more sadly for egoist interests and presumption.

The internet guaranteed a new faster way of communication and links and the experience kicked in well and led to the organization of a couple of major events in Venice, the "Hazy shade of winter" in particular, starring The Music Machine and a fresh djs line up with Tony Sanchez, S. Golowka and Steve Bowstead all of them well established faces and great people.

My attempt by the long terms was quite foolishly ambitious and ingenuous...the scene split in some ways was even going wider...with the purists fringe of the early mod taste pushing towards the 50s RnB and on the other side the regency Carnaby dandy style dying for more outrageous challenges of early 70s funk and hard rock. My generation also was starting to settle down, some left, some made families, some decided to become "adults". I didn't.

By mid 2000s I was keeping on wandering around in my satin shirts, damask ties, hipsters and Victorian like chisel toed shoes. Still looking for records, still fancying chicks, still travelling, still refusing the way somebody else wanted to decide right for me. In 2004 I was privileged to be in the dj line up for the new Modstock, this time hold in London, along with many cool fellas and overall aside the names of Pretty Things, Yardbirds, Prisoners, JTQ and The Creation. After ten years from the Saarbrucken event it was for me the bestest recognition of my lifelong service to the scene. Certainly not the final act.

Later that year I moved once again to London. Despite the help and support of Irish Paul, unlucky circumstances forced me to a just few months stay. The scene in the meanwhile evolved again...Ebay and social networks became fundamentals assets for the movement as long as low cost fare flights made the scenesters gathering at events held all around Europe and the success of this new trend overwhelmed the old traditional mod monthly clubs appeal. Everything was easier by one way now though that doesn't mean better.

Today the fever for me is still high, I don't miss any 60s acts reunion, I saw The Fire, Chris Farlowe, the amazing Fleur De Lys complete with Sharon Tandy, The Birds, Dean Parrish and The Seeds. The new tech means give me the chance of meeting old legends by the like of Eyes, Syn and Kaleidoscope singers. I still spend all my spare money in records and clothes. I dunno about tomorrow, life is hard for everybody...we just have chosen to taste it in deep and to keep ourselves busy looking good.
Carlo Sesto

8. **Steve Sparkes** account of Raving in the summer of love.

Sometime in about March or April 1989 three friends and I were keen to see what all the fuss was behind this acid house phenomenon that was sweeping the U.K. by storm.

Yes before you say it, "Fucking '89? We were raving in the summer of love, '88" I know there some of you out there that can lay claim to being one or the first 'cheesy quavers' on the planet I've heard it all before but for us four this is our story.

The four of us being Ian, Richard, Steve (Richard's older brother) and myself. We were all down the pub, which an old school friend happened to live in, doing our usual thing playing pool, drinking Kronenburg 1664 and nipping out for the odd spliff now and then and listening to the Deep Heat album and Adamskis' *Live And Direct* on the newly acquired CD juke box.

House music had been around a while and I myself can remember going to the Kent Hall discos on a Monday night (under 18's) and Saturday nights (over 18's) and listening to this new house sound, hearing the likes of Russ Browns *Find A Way*, Razes' *Jack The Groove* and Steve 'Silk' Hurley's *Love Can't Turn Around* amongst others thinking this has got something this new sound. So much better than the 'Shit factory' stuff that was also getting played at the time like the Bros and Rick Astley bilge.

There was the four of us in the pub when a few of the others started to turn up, Mick and his ever trusty side kick Rusty, Daz, an old mate from the village I grew up in Jason, (lifelong friend to me) plus a few others. This was a Friday night and people were making plans for the weekend, bit of billy and an 'enry, sorted!

It wasn't long before discussions started to turn to this rave thing that was taking over a lot of peoples weekends. There was talk of a Biology party taking place the next night at a secret location all we had to do was get tickets and find out where the venue was and we were away.

Plans were made to meet up the next morning to get up to Oxford Street and Soho market to suss out this scene. So it was that I picked the other three up in my trusty, no rusty, old MG Metro and we set off up the M20 to London. All the way up there, with the tunes blaring, we were buzzing with the excitement of finding out what the shops and market had in stall for us, records, clothing, fliers and the chance of securing a ticket for the Biology rave happening (somewhere) that night.

On arrival in London we made straight for Soho and found somewhere to park, yes you could quite easily back then. We had a mooch around Berwick Street Market and found our way to Black Market Records store where Ian got a copy of the Frankie Knuckles album on the Trax label, a true classic which I'm also privileged to own.

While we were in there we enquired about the aforementioned Biology rave that night, the guy behind the counter was a bit cagey to start with but eventually sold us tickets for the sum of twenty quid each, bearing in mind this was 1989 and twenty quid was quite a bit then but "fuck it" we all said and bought the tickets. We all came out of that shop beaming from ear to ear at the thought of going to a proper rave and not the usual clubs in town or house party or village hall disco.

Next we made our way to Mash clothing store, which was one of the reasons I wanted to go, eager to acquire some new clobber. Once finding the shop we had a good search through the stuff in there, taking the piss out of some of it shouting "here moosh, who the fuck would ware this" much to the annoyance of other shoppers and staff. While in there I bought myself what could only be likened to a hippie hoody, for want of a better description, I must've looked a right cunt in it but at the time I felt like the 'mutt's nuts'.

After spending the day in London we were buzzing back down the M20 to Maidstone and after dropping the lads off it was in, dinner, shower, change and back out again round to Steve and Richards house to meet up with Ian and get to the pub. We eventually set off back up the motorway, it was well into Saturday night by this time. The thing to do with these illegal parties was to tune into one of the pirate radio stations and listen out for meeting points, our choice being the great old station Sunrise, which everyone used to tape the sets by the then up and coming DJ's of the time, some of which went on to become household names, and play them back in their cars. This was quite difficult to do living at the bottom of the Downs and London being up over the other side, you either had to know someone who lived quite high up or drive around listening out for a good signal and try to tape it on a 'wog box', something I used to do a bit later when I worked in a bakers as a night packer in Bermondsey and still have a friends FM tape from Christmas 1990.

We eventually found out our first meeting point was Blackheath, actually on the heath, so after shooting about all over London we headed for there. Thinking back we must've really caned the petrol driving here, there and everywhere but we were still buzzing with the excitement and anticipation of getting to this Biology do, with our new clobber on and the distinctive 'diddly diddly diddly diddly" opening bars of Frankie Knuckles *Your Love* a sound that still gives me tingles on the back of my neck and memories flooding back, it was like a 'pied piper' type sound calling all us teenagers to some far off field to trudge around in mud off your face.

Once at Blackheath quite a few cars had started to gather and there was people standing on bonnets of cars dancing to car stereos pumping the acid beats, obviously on the gear already, we met up with a few like-minded people from different areas and all got chatting, the thrill of going raving in everyone's eyes. After a fair bit of socialising someone shouted to hush up a bit they were going to give out the next meeting point. The word soon got around that it was to be in front of Charing Cross station on the Strand so into the cars we piled and shot up the A2 to central London where, again, quite a few cars had gathered and the people there looked like the real hardcore ravers who'd done this many times before, I can remember admiring these two dudes with their long, centre parted, hair and almost hippy style clothing, thinking they looked cool.

After a bit more banter the next meeting point was announced over the radio, Liphook, fucking Liphook? Where the fuck is that? turns out it's down the A3 in Hampshire, for fuck's sake! So in we get, find a petrol station, fill up and we're off across London to pick up the A3 and before long we're going past Tolworth Towers and on our way, the novelty rapidly wearing off, well for muggings here anyway, as I'd stayed sober as the designated driver. We finally get to Liphook, or the outskirts anyway, and by now quite a convoy of motors had built up and there we are, like the blind leading the blind, trying to find our final destination.

We ended up driving up and down country lanes looking for sign of lasers in the sky or the boom boom of the bass of a big open air party in a field, each time following a different car saying "*here we go these look like they know where they're going*" fat fucking chance of that and couple with the growing interest of the local old bill and me panicking as I knew at least one person in the car was 'holding'. We ended up taking stock of the situation franticly searching for a signal from the pirate station when all of a sudden its announced its not in poxy Liphook and we've got to get to South Mims Service Station as this is the next meeting point, I gotta tell you I was ready to say bollocks to it and piss off home there and then, but, being the driver and seeing the others wanting to get to this party I soldiered on so it was back up the A3 onto the M25 and off to South Mimms.

When we got there this whole fiasco of a night seemed like it was all going to be worth it as the car park was packed with hundreds of ravers dancing on car bonnets and generally having a blinding Saturday night. Everyone was waiting for that radio message to let us know where this party was going to be but to be honest I was glad to be out of the driving seat for a bit and mill about South Mims Service Station chatting to people off their tits (and having a good gore at the copious amounts of fanny some of the geezers had in tow).

Time was getting on now and it must've been about 3AM when word started to get out that it had been given out on the radio that the Biology Rave had indeed taken place in Liphook but had been shut down by the police, selfish cunts did they not know we'd spent twenty quid on a ticket? They probably did and had a good laugh about it, as did the organisers of this rave as they must have earned a good few quid on ticket sales. So to the organisers of Biology thanks for fucking up a Saturday night for us four!

We ended up getting back on the motorway and home in the early hours completely shattered but it never dampened our spirits as the next day we all had a good laugh about 'what could've been'. We ended up going to copious amounts of raves together in the end and had a fucking good few years at it going to parties all over the place and some right seedy ones at that, not to mention some right dodgy East London clubs and warehouse parties and nearly every time someone had their car stereo nicked but I could be here all day reminiscing and I'm sure you've all got your own memories and stories to tell but to me raving was a great time to while away my late teens and early twenties.

Steve Sparkes

THE FAN CLUB SECRETARIES
"THE SMALL FACES FAN CLUB"
52-55 CARNABY STREET
LONDON, W.1

18th June 1966.

Hi fans,

Well here's your chance to put the Fab Faces at the Top, where they belong.

All you have to do is, buy as many Melody Makers as you can afford, and get all your friends to buy them and enter the Poll Contest for the best Top Group, which we all agree is the Small Faces.

And of course we also agree that "Sha La La La Lee" was the greatest disc of the year. And fans, here's your chance to show, Stevie, Mac, Plonk and Kenny exactly what you can do!

Love Pauline

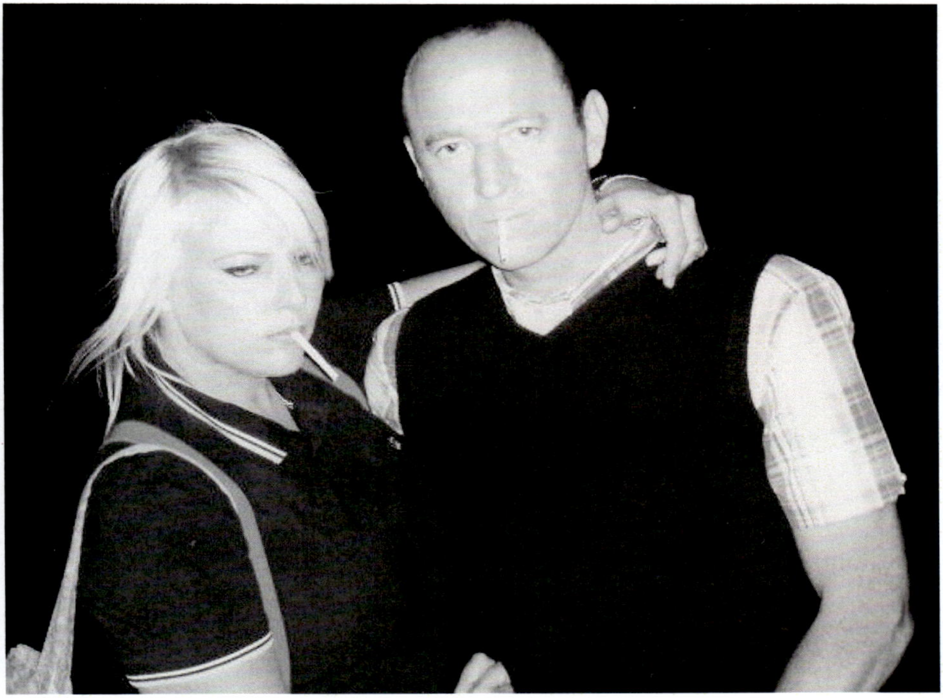

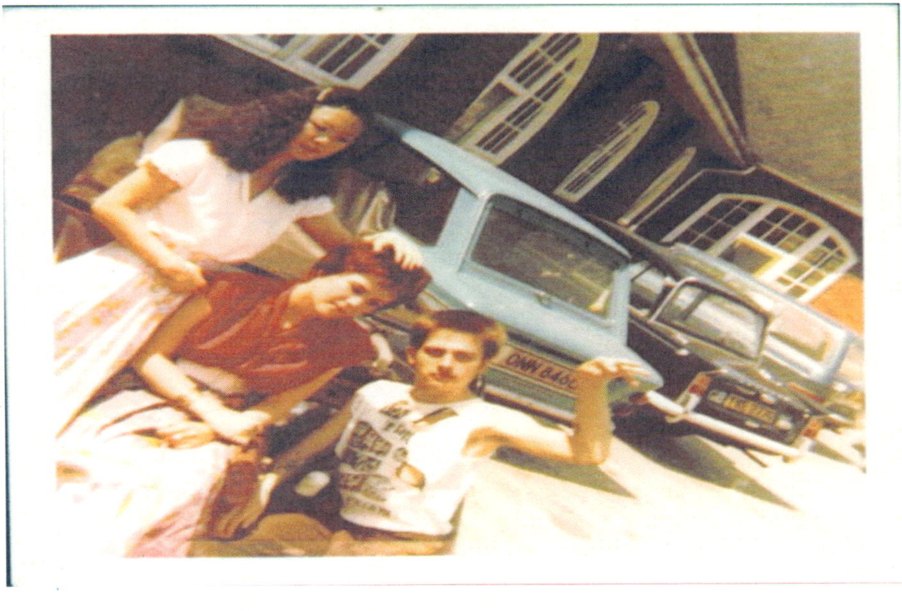

9PM - 6AM

THE ASTORIA,
157 CHARING CROSS ROAD,
LONDON, WC2.

FANTAZY FM

PRESENTS
THE RAVE PART 1
BANK HOLIDAY WEEKEND
SUNDAY 26th/MONDAY 27th MAY 1991

10. Another Soul account from **Chris Harris** setting off in the early 80's.

When our love for Northern Soul really began it was back in '81. We had done the Mod revival thing for 3 years and had obviously had been well into 60s Soul, Stax, Motown, R&B we all collected Sue singles as well as a lot of the American blues stuff from the sixties. I also collected a lot of Ska stuff on Blue Beat, Ska Beat, Island and other labels although this tended to be frowned on by a lot of people as not serious music.

We had just spent about a year in Mods Psychedelic phase going to clubs like Planets that were very 67 a lot of early Floyd, Double breasted jackets, guardsman jackets, joss sticks, back combed hair and paisley shirts and by mid '81 we were becoming fed up with that scene as it became more swinging sixties and less clothes orientated. One of my friends Mike who later became a really good northern soul dancer even started doing yoga and transcendental meditation, it was time for change.

One night after a club three of us were round my house and we started playing stuff by the Sims Twins, Jimmy McGriff, Billy Preston, Gene Chandler, Phil Upchurch, James Brown, Wyder K Frog, The Impressions, The Alan Brown Set, Jimmy James, Geno Washington and lots of Motown all the mod stuff we had stopped playing in favour of the psychedelic music that was the then mod fashion. We all agreed even if everyone else stuck with it we were going to ditch the psychedelic and go back to basics. The next week we all had college boy hair-cuts we opted for a new dress code of open necked high collared Ben Sherman's or Brutus shirts with mohair suits or Roberto Carlo tops with tailored trousers with split or stepped seams with buttons above. Worn mainly with Brogues or flat leather soled Italian basket weave shoes. All we needed now was somewhere to go that played the sounds we wanted to hear.

We heard about the 6TS Club from the East London Soul and R&B DJ Dick Combes he ran The Southend Rhythm and Soul Society much loved by the East London Mods and had a small record shop down Carnaby Street he could get most tunes for you. So the next Saturday me Chris, Bobby and Dillon who we used to call Jim because he thought it sounded more mod made our way to the 100 club for our first all-nighter we loved it and danced all night to the smooth soul of Major Lance, Jackie Ross, Candy and The Kisses, Chuck Jackson etc. We thought the music was the smoothest, coolest most mod we had ever heard. As the night went on we learnt a lot of new dance steps that we more intricate than "The Block". I noticed that the best dancers didn't leave the floor with there feet except when doing an athletic move or something they seemed to glide effortlessly. Bob Morris, Smooth and a few of the other East London lot were down there but most people were older than us and either Northern Soulies or from other club scenes.

I bought five singles that night *Out On The Floor* by Dobie Gray (which became the London Mods Anthem that year) *Aint No Soul Left In These Old Shoes* by Major Lance, *The Sweetest Feeling* by Jackie Wilson, *Our Love Is In The Pocket* by Darrell Banks and *The Right Track* by Billy Butler which we liked so much we called our scooter club after it.

So after a week of non-stop dance practicing and with our handful of soul records we headed down to our local weekly dance which was on a Thursday night at the King Charles Hotel in Chatham. At that time the order of the day down there was Yardbirds, The Who, The Kinks, some revival stuff with a splattering of well known Stax and Motown. We asked the DJ to play our records and he did I remember how nervous we were before we started dancing when we started everyone stopped dancing on the first song and watched us then by the second song people were copying us they loved it by the next week people only wanted to dance to Northern Soul and Motown although now some of the songs may seem passé the big tunes then were *Give Me Little Sign* Brenton Wood, *Agent Double O'Soul* Edwin Starr, *Lover* The Delites, *Fortune Teller* Benny Spellman, *Right Back Where We Started* from Maxine Nightingale, *Everybody Is Going To The Love In* Bob Brady and The Concords as well as Chairman Of The Board, Dean Parish, Gloria Jones, all the Disco Demand, Inferno, Black Magic and Casino Classics stuff. There also always seemed to be someone with bootleg copies of the latest biggie at the London clubs so our musical intake improved even in deepest Kent.

I was working in the city at the time and pretty soon had a club to go to every night of the week except Monday. There were Northern soul nights at the Whisky a Go Go , The 100 Club, Barons , The Greyhound in Chadwell Heath as well as in Kent The Springhead Tavern. run by some of the Gravesend Mods and Bogarts in Strood which played some of the best music I ever heard anywhere the DJs were Graham and Keith who were two mods from the sixties. Keith had a legendary record collection and was an Art Teacher from up north who was a regular at the Twisted Wheel.

Then there were the Thanet Coasters dos run by Martin and Joanne which were excellent.

By January 1982 we were all into Northern in a big way our clothing had changed it was the beginning of the Scooter Boy thing and we were running round in baggy army greens and boxing boots. But at night we tended to dress in tailored or high waisted pleated bags that weren't flared but had turn ups we wore these with flat shoes but still with button down shirts and white or red socks. We all carried bags covered with patches.

After our local dance finished that Easter Thursday we all rode our scooters to the rally in Scarborough on the first night we danced to Northern in a giant Marquee on the camp site and the next night though we went to a club in the town everywhere you went all you heard Northern Soul .They said there were around 15000 there that weekend it was great.

Later that year Barry one of our friends started to out shine the rest of us on the dance floor with longer and faster spins, back drops, splits, flips, high kicks you name it he could do it. I was round his house one time and his Mum said you like this Northern Soul don't you I said yes she said well come and look at this. We all trooped up to Barry's bedroom where she showed us a six foot by three foot hole in the carpet she said he just practices dancing every night we then knew why he was so good.

Around this time I can remember about 70 of us taking over a car park just outside Great Yarmouth and with the help of a loud car stereo dancing to Northern Soul for about 3 hours all trying to out do each others moves. The locals were amazed. We liked Reggae, Rocksteady and R&B but it was Northern Soul we loved.

By late 1982 our scooter club had all become casuals with wedge haircuts although we still went on the scooter runs we now dressed for daywear in Lois jumbo cords, Diadora trainers, Pringle jumpers with Burberry fly fronted macs and jackets. For the soul dos though it was still pegged or pleated trousers with a La Coste polo top .This look lasted until about 84 when we dropped the obvious designer gear around this time we would travel to clubs up north particularly if we could go and see a footie match as well. Of course later on we got into rarer and better sounds and travelled to some of the classic all-nighters but the youthful energy of those early days will always be what made Northern Soul No1 in my heart.
Chris Harris

11. An interview with **Paolo Hewitt**. Paolo has written countless words on British youth culture and in this interview he speaks about where his passion for the subject came from.

It's 1963 and a young boy is humming and singing the words '*She loves you yea, yea, yea*' all day long. The young boy was a certain Paolo Hewitt later known for his youth, football and Mod culture related books like Beat

Concerto, The Soul Stylist and the Fashion of football to name just a few. The aforementioned Beatles song was Paolo's earliest memory of being captivated by music. The boy was five years old and I am certain he would have not been the first toddler to hum along to the fab four in the 1960's.

At the time Paolo was living with his Foster mother with whom he lived between the ages of four and ten years old before moving onto the Burbank Children's Home in Woking, Surrey. Paolo does, however, recall being awestruck by watching The Beatles on the London Palladium. As the years in the children's home rolled by and the small boy grew into his clothes so did his passion for music grow in his heart. This passion would later manifest itself alongside his other love. The other mistress was reading and writing. By the age of seven Paolo was submerging himself in what he termed 'Escapist books'. Examples of these books were "Treasure Island" and stories from Greek Mythology.

Paolo recalls a local shop owner would occasionally donate unwanted records to the Children's home and because of this Paolo was exposed to a wide variety of musical genres. The Dubliners would get played in the home alongside the Woodstock album (a prized possession of his friend Colin who also lived in the home). Having access to many styles of music and many bands was a 'good education' say's Paolo.

Other memories of the music of the day were Bowies *'Space Oddity'*, a bit of Motown and a Faces album that 'got under' Paolo's skin. Everything about the album thrilled and excited him. The band members represented the kind of things that Paolo aspired to 'Fun, girls, freedom'. The album sleeve says it all. Several years later another boy from the neighbourhood called Paul Weller gave Paolo a tape cassette with six Small Faces songs recorded on it. In return Paolo gave Weller a tape with Faces songs. That is how Paolo discovered The Small Faces. He would later go on to write "The Young Mod's Forgotten Story".

By the time Paolo was attending St John The Baptist secondary school in 1971 the Brutus shirt, Loafers and Sta-prest look of the Suede head dominated the playground. Sadly Paolo was only getting two shillings pocket a week so he was not in a position to buy the clothes he longed for. Paolo does recall sporting a tartan scarf that he loved which he wore in honour of Rod Stewart. Paolo remembers Pete, his mate from school arriving at school one day with a £40 Crombie on that his dad had bought him. The headmaster told the boy to go home. The boy went home only to return later with his angry father who gave the headmaster a bollocking.....and rightly so.

Nineteen seventy one meant the radios and local disco's played Trojan alongside Prog rock bands like E.L.P and Yes and then Bowie, Bolan and Roxy music. Paolo commented that he liked the early Genesis stuff and has fond memories of a song originally recorded by the Young Rascals and later by David Cassidy called *How Can I Be Sure*. Paolo also retold the story of the chatter in the playground the day after Top Of The Pops showed Bowie put his arm around Mick Ronson during a performance of *Starman*. The teenager's questioned the mystery of Bowies sexuality. The shocking seventies eh! One day Paolo arrived at school with a copy of *Alladin Sane* tucked under his arm. The headmaster considered the semi naked body of Bowie to be offensive and inappropriate. This resulted in a three canning 'Bend over boy' session from the head.

By the age of fourteen Paolo was an avid reader of the New Musical Express (NME). '*The NME was my bible*' remarked Paolo. He had also decided that writing was what he wanted to do and in nineteen seventy eight enrolled in the North London Polytechnic to study English Literature. During this time he wrote for the student mag called Fuse. It was also around this time that Paolo returned to listening to the soul music of Motown and Stax. One night his search for soul led him to discover a small club near the Belsize tube station, with only twenty young people in it. The only music they played was soul on the type of labels that Paolo was listening to.

Paolo spent a large part of the seventies going to see bands like The Faces at Reading festival, which was '*a very disappointing*' performance from his beloved band. He also saw The Who at the Valley which was and still is the home of Charlton Athletic football club. Paolo saw The Who again at Hammersmith Odean where they opened with *I Can't Explain* and "*are still opening with it*" he said. Paolo also nearly saw Led Zeppelin at Earls Court but he fell asleep three times. A local band from Woking called Squire also had gigs attended by Paolo. Squire would go on to be included in the list of Mod revival of the late seventies.

Paolo informed that he would go and see any band and would often frequent the Guildford Civic Hall on Sunday afternoon. Additional to Paolo's list of bands seen were Dr Feelgood, Bob Dylan, The Rolling Stones and another Woking band with local lad's called The Jam. "*Music was my life blood, I was obsessed with music*" says Paolo. This passion must have been evident because one of his teachers once said to him that "*if you knew as much about maths and English as you do music you would be Einstein*".

It was 1976 and Paolo was into the punk of the day. He wore Levi jeans from Milletts and White tee shirt and looked like the Fonz from Happy Days. Paolo was listening to The Clash and The Sex Pistols. He remembers going into a local record shop called Aercos. He asked the girl behind the counter for a copy of *Anarchy In The UK*. The girl collected the record and *"threw it on the counter in disgust"*. This was why Paolo liked punk.

Paolo was just another boy about town and one day another young male called Enzo introduced him to one of his friends whose name was Paul Weller. Paolo would continue to see Weller around Woking and their relationship built up over the occasional nod and a *"you're alright, you're Enzo's mate"*.

The Jam gigged their way around Woking and Paolo followed them around. One day Paolo entered a local pub called 'The Cotteridge'. He spotted Weller sitting by himself. Paolo was faced with a dilemma go and speak to him or avoid him. The problem was that only recently The Jam had been pictured on the front cover of his bible, the NME. Paolo thought if he talks to the lonely Weller he may think it's only because of the NME but if he doesn't talk to him it could also be taken wrongly. In the end Paolo did speak to Weller and they spent the evening getting drunk together.

In 1979 Paolo, who was now living in London got his first writing commission. It was a two hundred word piece for the Melody Maker on a Mod festival at The Marquee. Squire were amongst the bands performing. Paolo informed me that recently he rediscovered and read that article whilst doing some research for his latest book on the clothes The Beatles wore in the British Library. So, Paolo started to get a wage. Now he had money to buy the clothes he had been deprived of during all those years living under the roof of Children's homes.

Paolo's writing career progressed and he interviewed The Jam countless times and found a new job in working for his bible of the past decade the N.M.E. I for one spent my youth reading Paolo's words in the music mag. Paolo say's the office was a strange place to be. It was an office with divided loyalties because of the music that the employees favoured and championed.

Throughout Paolo's youth he interviewed the likes of Marvin Gaye, Stevie Wonder and Nina Simone. Of Marvin, Paolo says when he interviewed him *"I didn't know my music"* he referred to being too young (knowledgably) to really make the most of the opportunity. Of Nina he said he had to *"past the test"* before she would even allow him to interview her. Paolo owned twenty seven albums by her. He was clearly a massive fan and still is.

Another memorable interview was between Paolo and Steve Marriot. It was 1984 and they met in an old haunt of Marriott's in Denmark Street. On Paolo's arrival Marriott said *"Shall we go somewhere else this place was a shit hole then and it's a shit hole now"*. Paolo did however buy Marriott a drink before they left after Marriott said "*I'll have a Brandy and a Whisky coz you get expenses and I don't*". The interview was then conducted sitting on boxes outside a music shop. One of the questions that Paolo asked came from Weller. "*Why don't you make blistering R&B records anymore like you used to do?*" Marriott's reply was "*Tell him why don't you come to one of my gig's you cunt*".

The interview continued with further discussion around music, bands, football (Paolo chose Spurs after telling himself that whichever team won the semi-final game between Spurs and Derby he would support. This was 1967) the Hip Hop of 85, Acid Jazz and I asked two more burning questions. I wanted to know what Paolo preferred leather shoes or suede shoes. He answered Leather tongue and tassel loafers. When asked of a favourite shirt he said a Blue and Black tartan check Brutus that he once owned.

With that he gulped down his Perroni, I sipped my Red wine and we both headed off in the directions of our required tube stations. On my journey home I reflected on the time spent with Paolo. It was a pleasure chatting with the man who evidently has a deep rooted love for music and youth cultures. He knows his stuff too.

Paolo Hewitt interview

12. **Dick**, who attended many Untouchables Mod Rallies in the '90s account of scooters, mates and trying to pull.

We didn't really have a plan Lee and I, all we knew that there was a scooter rally in Weymouth at the weekend and we were going. I had only ever known the local scooter ride outs and the mod rallies to Margate before and were hearing the stories of the big scooter club weekends around the country and thought this is where all the mods go, not just hop on the train to London and hang out in Carnaby Street or Kensington indoor market then wait until somewhere like the Groovy Cellar opened and stood at the back looking at all the much cooler than ours clothes they were wearing. We wanted something bigger, a couple of hundred scooters in a car park in Margate was nothing, and we wanted to see thousands.

We didn't have much money between us, so decided to save costs and go to Weymouth on just the one scooter, mine. So that Wednesday morning we spent cleaning the scooter and bolting a few more lights and mirrors on and made a sign for the back, "The Arrivals scooter club, 1983 Margate to Weymouth Trans Global Express". There wasn't a scooter club as such, just Lee and I, we were sort of between clubs, the Triple S scooter club had recently sort of dwindled away (still have my patch though, and that of the Kent Coasters before that) so started we one ourselves that morning, and we thought it sounded cool, a bit like a name that could be used for a mod band, and the Trans Global part was from The Jam track.

The following conversation took place, but I can't remember now who said which line

"*So what shall we do now*",

"*Let's just go*"

"*But it's Wednesday*"

"*Yeh lets just take our time and see who we can pick up on the way, we can go up through the Medway towns then across to Maidstone and across country, bound to be lots of mods going and we can crash out wherever*".

So off we went, tent and pack on the back and modded up. Late afternoon on a Wednesday isn't really a hive of mod activity in Chatham town centre, (we had always thought of Chatham as a mod mecca around that time, so many people from there used to come down to Margate at the weekends) the scooter was parked up behind the shopping centre and we just wondered about from café to café looking for the local mod hang out, there must be one we thought, every little town had one and this was a big town, must be one, then we met Tracy. Don't know who saw who first or where exactly, but this lovely girl in green trench coat and ski-pants and short blond French crop asked if we were in town for the gig tomorrow night, "*going to be lots of mods there*"

"*Yeh of course*" we replied together, our chance to meet up with loads of others for a big ride down to Weymouth we thought.

"*Just need somewhere to stay tonight*"

"*You can stay at mine*" we couldn't believe our luck.

"*Wow is that your scooter, will you take me for a ride in the morning*"

"*Of course*" I said, Lee was not amused and gave me a scowl.

So the next morning we told Lee we wouldn't be long, just nipping over to Maidstone so Tracy could pick up some new shoes for the do that night.

He wasn't amused when we got back six hours later, he'd been dressed up ready for the do for hours, but we had just got on well and were enjoying each other's company, oh well he'd get over it, he didn't.

There were a lot of mods at The King Charles Hotel in Gillingham (venue that was used so many times over the years, and I have great memories of so many bands there, best of all though was the one off Christmas show that The Prisoners did there when they reformed for a couple of gigs in the mid 90's, was very privileged to have been there for that) that night and we had a great night of dancing and drinking, not so much Lee though, but oh well I'd met a lovely girl, I know selfish, but hey ho!. I'm sure it was Geno Washington that night, but can't say I took much notice of the band, was too busy chatting with Tracy and having fun.

Only problem was, we hadn't met anyone that was going to Weymouth. So Friday morning it was kiss Tracy goodbye and a somewhat annoyed Lee climbed aboard and we were off on our way to Weymouth, be there in a few hours we thought, how wrong we were.

Somewhere near the Kent border we were travelling down the main street of Westerham (I think it was called) a narrow street lined with shops and a narrow pavement, with a bend in the road, I took the bend only to find a zebra crossing and on that crossing a little old lady being helped across by a police woman, up and over she went leaving a trail of Brussel sprouts from her shopping. I parked the scooter up looked back at Lee who was just sat there with a shocked look on his face, looked over at the gathering crowd round the old lady checked to see if I could do anything, then re-adjusted my mirrors back to where they were, Lee was still sitting there, a shopkeeper came out, "*you all right son, want a cup of tea?, don't worry it will be all right, been trying to get that crossing moved for years, so dangerous*" the thought of the poor old lady on the floor upset me for quite a while after.

We spent the rest of the afternoon at the local police station, and was quite late by the time they let us be on our way, they did me for a faulty brake light bulb and a few months later three points on my license for driving without due care, but I wasn't fined because of the mitigating circumstances that the crossing had been put in a dangerous place, the poor old lady and her shopping all over the place is still etched in my mind.

It was way after midnight as we saw the signs for Weymouth 5 miles, there were a few scooters parked up in a layby and a stall set up selling scrumpy in five litre plastic containers, the sort you bulk buy washing up liquid in for restaurants and hotels, but it was bloody cheap and as we couldn't afford much else a couple of these were bungeed on to the scooter. The drive into town was uneventful and we followed the signs for the so-called campsite, this was a tarmac car park next to a go-kart track, people had tried to pitch tents as best they could, we were walking through the dark, were very down and looking for the best place when we heard "*Dickie over hear mate*" it was Jay, one of the Herne Bay crowd, "*there's a patch of grass next to our tent, it's on a bit of a slope though, but it will do*"

After our feeble attempts putting up a tent on 45 degree slope we sat with Jay and others listening to music and scooter engines, downing Scrumpy (with a rather strange after taste, never buy from lay by sellers). It wasn't long before we found that we were in the minority on this rally, the minority being mods! It seemed that every other type of person rode a scooter here, this was new and strange to us young mods, Skinheads, Punks, people in denim and leather, looking like the rockers that chased us and we chased back in Margate, but on scooters, but scooters the like of which we had never seen, little or no panels, extended forks, matt black or camouflaged, we didn't realize at the time how much this would affect us. The rest of the weekend went by pretty uneventful and we left for home on the bank holiday Monday morning with about three pounds between us, which meant we ran out of fuel in Brighton and had to syphon petrol from somewhere, this done we made it home coasting the last few miles on fumes. I only ever saw Lee once again after that weekend, don't blame him really, I wasn't much of a mate abandoning him for the day and then putting him in shock, guess he'd had enough.

As for me the scooterist had arrived on the scene , and gradually over the next few months the mod scene had pretty much died out around us, a far cry from the days when we were bolting as many accessories as we could on our scooters, people were cutting down their scooter panels and out came the matt green paint, and scooterists we became, although I kept my scooters pretty much whole, I still preferred that look and instead of customizing with accessories I found I loved custom paintwork and engraving, but the scooterist rallies were not for too long for me although I went to quite a few and had a lot of fun to with some great mates, something in me missed the mod scene and the smarter clothes and to my mind the better music, by 86/7 I had started going to the CCI mod rallies, first of all in nearby Hastings this is where my heart was and then came The Untouchables weekenders, much better still, I had found my place. Another couple of years and it was then The New Untouchables [Nut's], perfection for me, the music scene had shifted for me

74

from soul based to the music of '66 and beyond and my love of all mod/60's style of music was growing more and more and I couldn't get enough, it was like feed me more tunes, I tried to make it to every Nut's event I could, regularly leaving work on a Saturday afternoon, driving to the Purple Pussycat or The Electric something or rather, Mousetrap etc. partying all night, crashing out for an hour or two then driving back to be at work on a Sunday morning, the mod scene was designed for people that worked weekends.

I became a regular at the clubs in London, so much so that I soon found myself talked into working for them by my old mate Rob, even let me do a bit of Dj'ing a couple of times, and that was that for the next god knows how long, travelling to every all-nighter, weekender, here, in Europe (where I met the lovely young lady that became my wife on a mod party on a Rhine boat cruise) and even to the States, with a wonderful bunch of mad eccentric crazy lovable friends, seeing the most amazing bands, to many to list here, but bands of young and some not so young people playing covers and their own material, with fantastic tunes and now highly sort after records, or trying their best to sound like their heroes from the 60's, and seeing some of those very heroes live (or in some case almost live), and for me meeting many of them at sound checks or before and after shows, that was my life, the Nut's, and I bloody loved every minute of it (well nearly).
Dickie, (Nut's retired.....mostly)

13. The books first Skinhead account from **Nigel Harris.**

First year of secondary school (year seven in modern speak) 1969 there was no other fashion, alright you had your Grebos (Rockers) and your Wallies (Hippies) but they were very much in the minority, your "High Street Fashion" catered for us! Frank Wright Loafers, Silver Stud Brogues from Featherstone's or Pyes in Rochester, Ben Sherman and Brutus slim fit Shirts, Levis Sta Prest, Tonics from Silvers in Chatham (they had a closing down sale that must of gone on for about 20 years) and we had Rochester Market, where we bought our Harrington jackets. Burke and Hare was an unknown or long forgotten label that used to produce some lovely quality gear on the markets, (probably knocked up in some East London sweatshop) Dog tooth check, Prince of Wales check, Tonic, trousers and suits, then we had the Guards Factory in Strood that made Crombie's, cheap enough especially if you knew someone who could get one out the back door!

My first pair of boots came courtesy of my Dad, his old work boots, Doc Marten Astronauts, well they were once I'd cleaned them off chipped off all the cement and concrete and diligently sat there polishing them till I could see my face in them, slightly too big but this was sorted out by stuffing the toes with bog roll! Levis or Lee Jeans (Tesco's had just opened up in Chatham and my Mum kindly bought me a pair of Delamare jeans, I was devastated I never wore 'em!) rolled up just enough so that when you walked you flashed just a half inch of bright red towelling sock or some such other bright primary colour!

Shirts, quite a controversial subject these days, as I remember plain Oxford weave or striped fitted button downs were the order of the day, Ben Sherman, Brutus and Arnold Palmer were the ones to have! A few years later these button downs changed to penny collared or jumbo collared shirts. Jaytex and the big bold checks came a lot later in my opinion? Of course Fred Perry's were worn back then too, smart, casual, comfortable and would go with anything! My school uniform at the time was a bit special, white Ben Sherman button down, school tie with a somewhat impossibly large knot, black tank top, Barrathea blazer, black Levis Sta-Prest and black loafers. Thought I looked a bit 'arry and of course I had the attitude to match!

Like I said I was in the 1st year, the 3rd, 4th and 5th year students looked like men, proper grown ups with facial hair, and what seemed like loads of money to spend on all the latest gear, to go to any of the many "Unisex hairdressers" popping up in Medway rather than just going to the barbers like the rest of us (I'd only just got out of being dragged to the barbers by the old Man about a year previously, (short back and sides with a large dollop of Vitalis to smooth the top in place)). The Hygenic in Bachelor Street or Chatham bogs was where I got my barnet cut, seemed ridiculously short at the time but not by today's standards!

All this happened about the same time as I gave up playing football and making Air fix model kits because all of a sudden all I could think of was girls, not just the way they looked but also the way they smelt, everyone and I mean everyone that was anyone, male or female were smothering themselves in Brut 33 and I was no exception, this was before they did the gift packs and the soap on a rope and the deodorant etc etc. all they did were these little bottles of aftershave that didn't seem to last very long for some strange reason? (We were literally bathing in the stuff) (later on Henry Cooper told us to *"splash it on all over"* not a good idea because before one less than memorable date I splashed it all over and nearly burned my dick off with it!!!).The girls back then, apart from the tonic skirts and the tights with the patterns down the sides wore pretty much what we wore, but they looked so much better in it than we did. The fitted shirts fitted better, the sta-prest seemed to show off their curves a treat too! But it was the hair that did it for me, feathered hair; I don't mean the Chelsea crop of latter years but the proper long feathered hair! It was a much softer, girly look back then, one that I've still got a soft spot for all these years later!

Couple of things I do remember from back then but I don't know if they were localized or a national things, I've never heard anyone else talking about 'em? Loafers, you'd go and buy a brand new pair and take them straight down the local snob and have extra leather soles put on with quarter plates front and rear making them very heavy and very noisy especially if you'd gone to town on them and nailed loads of Blakeys in the bottom of them too! And the other thing is about Crombie's, Girls used to go down to Woolies and buy cutsey patches, butterflies or teddy bears or bunny rabbits and sew them on the breast pocket below the handkerchief and tie stud. Us Chaps, (remember this was back in the day before you could buy your favourite Football club shirts, you could buy the shirt colour of choice (mine being of the claret and blue variety) but they weren't badged up like they are today) you could buy some football badges (the larger more popular clubs) from certain sports shops, these were embroidered on a piece of white cotton about 5" square, these were sewn (in its entirety) onto the Crombie breast pocket, again below the silk hankie and tie pin.

First record I ever bought was the *Double Barrel* album by Dave and Ansell Collins, my Dad went absolutely garrity, *"wasting your money on that rubbish!"* this was closely followed over the next couple of years by the *Tighten Up* albums, the *Reggae Party* albums and the *Motown Chartbuster* albums, these were like the *"Now that's what I call Music"* albums of their day. During this time I was buying singles too, nothing particularly memorable, *Double Barrel*, *Monkey Spanner*, *Wet Dream*, *Liquidator* etc etc. but the one thing I do remember is the day it all changed.

One lunchtime one of the older kids had been into town and bought some new records, I remember him pulling out from his bag the latest *Chartbuster* album and the latest *Tighten Up* album, he then pulled out a single which we all looked at rather quizzically ....
Rock 'n' Roll pts 1 & 2 by someone called Gary Glitter?
Nigel Harris

14. The books second foreign contribution from Spanish Mod **Edu**.

Let's go back in time to 1996 when the boom of Britpop arrived strongly to our normal lives in Barcelona, it's the moment I got trapped with music that defined me for the rest of my life.

As far as I remember first time I recognized the word MOD was in a Paul Gallagher's book talking about the likes in music of himself and his famous brothers, there appears The Jam, The Kinks, The Who and The Small Faces. I had no idea at that time I was going to get involved in that 60's thing far away from just the music. There was something hypnotic in that blue, white and red target, I had to investigate more about what MOD was and so I did. Reading about the influences of the bands I adored at those days were The Beatles, The Kinks and Paul Weller himself and The Jam, of course.

The Jam had the punk attitude and the right vibes you need when you're young and want to have fun feeling yourself the king of the world in the presence of strong raw power pop you can feel it running through your veins. At the same time the better way to catch that info was buying MODZINES because music is for hearing but also for reading.

Trying to get more info about that sound, later I'll know it was called revival MOD and its higher point happened when I was born in 1979. So to me the door to the movement was revival thing through Secret Affair, The Lambrettas, and Merton Parkas, Squire, The Prisoners and so on. Best live act in that style to me in those days were the 3 piece combo ART SCHOOL, from Murcia. Their first LP was the first piece of vinyl I ever bought in my life.

Step by step I listened to other genres like Motown classics, Northern Soul, R&B or what I founded more genuine, blue eyed soul from the 60's, white guys wearing cool clothes trying to imitate black music sound, bands and artists like The Action, The Pretty Things, Spencer Davis Group, The Birds, Georgie Fame, Brian Auger, The Yardbirds and stuff.

I remember myself walking by Tallers street and watching that big guy hanging posters on the walls. I stopped there in front of one and that guy invited me to go to the party they were going to organize, not so far from where I live which was first MOD/60's party I ever attended. Red Fred Perry polo shirt, tight pants, grey 2 buttons jacket and loafers, with no idea about how to dance , with no idea about the music it was played, without knowing anyone and just having a good fun watching Les Cactus playing live and enjoying the most with every song sounding through the speakers.

I met kind people in there who saw us young and new ones, talking to us and treating us like if we were friends for a long time made us, my little sister and I, feeling comfortable in the middle of that entire new thing, an all-nighter.

That was just the beginning, after that one I attended to every single party I realised was organised in town, I especially liked the monthly "Magic in the air", including live acts and guest Dj's from all over Europe.

Some months later I read something about pop art music, garage and the weirdest name I had heard of at that time, freakbeat. Another turned point was listening to Los Flechazos from Leon, probably the most recognized 6o's oriented band in our country, sadly I never was able to see them live but the words and the sound bring you to the time where POP was fuelled by colours and where being young was writing the future in big words. I was immediately interested in Swinging London and London underground '66/'67 counterculture thing. Freakbeat? What Freakbeat is? may be is a question I'm not able to answer nowadays, I'm talking about The Attack, John's Children, The Creation, The Smoke, Fleur de lys, The Move, The Eyes, Powder and stuff. It was awesome attending to The Flake gig at "Magic in the air" club, a band from Saarbruecken (Germany).

Especially The Attack trapped me more than any other band I heard before, let grow my hair and tried to get clothes more oriented to late 6o's stuff, coloured shirts, flare shaped trousers and foulards, next step was discovering Psychedelic, specially UK psych with bands such as The End, Tomorrow, July, Pink Floyd, Tintern Abbey, Factory, One in a million, Kaleidoscope.

One more step, trying to get myself and a small collection of original singles and LP's I like and those ones I can afford. The Elephant Band from Coruña and Londoners Neil's Children were the bands that freaked me out the most on stage in those days.

It is brilliant being dee-jaying your fave tunes to an audience and make their dance to the music you like, you alone with everybody.

Best of being part of the 6o's scene is sharing your passion with other weirdo's you find thanks to the big meetings or weekenders in Spain and in the abroad, special to me is Gijon's Euro Ye Ye where I've attended every year since I was 18 until present days, Leon's Purple weekend was ace, London's Le Beat Bespoke is massive, small ones like "All Saints" in Lavarone, "Cloud 9" in Rimini were charming.

From my point of view people make the scene, looking for the points in common more than the differences of likes and dislikes in music or style, sharing laughs with friends you make there with people from different places and accents is priceless. Being in an all-nighter listening to the music you like sharing with other freaks, just like you, that want to party till the end even not knowing their names, their faces or anything at all is just brilliant, I think there are no words to explain that feeling.

Being part of it is more than the music or the style in concrete is more like reviewing the 60's at your own way keeping that feeling alive. When you are trapped by 60's you love art, films, literature, furniture, everything. Living your own 60's bubble means stopping the time and the space and express yourself the way you feel, that's to me real life being part of this wonderful unreal world.

Actually nowadays my main interests in music are late 60's and early 70's stuff: freakbeat, USA garage psych, euro beat, folk psych, early 70's prog rock, popsike, funk rock, hard psych and Spanish prog.
Edu Lazaro

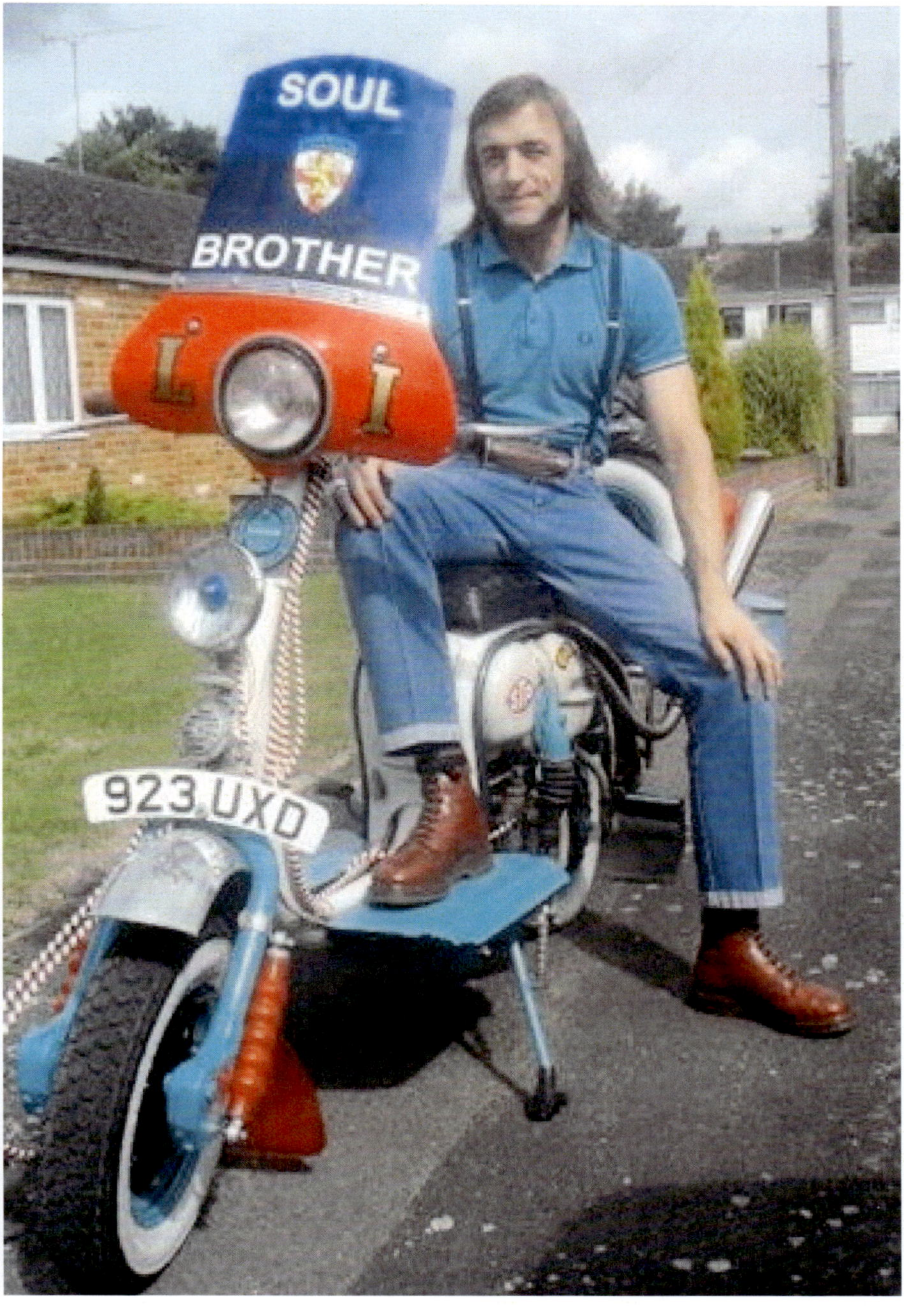
SOUL
BROTHER
Li
923 UXD

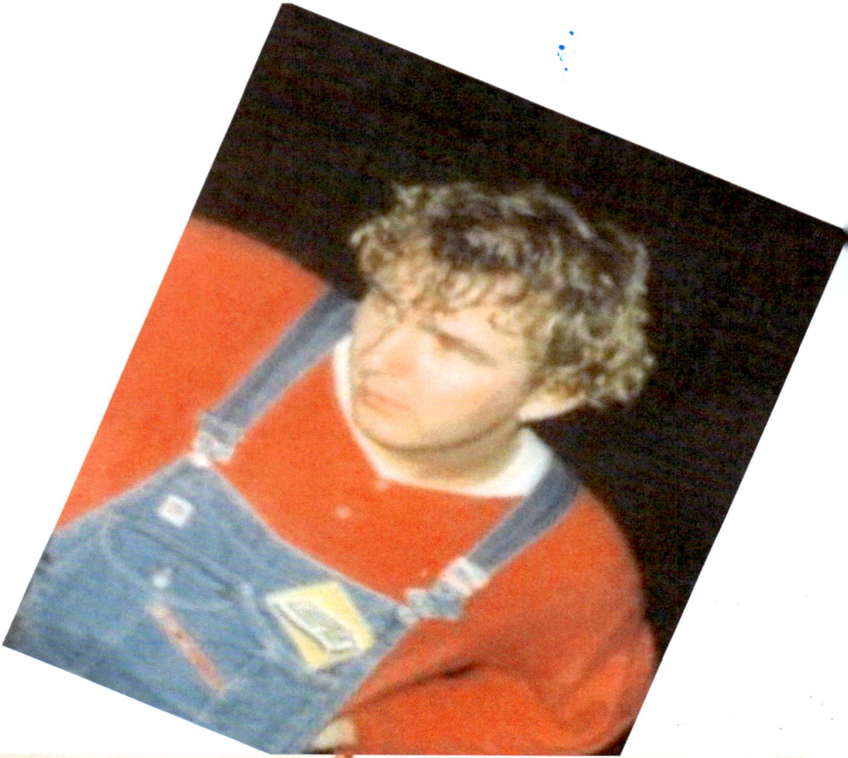

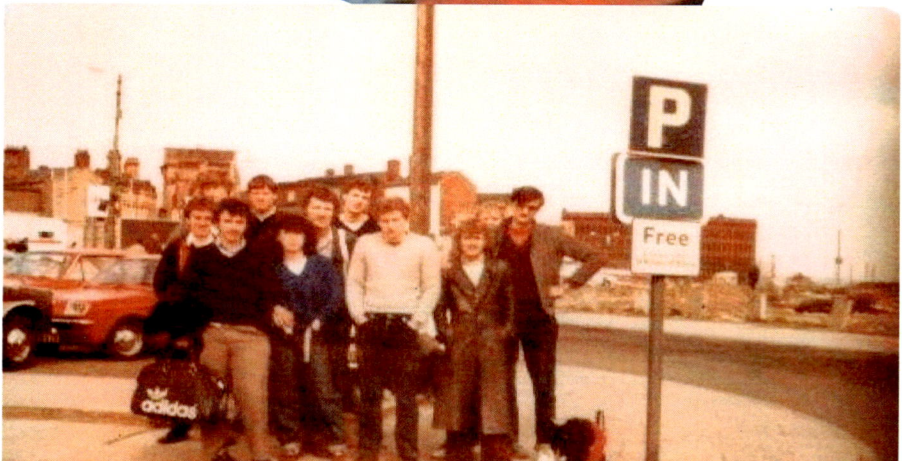
P
IN
Free
adidas

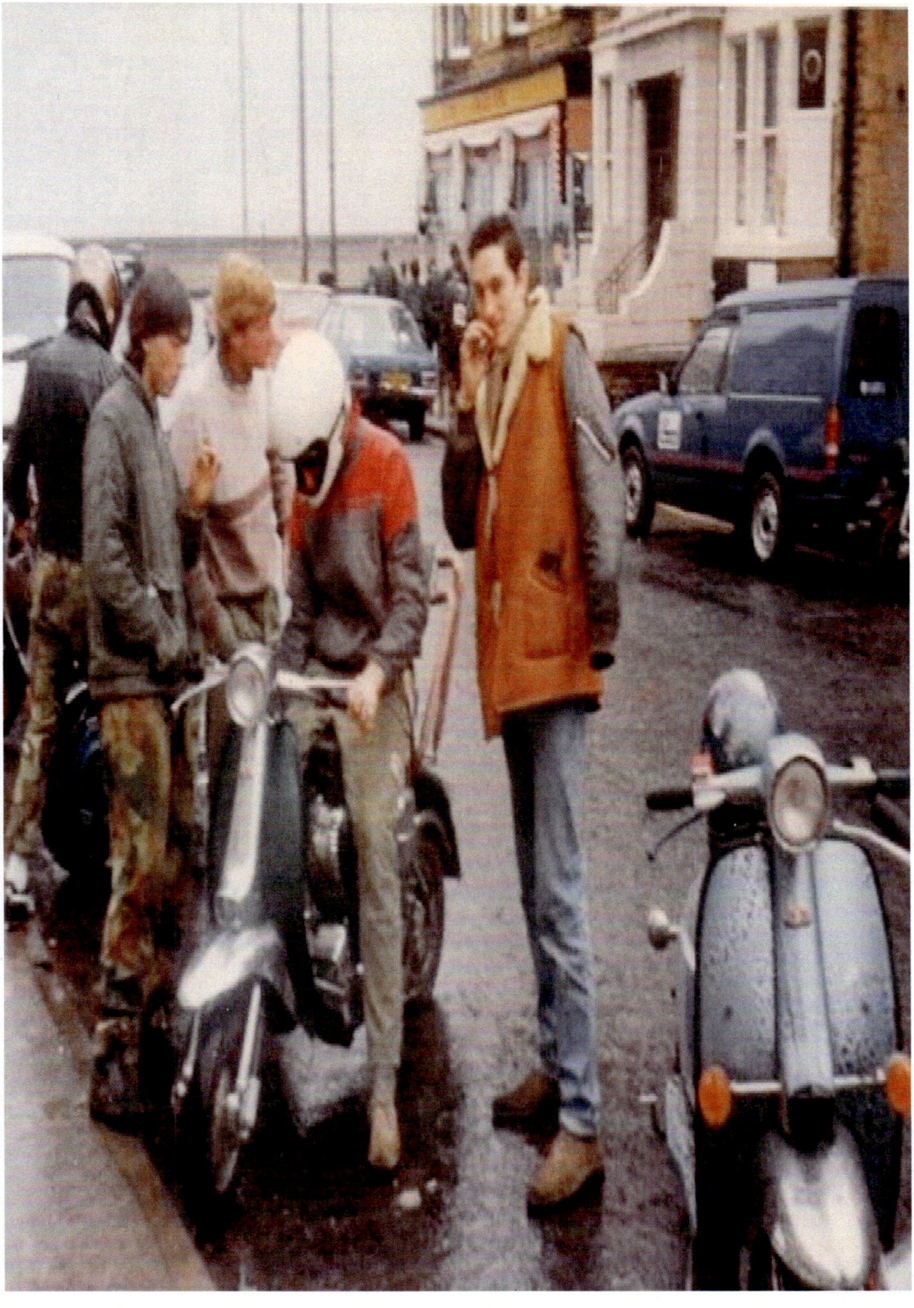

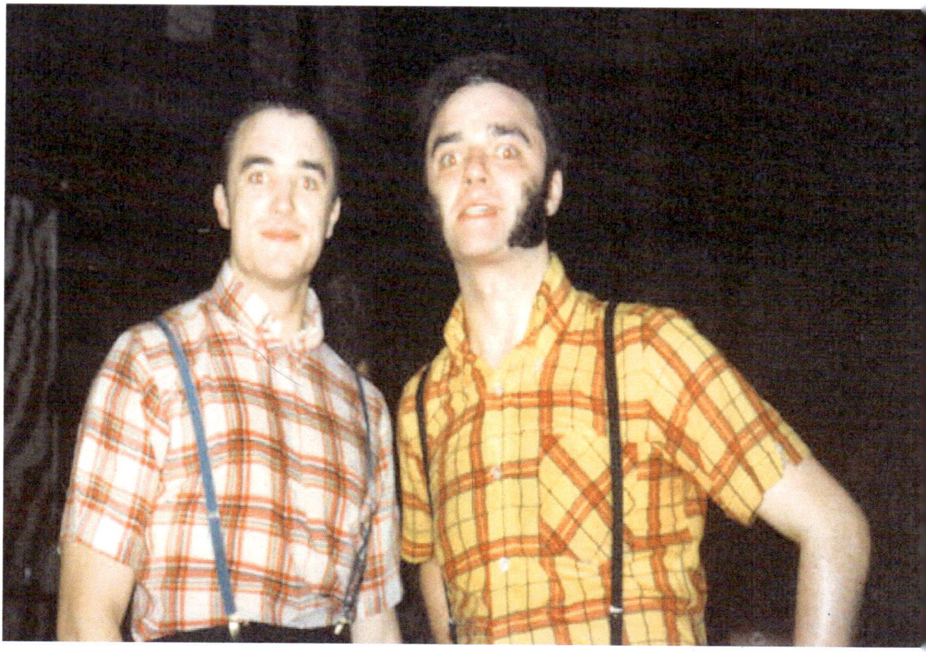

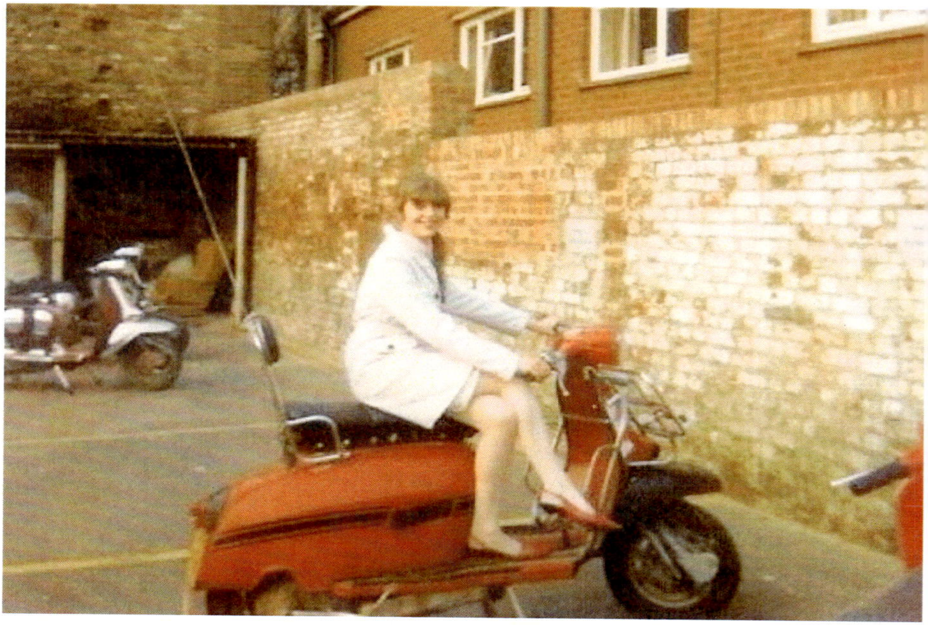

15. This is an article donated to the book from noted author and music journalist **Garry Bushell** which he originally wrote in 1979. He provides a feel of what was happening at the time.

Changing trains at Leeds from the relatively plush Inter-City to the archaic Huddersfield link, the last Cockney voice I'd heard echoed round my brain again. It was a Southern Mod grimly repeating old prejudices about Northerners and their alleged obsessions with Stranglers stick-ons, 40-inch flares (referred to in hushed tones down here as *"the trouser problem"*) and parkas covered in unsightly beer mats.
With reservations mounting like a pay-per-screw porn star, I recalled my mate's shaking head and his solemn warning that with my CAFC and Secret Affair badges, my Harrington, straight jeans, snow white almond rocks and functional Fred Perry I'd be about as welcome "up there" as a dose of clap on honeymoon, not to mention an ideal target for Northern retribution for supposed Southern crimes.
Sod it, I thought, I ain't getting paid danger money, why didn't I just jump back on a homebound train and go on the Tom and Dick for a week? But don't fret faithful readers, your Sounds scribes are made of sterner stuff and hiding behind Ms. Turbett's skirt I trundled on, only to find that the Southern Mods had got it all wrong, their false impressions stemming from premature sightings of their Northern counterparts. From last May in fact when Secret Affair brought a coachload of Londoners up for a gig with The Killermeters, the Huddersfield band who form the musical mainspring of the whole Mod scene.
For the first time that night the local scooter clubs decided to turn up in force, and it was by their, at that time, alien presence that the Southerners had pre-judged the Northern scene. And as my piece on the history of the Southern scene two months back had repeated their prejudices as fact, this report is an attempt to set the record straight.
Although very similar in essence now, the two scenes are historically miles apart. Whereas the Southern scene didn't really begin till February this year with the embryonic roots back to mid-'77, the North, where the scene took off properly in May, claims with some justification to be more directly descended from sixties Modism.
By their own admission, the North caught on to Mod later, but hung on to it longer; although some would argue more as a parka and scooter thing than a posey/state of mind affair. In the South Mods split into hippies and skinheads, and scooters fell rapidly from grace; but in the North change was slower and

different, and the scene was still flourishing long after trendsetting London townies were immersing themselves in acid or aggro.

Mod DJs everywhere had prided themselves on their ability to search out new artists and new labels, developing beyond the standard Mod soul music on Tamla and Stax to lesser known outlets. Naturally when Mod persisted in the North, DJs continued this trend, and (I'm oversimplifying like crazy) this search eventually evolved into the distinctive sound of Northern Soul, fast, brassy and often bootlegged.

Based round all-nighters in Wigan and surrounding areas like Cleethorpes and Manchester, Northern Soul developed in the early seventies as a Mod off-spring with marked differences.

Primarily the cult made such a fetish of obscurity that musical values arguably started to go increasingly by the board, while for practical reasons suits collars and ties were replaced by vests and wide bags (the new scene was also a lot straighter that its predecessor, less the prerogative of the sharpest kids).

Aside from soul music the other constant in the North's evolution were the scooters and the scooter clubs for whom Wigan all-nighters were a danceable alternative to the staple diet of cross country scooter runs. These clubs span the years between Sixties and Seventies Mod, and even though at times the clubs' membership might have been down to five or six enthusiasts, the tradition was not allowed to die.

New Mod has swelled their ranks again and one informed commentator claims there are currently 2,000 scooters north of Birmingham organised in clubs like the Fugitives and Revival in Huddersfield, the Red Lion Club in Heckmondwicke, the Yorkshire Roadrunners, the Scunthorpe Road Rats, the Preston Wildcats, the Crewe Jaguars...and many more (The South's 5-15 Club from Sevenoaks in Kent aren't too well respected it would seem, however, and prejudices abound along with tales that they bring their scooters on runs in the back of lorries etc).

In May, the Scooter clubs discovered the New Northern Mod scene and for the most part fell in love with it. Many of them have now discovered the fashions too and a casual observer would be hard pressed to tell the two tribes apart on the clothes front. (One club incidentally is completely infatuated with the Jam and have customized their scooters with the 'Strange Town' single sleeve pic).

At the same time, much more so than in the south, Northern Mod music fans have shown a corresponding interest in the scooter clubs. But where, you might well ask, did they come from?

The answer in a word is The Killermeters. They began life in mid-1977 as a straight forward thrash-'n'-bash punk combo, lasting until a disillusioned break-up at the beginning of '78. They were reformed last October by bassist and vocalist Vic Vespa, lead guitarist Mick Moore and drummer Graham 'Jez' Jessop, who, along with the guitarist Ruttle brothers Sid and Tony, form today's very different Killermeters.

Jez explains: *"We were all pissed off with straightforward basic punk material which is why the band split up, we wanted to play something with a bit more melody and technique hence the type of songs we started doing in October."*

Coinciding with their change in musical direction, was the band's increasing association with Paul Nicholson, a Sixties Mod who'd never lost his cool and who would talk at length about Mod as he'd lived it.

Nicholson had never had any timer for Northern Soul. *"Mod didn't die here till about 1969,"* he explains *"and Northern Soul to me didn't have any identity, stupid baggy trousers and... well I never had any time for it."*

So a combination of Nicholson's recollections and their musical direction led the 'Meters to decide that Mod was the image they wanted to adopt and this at the time when The Jam aside, only the Purple Hearts were blazing the parka trail darn South.

In other words, they began totally independently from the Southern scene, playing their first gig last December and gradually building their own following, and perhaps more jocularly than the South their own movement in the shape of - don't laugh - the Jolly Boys.

Appropriately Paul is known as King Jolly but I spoke to one of his deputies a guy by the name of Evil Roman. It's the truth! He had his name changed by deed poll, and moved from fanzines and poetry to being the Killermeters biggest fan, walking ten miles to one gig and actually taking 120 Anadins the one time he missed a performance (which by coincidence, is the recommended dosage to take during a Boomtown Rats performance).

Leaving aside such suicidal dedication, Evil explained that the Jolly Boys had one aim in life - to get steamed out of their boxes every time they go out; in other words, inebriated, legless, pissed, in short well and truly jollied up. (Blues incidentally are virtually non-existent up here).

Of all the bands to have emerged in the North in their wake - The Name in Peterborough , The Moving Targets in Leeds, The Scene in Bradford, Handsome Jack And The Casualties (cough) also in Huddersfield, and the punky Two Tone Pinks in Manchester - the 'Meters have undoubtedly established the biggest and best scene around them, as simply illustrated by tonight's gig at Huddersfield one Mod venue, The Albion (the one time location for a punk disco that was dropped as punks became virtually extinct up here, replaced by a Mod movement which has been expanding steadily ever since the 'Meters bridged the gap between Mods and Scooter clubs in May).

Fact is Mod is far bigger now in Huddersfield than punk was at its coinciding stage of development. It's also a solidly working class movement, as reflected in the 'Meters own day jobs - two engineers, one carpet fitter, one cabinet maker and one building labourer.

Tonight's audience is missing many faces. The bulk of the scooter clubs have shot off to Wigan tonight for the first all-nighter for about a year; but there's still enough eager punters to pack the place out and I take the opportunity to chat to fans, the band, King Jolly and Scooter boy Bob Monkhouse (no relation) a member of the 15-strong and growing Fugitives Club.

Bob's been riding scooters for six years now. He lives and breathes them. He formed his own club back in the mist of time and currently owns ten of the beauties, all of them personally customized by his own fair hands (he intends entering one in the Ally Pally Custom car show next year.) Bob's eyes glaze over at the mention of the Arthur Francis Extra S-type 200 and he affects a heartfelt sneer at the mention of Vespa's ("*Lambrettas are scooters,*" he says, adding dismissively: "*Vespa's are Vespa's.*")

"*I used to listen to Northern Soul,*" he admits. "*But I didn't start going to Wigan till '76. I started listening to the Killemeters about two months ago. I don't really rate many new Mod bands but the Killermeters are definitely going places. Now you've got Northern Soul one way and Mod bands the other and Scooters are in the middle linking the two together.*"

The worst aspect of the current Northern scene is the growing police interest in scooter riders, and just as many people testify to police victimization as condemn violence between North and South, something Paul Nicholson gets particularly up-tight about.

"*It's ridiculous,*" he opines. "*A load of shit. North or south, it's all working class kids, that's what it's all about and what's the point of working class kids punching shit out of each other?*"

None at all I'd say, none at all. I wondered how he felt about now and the sixties, being part of both and all. "*Well it's different; it's not the same all now really. We used to blow all our wages on clothes and now it's all second hand clothes, and they've got their own thing now, their own music which is great, especially Secret Affair, The Teenbeats and The Killermeters. The only bad thing when the Southerners came up was you had some of these Glory Boys wandering about going 'Sieg Heil' and that really annoyed us here.*"

And that is another gratifying thing about the North - there's no obsession with violence, no hint of suspect politics. DOWNSTAIRS tonight the dance floor makes Wembley on cup-final day look like a two man audience in the Albert Hall. I wouldn't say it was packed but it took me six attempts to reach the bar and then only by yelling "*Fire*" in a strange high-pitched voice.

The first chilly fingers of lager were just finding their way into my Derby when stage front the pilchard-packed mob's chants of '*joy-joy-joy-joy-JOLLY BOYS*' reached a crescendo and the fiver Killermeters trotted on stage to a riotous reception. Yeah, I know it was a home crowd and all that but no way was the crowd's ecstatic reception the result of excess beer or misplaced loyalty.

Simply the band play one hell of a fine blend of sixties-derived (cynics in the office claimed my tape recalled everyone from George Harrison to Wayne Fontana) modern pop; a creamy twelve song recipe that by my humble reckoning puts them well up in Mod's Division One.

Best number is the next single (either on Psycho this month or EMI/Din Disc/Phonogram etc if they've got the suss to sign 'em snappy) called *Twisted Wheel*, a superb hymn to Manchester's famed early sixties Mod Mecca. That's going to be coupled with the fast scooter song *SX225* (and up till '68 that was THE scooter to have.)

An unhealthy fixation with the past, sure, but it doesn't permeate the whole set where matters of the heart predominate (like it or not Eros is replacing Anarchy on all the best-selling banners these days).

Basically the songs are strong and well structured, oft-times perfect pop having none of the 'wimpiness' live that is sometimes wrongly attributed to their recorded work, the fine Psycho single *Why Should It Happen To Me?/Cardiac Arrest*. Their fresh pop sound finds a receptive sea of clapped hands and hungry, joyous faces bucking about in a sweaty human mess in front of me. It's exhausting even to watch. Edwin Starr's *SOS* and The Who's *Legal Matter* are covered particularly well, while the tender *Rhona* sees their first proper exercise in dual guitar play.

The band manage two encores till bomb hoaxers close the place down and I'm left pondering how much further they would have got by now had they been based in the Smoke instead of grimy old Yorkshire.

The band talks with a genuine excitement about their music and their movement.

"*We're totally into the idea of Mod here,*" Jez enthuses, "*having a good time and looking after yourself, it's great. The punk thing was defeated by the commercial market. It started as a reaction but ended up business.*"

"*But the Mod scene up here is really healthy. No way is it a business thing. Up here its ordinary kids and Oxfam shops and everyone is into scooters, and the music and the look.*"

"*Obviously it wouldn't have happened without Punk,*" Vic Vespa intersperses. "*But it's a new movement. It's more melodic and danceable. And we're building something of our own. Something new*".

"*Usually something happens in the South and the rest of the country follows, but with Mod the Southerners seem to be trying to change something that's our own, and that won't happen because we've got something special here*".

"*But thankfully the antagonism between North and South is starting to cool down now and I believe it's got to, otherwise the whole movement will collapse.*"

What d'you reckon will happen with Mod then?

"*Obviously it'll go the same as punk eventually*".

Anything that comes from the kids on the streets is taken over and made commercial but at the moment the whole scene's going well."

A glazed look comes into his eyes. "*Someone said last year that 1979 was gonna be the year of Mod*" (I did - GB) (And me - Ed) "*but I reckon 1980 will be the real year of the Mod and the year of the scooter. Next summer it's gonna be massive.*"

"*You know what my ambition is now?*" Jez asks rhetorically, "*It's to play Manchester Apollo and pack it out with Mods instead of Rush fans. That'd really be something to achieve.*"

And I'll see you there Jez, I'll see you there.

© Garry Bushell, October 20th 1979

16. The books first female contributor is Northern Soulie **Jane Harrison**

It was another oldies night at The Casino, a time when old faces turn up out of the Blue and check out what they've been missing or haven't. It must be early 1979, and someone has actually bothered to take a camera this time, I don't know who, as it only came to my attention in 2006. I remember the night well, we could not get a coach together any more in Wolverhampton as the friendly neighbourhood squad had scared the coach companies off, and with the demise of the longstanding freedom bus, we had no choice than to plan for it to run from out in the sticks.

The problem was that we would all have to make sure this coach never came off the motorway and ventured into Wolverhampton as it would never make it out again.

So we met the coach, which meant we had to get to junction 10 of the M6. And instead of meeting up in town we should meet in Willenhall nearer the junction.

It was also decided that we should meet in separate pubs as the paranoia had set in within our circle and many of our number had recently been either been lifted or scared away.

It would look a bit odd when we all took the same bus to the motorway though!

Nine thirty this coach is supposed to be here and it's late, strange looks are a plenty, from the passing cars, why would a group of 30 people be stood on a motorway junction in the dark at night? Are we waiting for the Queen or is it some mass hitchhiking exercise, in fact I've took part in a group hitchhiking contest to Wigan, the night Billy Butler played The Casino, I made, it but my two mates only got as far as Knutsford services.

Here it is, when it pulls up there are as many jumping out the coach as trying to get on it, old friends, long time no see friends, friends who I still see today.

Its mayhem on the coach, caused by either excitement in anticipation of good night or we just happen to bring this behaviour out in each other. It's a bit of both spiced with a bit of added chemical content.

First service stop, Hilton park hang on we've only just got on, this is still to near to town and some of our own number have decided to get off the bus and hide in the shadows, until we set off again. We are off again no more service stations we've agreed, then we disagree so we stop at Knutsford We hit junction 25 and were nearly there, navigate through town and onto station road bang on twelve. I'm off and into the throng; I need to see someone, who unknown at that time would be the last time for a year, as he will be modelling her majesties latest work wear soon I bump into people I haven't seen in a while 'last time I saw Andy was when he was being led away by the coppers after jumping the train to Wigan on a platform ticket and as a result was forced to move back home to Lancashire.

Little was I to know then but my chance meeting with him outside Boots in Blackburn 18 months later would re-kindle our friendship to the point that I would become his best man and he would become mine. Back to the night, its typical oldies, full hot and loud, I loved the oldies; the music gave a reminder why you fell under the spell of the sound of black America .The night seems to whiz by in more ways than one, and before I know we are out, squinting in the cold early daylight. The coach back is subdued; most people just want to get back home for some peace and shuteye, but not us if we get back at the usual time it means there is only one hour before the pubs opening.

Some of us decide that Sandbach services would be the best place to stop, for 2p you get a shower complete with towel. The coach drops off back from where we were picked up the night before, most go their own way but some of us we decide that the Vic is the best option. We don't have long to wait for the bus, it's Saturday morning and the bus is full of shoppers totally uninterested in this bedraggled bunch climbing the stairs to the upper deck.

The bus pulls into its destination and everyone piles off, and that's when the camera came out, no smiles no hugging just stood there. Some of that crowd are no longer with us, the others have attended each others 21st's 40th's 50th's, weddings and so on, brought together by chance and friends forever.

"*I've got us a lift*" said a Jill, oh god my heart sunk "*It will be ok. When the parties finished we have a lift*". The lift in question was the Clitheroe lot (affectionately known), having seen them down lager, Mild Guinness and a few smarties I was not looking forward to the journey. Our lift was in the van. The van in question was an old post van so I'm told but can't remember whose van it was but the company was excitable to say the least. There was Barney, Pogo, Brian, Fred and Craig. Me and Jill were the only girlies. I thought I know these guys so I'm fine. The van was an original I believe it's an open floor style new to the scene. Then those words you don't want to hear "*I feel sick*" and then having to watch the contents of Eric's tummy fall to the floor. I should of got the bus or thumbed I thought to myself.

We got to the oldies, to Mr M's to hear *Sly Girl* for Jane on her 18th birthday from the Clitheroe lot and all was forgiven. But I still wished I had got the bus.

The bus journey (see pic) whilst doing my travelling from Accrington to Blackburn to get the next 10 to 10 bus to Wigan oh hell its cowboy time...you had to change at Chorley. I was ok; I knew a few faces at Blackburn. I had a lager and black and I'm on my way. I was on my own, my mate Jill was on her way to Morecombe.

At Chorley I was met by the rockers (I knew a lot about other music besides soul) so after you got over the pill head fuckin shit soul and the beer wore off you talked, its funny how many rockers like Tamla Motown. After all wasn't Gene Simmons girlfriend once in a soul group.

So I sat on the bus hoping for a bit of peace and not to be noticed...after all no leather just my bright Red coat, two jumpers, scarf and hat (not an Accrington girl so need to be warm). Then I heard "*sit with us sweetheart*". Oh god, what now? Oh yea the cheeky boys, the lads from near Manchester, Steve I think. Having just got over the rockers I didn't need any more hassle. '*Come up here, see what comes up*'. Oh change the record. Was going to Wigan worth it? Cold, three lagers, no toilets and now this lot could be worse than the punks at the end of the arcade in Wigan. 'Oh well Jane, head down, let the others go ahead for a battering. I went the long way round. Bad move I was met by six punks, '*fucking soul shit*'. Oh not heard that before but how can I run on my own in these boots. How could they tell I was off to The Casino? Oh yea the big overnight bag gave it away. I tried to ignore them then it got the better of me '*Just because you look and like different music means I don't understand your taste or style of music. After all if you don't want to fuck me is a classic the electric chair will do it grand*'? I can't remember running all I know is I really confused those punks. After I slowed down I ran into my mates and had one of the best nights in Mr M's. They even played all the tunes I wanted to dance to...

Jane Harrison

17. The books second female contribution from a Scottish Mod and event organiser **Jennie Baillie**.

In the summer of 1982 I was 12 and a half, lived in a crappy small town on the East of Scotland called Carnoustie, I'd also just started secondary school and musically, up until that point, the records I was buying were either by Adam and the Ants or The Police. By 1982 the Mod Revival in my town was in full swing, but it was starting Secondary school which exposed me to all the other music out there – I'd been listening to 60s stuff for years, thanks to my Dad having fairly good taste in music – but it was all clicking together, The Who, The Animals, The Yardbirds, Rolling Stones all playing a medley in my head, and then I heard The Jam. I must've been aware of them over the years, in fact I remember religiously taping the top 40 every Sunday and Going Underground being number 1, that was probably the song that "*Jennifer, your tea's ready*" is recorded over, with "*but I'm taping the charts Mum*" making an appearance too. So, *Just Who Is The 5 O'clock Hero*, *The Bitterest Pill* and *Beat Surrender* and then that was that. Bugger, whilst I was listening to The Police and *Ghost in the Machine*, I should've been listening to *The Gift*, arse!

So it was a bleak start to 1983, but all was not lost. I managed to pick up a few after school jobs, a paper round, a Friday evening milk round and weekend waitressing, so I had cash. On Saturday afternoon's I headed to Dundee for the record exchange shop Groucho's. Oh, what a shop, hundreds upon thousands of records, and a couple of very helpfully categorised boxes labelled "mod and soul". This continued for a number of years, every Saturday you'd find me rummaging in the boxes buying up the back catalogue of The Jam and The Specials and bits and pieces by 60s bands I'd heard of – I hate to think about all the tunes I overlooked, because I'd not heard of them. There were fanzines too, Groucho's stocked "007", I was buying clothes from Cavern, not very good quality, but I thought I was fab.

It was difficult being a Mod aged 13; none of the girls in my year were really into it, the musical interests of the group I went about with ranged from Duran Duran (blah), Shakin' Stevens? and Simple Minds, so not really any chance of us learning from each other. I expect throughout first year I was still discovering the sounds which would stay with me, and then one year on from starting secondary school, The Style Council came on the scene. I'd been reading about Paul Weller's new group in the likes of Smash Hits, but for some reason I took an extreme dislike to Tracey Young. I'm sure she's a lovely girl, but I'd read an interview with her which really irked me, and out of principal (or bloody mindedness) I refused to entertain the mere suggestion of listening to, never mind actually enjoying *Speak like A Child*. It was my Dad, once more, I can thank. He reckoned I'd really like them if only I'd give the song a chance. So I did, and that was that, a life changing moment, sounds dramatic, and it probably is. I loved the song, loved the look, I was a Mod. The band opened my eyes and ears to something new and magical. And as the Style Council years continued, I'd buy everything I could which featured the band, taped every programme they were on, I still have a few VHS videos worth of performances ranging from Wigan to Saturday Superstore to cooler TV programmes like The Tube.

The Mods were all the older guys 2 or 3 years above me at High School, who were so cool riding up and down the High Street on their scooters, but it wasn't the done thing to hang out with them. It was kind of crap really, when I hear folk talking now about how fantastic it was being a teenage Mod...back then, the camaraderie, the friendships which have gone on to last a lifetime, it wasn't like that for me. In fact, it was quite isolating, me in my dog tooth ski pants, polo neck jumpers, little dresses and pointy shoes, but I persevered, kept buying records – I was still following the Style Council and listening intently to the words of Paul Weller, getting into Red Wedge and the Faith Brothers, but I had also started listening to Soul, more specifically the sounds of Curtis Mayfield and Otis Redding, although for some reason it was 70s Mayfield I was digging, The Impressions would come along later. I remember one of my favourite albums at the time was *Otis Blue* and kicking around somewhere in my house is a very badly recorded cassette of The Action's *Ultimate Action* which I played to death. I was reading what I could about the 60s, quizzing my folks about what to wear, and then like a miracle from above, "Ready Steady Go" was repeated on Channel 4. It was shown on a Friday evening, 5.30pm rings bells, and so I'd head out on my milk round at 5, do half the round, come home for tea and watch RSG. It was fantastic; it gave a focus to everything I was doing. Now I could actually see what the girls were wearing, what they were doing with their hair and the music that was being played. That would've been about 1985 and I continued to have my own wee scene in my bedroom, probably went to some parties, and remember going to a Mod ball in Dundee in 1986 once I'd turned 16 and was "apparently" a bit more responsible. The music being played then was very much the Wigan Casino compilation album, you know... *The Snake, No 1 in my heart, Ski-ing in the Snow*, to be honest, it didn't fill me with inspiration.

In the summer of 1986, four years on from my epiphany, I moved to the arse end of nowhere, commonly known as Pitlochry for four months to work, when I returned home, the mods had disappeared. Everyone was either a Scooterist or a casual and then finally mere months before my 18th birthday when I could actually go out and drink, the tunes had changed and the clubs would play a solitary half hour of northern soul – *Nine Times Out Of Ten* anyone???

Through my late teens and early 20s I was listening to other tunes and sounds, saw The James Taylor Quartet in about 1989 at Fat Sam's in Dundee, they were fab but nobody seemed to dig them, there was no Style Council then, and I probably became a bit more influenced by the sounds of my then boyfriend. He was into grunge, which wasn't my thing, I was dabbling with a more 50s look, baseball jackets, quiff, turned up jeans with DM boots, I thought I looked great. Didn't really do the Acid Jazz thing, I bought a Galliano album because I read somewhere that Mick Talbot was involved with the band. The relationship with Grunge boy fizzled out, but my first love... Paul Weller came back into my life with his debut solo album, and finally, in 1993 I saw him live at the Barrowlands in Glasgow, YES!!!!! I'd never got a chance to see the Style Council, a combination of overprotective parents, and well... overprotective parents meant I couldn't go to Glasgow or Edinburgh and when a gig in Dundee was finally announced, I quickly bought my ticket, and then it was cancelled. Nae luck!!!

I wasn't doing the all-nighters and rally's like so many of my now peers were doing, I didn't know anybody who had been or still was a mod, so like the 80s, the 90s were spent following Paul Weller, buying lots of Kent releases and getting on with life, work and kids.

The new century was a new beginning for me. We got internet access and I started contributing to some Mod forums, the early days of Modculture.com, Mod Revival and the first Paul Weller forum. I made friends, who are still friends now, there would be meet ups with the Paul Weller forums, I heard about club nights and gigs happening around Scotland, my now ex husband and I went to see The Jamm (Jam tribute band) on numerous occasions in Glasgow, met up with folks at Paul Weller gigs. I was astounded to discover that there was still a Mod Scene, it hadn't disappeared, only gone a little quiet. I had two young kids at this point, so couldn't do as much as I'd have liked, but with the internet, I could keep up with what was going on.

There must be something about the summertime because in August 2003, I went to Goodfoot in Glasgow with my friend Jacqui – who I'd met on one of the Weller forums. Goodfoot was a long running soul night, I was nervous, this was the first scene night I'd attended in nearly 20 years, what if I'd lost my dance moves, was I dressed right? Bloody hell, people were up dancing ON THEIR OWN!!!!! I was so out of touch, there were Skins at a Soul do – my last experience of Skinheads was the Oi crowd of the early 80s, this was mad, but I loved it, the music was wonderful and I wanted to do this all the time.

Then I met Colin. He was a friend of Jacqui's, a Mod and was involved with Glasgow's Mod Club Friday Street. Colin is now my husband, and when circumstances allowed, we went to different clubs in Scotland, down to London for Crossfire, Leeds, Manchester and Rimini. I was hearing different sounds, bye bye northern soul, hello R&B; I got back into collecting records, and on occasion djing too. I organised a few nights and then started helping with Friday Streets PR and promotions. I helped book Andy Lewis for a Paul Weller after show party, through this involvement I met Andy Crofts, Steve Craddock and - it's only taken 25 years - Paul Weller.

A couple of years ago I started a mod fanzine with my friend Sharon Wood – Double Breasted Modzine is doing great and has been responsible for so many positive experiences. I've met many wonderful people through the fanzine, subscribers, advertisers and contributors, 'legends' like John Hellier, 'Mumper' Bax, Smiler, Dave Edwards, Guy Joseph and Eddie Pillar. My record reviews have put me in touch with Rich at Acid Jazz, Alex at Copasetic, I'm speaking to people all over the world, Mexico, Brazil, Hong Kong, hearing new music, interviewing bands and organising more gigs. Last year I put together a cd compilation of current Scottish mod/60s influenced bands (A Little Mixed Up), this turned into an allayer with 7 of the bands and I now have a record label which has released an album from The Laynes. I'm managing a band, and in 2010 A Little Mixed up 2 brought DC Fontana and The Universal to Scotland. Early in 2010, a chance meeting with Gary and Simon from the Purple Hearts at a book launch developed into me promoting both the Purple Hearts and The Chords gigs in Glasgow, the first time either band had played in Scotland for over 25 years. It's been amazing to see so many happy faces watching bands they worshipped as young mods back in the early 80s.

I remember having a conversation with a "grunge" friend about 15 years ago when I was 25. A guy drove past on a Vespa, and I turned to my pal and said, "When I was a mod, I always wanted a Vespa." his response, "Jen; you'll

always be a Mod." This conversation makes me think of what's being said nowadays about the so called "Mod Life Crisis." You never stop being a Mod, you might not be going to clubs, or being "Seen on the Scene," but just because you didn't regularly attend Club (insert name) in 1995 or a Rally in 2000 because you had a young family, doesn't make you any less of a Mod than the guy who did.
I'm 40, have 4 kids and having the time of my life.
Jenny Baillie (Double Breasted fanzine)

18. A dance music account from the 90's from **Spencer Vinten**.

After the Indie and Madchester scene fizzled out I was propelled into the Rave scene on the back of a random invite to a house party in Camden in late 89. It was twenty quid to get in but with entry came a free Love Dove. Little did I know how much that one pill was going to change my life. This party had no dress code and absolutely no attitude, just a very pleasant young man (who turned out to be an old school friend) with a wide smile who greeted us at the door. Once inside the lights were dim. There was very little furniture and in the kitchen three fridges full of bottled water only.

The music was a blend of warm smooth house music. There were DJ's upstairs and down which was totally new to me at the time. Each track melted seamlessly into the next creating a constant mix of wonderful melodic rhythms. It was impossible to dance to it. Izit-Stories (the Jackanory mix) is the tune, with its vocal loop, that just says it all about the night.

One of the big things I remember is the overall lovely vibe and the fact that it didn't matter whose eyes you met with or person you spoke to, it was always met with a warm smile and a pleasant response. Conversations flowed and new friends were easily made. I left there feeling like I had not only found the latest new thing but I had seen the light, I had awoken, been re-born and an excitement that I had never felt before had risen within me. From then on it was always about getting into parties anywhere near or far, legal or illegal and later on large Raves like Raindance and Reincarnation and many others.

The music was infectious and hypnotic. The party goers were all like-minded and non-judgemental. Sound people with the sole intention to have fun. There was no rascism, no class divides, all were equal and were there to party and smile in a driven hedonistic musical heaven. We lived for the weekend, the latest tune, a dis-used warehouse party, M25 convoys looking for Raves. It was a life changing scene. View points shifted. Ideals were forgotten. Compliance was not an option. It was all for one and one for all.

Tunes that mark those days for, me are Moby-*Go* (the woodstick mix), Orbital-*Chime* and Gat Décor-*Passion*. I was soon DJing myself and throwing small local parties to spread the word, the love and the fabulous music. The Rave scene in my opinion changed the way of the world or definetley in the Uk for good. It is now firmly placed in mainstream music and the staple diet for many party people young or old with so many variations and reflections of the original scene.

Long may it continue. Love and Peace.
Spencer Vinten

19. A 90's Skinhead with a passion for Soul music from **Matty Morris**

When I was greatly younger I remember my days with family down the local working men's club. Seeing my uncles and friends dress in skinhead outfits and lace up there 10 hollers and dance to Madness and two tone. There were different groups back then. Rock and rollers, new age romantics. Never any aggro just groups getting ready to dance there jig to there delegated time slot. I suppose I was so young my child roots had been break dancing, another classic of the day. However, with my ability to learn break dancing fairly quickly and then to change dances to rock and roll and then swing to Madness and songs like *Driving In My Car* stood me in good stead for the future.

My Mum and Dad were ex skins, my Dad even an ex mod however, I don't remember any of that only that I hated a red gingham check shirt that was soon to become one of my favourite shirts as a child and the monkey boots and flight jackets and the hand me down Fred Perry's from all my cousins to my brother to me. My Dad was an ex Skin Dj from the local area so maybe the music was going to wear off on me unknowingly. My Mum was more subtle disco and Marvin Gaye, Tamla Motown. You could say I had a varied musical background.

Northern Soul and the Scootering Scene started back in the day between leaving school and starting college 1992. Not long after getting my first scooter which was a dream of mine for half a year since getting in to the mod scene (me and my mates) via the great classic film Quadrophenia and the Scootering mag. A strange time to be getting into the scene. Music was dead for us in the charts and our escape was old music. A few of my mates saw a club scooterist do (The Medway SC) going on so we decided to go. I can remember some guy saying *"who are you lot supposed to be?"* I replied *"The reincarnation of the mods"* to which he laughed and walked on. Not knowing the scene then as I do now. We loved the mixture of sounds and heard and saw a kind of dance unknown. We wanted to dance but it looked so alien. We loved the music. It seemed familiar to soul and Motown yet different. Any way we tried. I can remember saying to my mates take the piss. Just dance and you will be doing it. We were all movers and somehow taking the piss or letting go we were pulling it off. Or we thought we were?

It felt good to let go and find a crowd of like minded people. A few months later I happened by chance to come across a couple of Scooterists. More Scooter boy and Girl. With a passion for scooters and Northern Soul. I was already greatly involved with old/vintage music from my child hood. It was their passion and guidance on music and record labels and giving me duplicates that they had bought that I started off. Of course going to boot fairs and rifling through old 45's and albums and comparing our finds. I obviously came off worse in terms of knowing Northern Soul records. Time progressed Rallies, runs, Scooterist northern soul. Many great adventures. I got married; my wife fell pregnant and gave birth to my daughter bought a house, moved house. Pretty much a scootering life. That is until Camber Sands rally kicked the scene from Northern connoisseurs to open top blow you away all-night dancing. That was the case for me anyway. My passion to dance to scooterist northern soul as I call it had been going a while. However, the scene was a vibrant dance floor of Northern Soul, Skin, Punk, Mod and Indie all in one room. As fantastic as all this was (drinking dancing taking the pi**) the all-nighters of Camber seemed to take me over. No longer was I doing the scooterist side. I was now going from Northern Soul to Reggae rooms. By now I was and had a been a skinhead for while since 96. Clothes became baggier Jaytex's were being worn again by a scene springing up. Hair longer, less macho some would say. It has a new feeling but old in essence. They looked and classed themselves as old... Maybe I had only just discovered it. Maybe I was part of creating the new look and passion within a small band of Northern Soul dancers from the skinhead world. These people were very like minded and sprung from the bad old days of youths finding there feet and not tolerating other youth group's gangs or musical tastes.

The scootering scene had whipped this up and shown the best of all cults. Perhaps we were a generation younger more tolerant that had enjoyed so many different musical passions that a new subculture was going to be born. Very similar to Suede head but a generation schooled on so much diversity and musical talents that to discover Northern Soul culminated this in a new generation wanting all night dancing to something we loved and related to. Something that although we had not heard directly had influenced our child hood music. Of the eighties and nineties where everything seemed to be a remix of old. This was Northern Soul and I think the birth for me of the Soul Skin. Not a big group of people. On the fringes you see them smart and shuffling. Someone influenced by Northern Soul with roots firmly in Reggae and the Skinhead way of life. But with passion and love of soul and dancing and partying hard. Somehow Camber made the Soul Skin for me.

My life in the scooterist scene had been going for a while when Camber started and I was an established shuffler. However, I left the comps and bigger move dancing to a chosen few. Camber introduced me to the Northern Soul Competition. Some would argue it isn't a proper comp. However, I disagree the amount of people entering from a shuffle to a somersault has grown and is growing. Bigger than some national dance comps.

I remember on an occasion when a friend finally striked up enough bravado to attempt Northern Soul dancing. After having a deep conversation with him he walked across the dance floor and started dancing only to realise it was in fact the change in record for the dance final. To which the DJ unceremonaly shouted at him to leave the floor. Thankfully it didn't deter him and he was shuffling about in the future. I did say to him fair play for attempting your first Northern Soul dance in a comp final. I said he had big bollocks for that!!! Lol.

My life was hitting the seven year itch, and not my itch. My wife's. A new outlet was needed. Scootering was a must but more was needed. Camber had kicked off a dancing passion. Although I was in a transition from scootering to Northern Soul. I started to attend the breakaway scootering movement that had started to do dedicated soul dos once again. The odd soul do was taken in around London, South Coast and Essex. I was loving the music. New records (unheard of from my prospective, that's the thing about Northern soul in 18 years of discovering it I am still finding and hearing records at do's on cd compilations it's a amazing) However, instead of helping the situ we were becoming more distant. Some one had caught the eye of my wife. Arguments and accusations were made. More dos and stolen looks. An admission that I was no longer loved and a feeling of despair from me. I had a conversation one time where I said after watching the dance comp I would enter. To which I was told "*I would never win*". You see my wife had regularly entered and come a decent 4th or 5th on the previous couple of occasions where I was watching or trying too through the crowds.

However, my marriage finally culminated in me finding out about an affair with the person I has initially thought it was. My mind set was horrible. I poured myself into Northern Soul; the music the dance the working out. Looking at myself as a whole and trying to better me! My dancing seemed to be stale, stagnant, unpolished and lazy. Just like me and my life. I video taped myself dancing once and said to myself you need to sort yourself out!! It was if I was somehow trying to change myself through dancing. Maybe a sad logic? But we all deal with our problems in a different way. I started changing my shuffles reflecting on past and present dancers I had seen and known. I tried to reinvent the dance and somehow me. I had a plan. Camber Sands. I would be ready for it.

Practising was easy. Whilst making dinner. Late at night in the house. Anytime was good. I was escaping and the music and working out to what you love is easy!

The time was approaching for the rally I rode down. I had a quiet Friday night in anticipation of Saturday night. I started Saturday night between the Reggae room and Soul room. Time was approaching for the real deal. I was sat in the Reggae and Ska room. I remember it well with some fellow Skinheads that were old skool and not into soul.

I was at a table drinking. As I had done most of the day. I am blessed with the ability to dance and drink. I don't do drugs. The passion and music take me over. Don't get me wrong I sweat buckets and get tired even knackered but I can carry on going or I could in the day. The comp was approaching and I said to the lads at the table I will be back in a moment. They said are you going to watch the comp. Might do I replied.

I walked to the dance floor and ask a friend to look after my braces wallet keys money. I wasn't prepared. My transition to Soul skin wasn't complete then and my tonic trousers were a little too tight but I had Loake brogue shoes for this but what the hell. The records flowed. My ex had also entered. By now the affair was over and a new person was on the agenda. A soul boy. They were trying to be discreet but I knew what was going on. It wasn't his fault maybe not even hers but for what I was witnessing. Life goes on I said to myself. However, I wanted some payback in a subtle personal way. I wanted revenge on her for the reason why my life was no longer what it was. Why I was eventually going to leave my home and my daughter. MY hard work. My laziness, my harshness, my nastiness. A good friend told me once to tell the fella of the affair to never show his face. He said to tell him if you turn up somewhere to put his pint down and leave. This guy heeded my words. My friend said once you kick him in and wreck his family he can turn up wherever he wants to and you will be in the wrong if you were to do it twice!!

I had chosen a peaceful path I had been handed the power to inflict damage by headcase friends and they would have done it. My thoughtful friend said think of your daughter. You will regret it in the future? How true that would have been. I never told his family I gave him the choice he never gave me. Although I am a firm believer that you make the decisions however tempted and my ex made her choice. I always said I would kill a man who robbed me of my life and family. It was close. I always said I would lie, cheat and steal for my family and unfortunately me ex did it for her lover of a couple of weeks! But something changed through dancing and partying. I had the outlet.

This was my passion; the comp. The words *"you will never win"* rang in my mind. Not for long the passion flowed the tunes rang out and I danced. It has been noted by some that I smile and really enjoy the music when I dance and that is true. I love it like a drug. Mad for it! People called my name in shock that I was in the comp. People were getting tagged out but I was alive in my mind, soul and body. On fire. I forgot everyone and everything. That is until the numbers dropped. The ex and new boyfriend were still in.

I had been knocked and barged earlier on Friday evening almost goaded by two guys dancing and showing off. I kept a lid on it! I just kept a lid on it. They were trying to show off earlier in the evening by my ex's. I think they thought they were doing her a favour but I wasn't biting then and now they got a taste as they were touched out. They looked on at me in amazement. They shook my hand after and congratulated me. It seemed very genuine and I thanked them. I think they knew what they had done on Friday and were perhaps a little shamed by it. People were amazed that my dance had changed or was I just imagining these feelings?

I probably was after the personal changing I had done through dance. How strange?

The old dancing splits came out. Leg kick, then down up on a twist. Or on to the other knee and back up spinning. Doing that move is always painful. The bruises are always evident on the knee after but I was having fun.

The moves I had learned as a child in the working men's clubs and practiced as a man in the kitchen and front room at home at every possible moment while cooking dinner and looking after baby of an evening. I was in there and in full flow. Then the new boyfriend went out. What a shame! But it inspired me. It gave me more confidence.

I now know him and there are no ill feelings its just life. We always say hello now. I don't remember how many songs went on but the ultimate happened the ex was tagged out and I think there were 5 of us left. That was it I had got my revenge. Strange and silly to look back but I still understand the feelings. Then the final came.

I was almost going to leave the dance floor my job had been done. I had done something and that seemed enough I didn't need to win it anymore. Then someone said come on Matty! "*You're the only one here who can beat Will*" Will was the champ at the time. They were kind words and inspired me. People were believing in the new me?? The final kicked off and only three of us left. High kicks drops. Luckily no split pants. Which I done a few times. Leg sweeps. However, the fatigue was setting in with us all. Everyone keeping an eye on the other secretly hoping that no one will throw another big move into the equation. Because you know you will have to equal or do better or you could lose it. The passion and free flowing dancing was oozing from me. The fun side that we all love was disappearing into a challenge to win and to please the crowd because of the cheering and to beat your opponent. This was not Northern Souling!!! It had changed. The champ from the previous two years was still in. I was still in but my fitness levels seemed better and that was going to win it for me I could sense. I hear the new song was coming to an end and I pulled one special move off at the end were I jump through my leg whilst holding my ankle with hand. (You have to see it) and I hopped I had done enough.

The song ended (*Do I Love You, Indeed I Do*) and it was a nervous wait. That was until I was announced in third. However, what I had not realised they announced the winner first and then second and third!!! I was ecstatic!! Third was good but I had misheard and I was the winner of the Camber Sands Northern Soul comp. I think it was the culmination of the new me forced upon by the powers at be. I had done it. People cheered and congratulated the people and dancing in the comp. It's all part of it I guess. A personal change, challenge and the icing on the cake.

In the celebrations after me realising I had won the comp I heard a pretty young girl ask my ex a question "*Who is that?*". My ex replied "*That's my husband*" To which I turned around step forward and promptly said to them both "*Not anymore*" After receiving the trophy (which was a gold scooter) I walked off back to the Reggae room. I walked through the large Soul room. I was having congratulations and back slapping from people I knew and didn't know. I met and became friends with a lot of people that night! Lots of hand shaking. I was the third or fourth person to win it in 9 years I think?

Any way I went back in to the Reggae room to the thunder of the bass and back to the table where my friends were still sitting. I put the trophy on the table. One of them read the plaque and said where did you steal that from? I laughed and said I won it! All of them didn't believe me and there were a few comments of "*FUCK of Wanker* "until the Reggae DJ announced across the mike that the Northern Soul champ was sitting in the Reggae room and that it was me. To which a big applause went up and my friend's faces was a picture.

I went home the next day and had a chat with my daughter (who was 5 at the time) and explained that the trophy was very important and that she should treasure it. She was impressed although it was a small scooter trophy. I said you must treasure this as Daddy may never win another again. I tried to explain my experience in a story about battling evil for good against adversity. I left her Mums actions out of it of course! I tried to explain that Daddy may never truly be able to recreate or feel the emotion to win. She would never understand or how I had related so much to the music. Life and hardships. The story went along the lines I had conquered my demons, fears and had won!

An emotional man who channels his feelings correctly and constructively is a powerful person. Too many stories are about destructive behaviour. The story I told her could become a Childs book. She loved it and hopefully taught her some life's experiences but I was telling the truth when I said I may never win it again because Soul dancing should come from the heart. You should flow with passion. Each song should mean some emotion and feel personal to you and your movements should reflect that. I don't think I will ever re-create the passion and determination to dance as I did that night. I chose a peaceful route instead of violence and it showed in my dancing. I turned my life around that night!

The chimp
Matt Morris

20. A Northern Soul story by author **Iain McCartney** who has penned numerous books on his beloved Manchester United FC.

The thump of leather against leather produced an echoing wall of sound, vibrating around a packed Stretford End, as the merlinic magic of Best and Law concocted another United goal and what was to be another victory on the march to glory.

Some seven hours later, refuelled with a decent portion of chips and the local delicacy, meat and potato pie, washed down with a couple of pints or so, the eardrums were once again subject to more abuse, but it was now a deep thumping beat, backed by a distinctive female chorus, as predominately male voices sang more tuneful anthems than those which had heard earlier. The venue had moved from Warwick Road and Old Trafford to Whitworth Street and the Twisted Wheel.

Finding my memories into the pages of a book is a little surreal to say the least. Had it been a volume on Manchester United, that could have been understandable, but Northern Soul is an entirely different matter altogether.

Many on today's Northern Soul scene have either been there for the past countless years, a lifetime indeed, known too many by either face or name. While others were regulars at one point, moved away to family commitments and returned again in recent years and making up for lost time.

Where do I fit in? Good question.

It would be best described as having viewed things from the outside, drifted away completely for many years, but more recently climbed back aboard the Northern Soul train, buying the ticket and going the whole journey.

CD's, books, magazines, concerts, night's, weekenders and even djing. Making up for lost time indeed! Coming from south-west Scotland, not exactly a hot bed for anything really, never mind Northern Soul, I was never really one of the crowd. Not for me a weekend in one of the local pubs, or supporting the local football team – the superbly named Queen of the South – or even one of the Glasgow so called 'big-two', nor did I listen to the same music as school friends, who went on about Captain Beefheart, Doors etc, although they did enjoy Geno Washington's *Hand Clappin' Foot Stompin'*.................'.

No, I did go to dances in the local town hall and ok, I did enjoy the odd pint, but I supported Manchester United, as they we the first team I can remember hearing about and my grandfathers uncle actually played for them in their early days when they came under the guise of Newton Heath. Soul music was also my preferred musical taste.

Enjoying music, I obviously bought the chart records of the day, but Motown, Atlantic and the likes soon took over. My first Motown record? The Supremes *Baby Love* on Stateside. But how did I get into Northern Soul as it was soon to be called?

Haven't a clue to be honest, 'cause as I said, no-one else was and I didn't have any older brothers or sisters to influence me (thank goodness). Obviously radio played a part, Radio Caroline and Luxemburg and I seem to remember a Saturday morning programme that would play favourable sounds. The Impressions – *You've Been Cheatin'* comes to mind.

I also, as mentioned earlier, went to local dances from an early age. I wasn't stupid. No sir, three O'grades and I knew that where there was music there were females and if you could dance......

The local promoter didn't simply go for local groups, (although a couple of them were good and well influenced by black American music, for want of a better description), with many travelling up the old A6 from Manchester and Liverpool and they would also play countless soul classics. Occasionally, there would be a coloured group appear who would give you 100% soul.

The seeds were certainly planted. I was by now also a member of the local Boy's Club, where we started having Saturday night disco's allowing me to DJ. Ok, I had to play the hits of the day, but you could easily slip in a bit of Motown.

The Boy's Club would go camping for ten days during the summer, with Whitby the first venture. I didn't go there as I wasn't a member then, but when they changed and decided to give Blackpool a go, I was a member, so it was off to the seaside.

Obviously, the Pleasure Beach was the big attraction and the first port of call, but approaching the main entrance, numerous females, and the odd male (but who cared), were making their way through a door at the bottom of what looked like a glass helter-skelter. Thoughts of the Big Dipper and the Grand National soon disappeared and where these short skirted females were going was of much more interest.

It turned out to be the entrance to the Casino and as it was Sunday, you could join their 'Sunday Dance Club'. Signed on the dotted line, parted with the money and up the spiral staircase. After about three bends, it opened up to a set of double doors from which music wafted out.

Walking through those doors was akin to a four year old walking into Santa's Grotto, as soon the already familiar sounds of *Stop Her on Sight*, *This Old Heart of Mine*, Heaven Must Have Sent You and the likes were bouncing off the eardrums. Other unfamiliar tunes such as *I'll Do Anything*, *Girls Are out to Get You* and *Seven Days Is Too Long* soon had me lost in a different world. Even the two go-go girls dancing at the side of the stage failed to grab my attention. Well, not too much of it anyway.

This was indeed the place to be and where I would spend most nights of the holiday and the road to the Casino would become a well worn path as I returned for the next two years.

One night, however, one particular song began to spill from the speakers and I was caught like a rabbit in a car's headlights. I had never heard it before, but from those first few bars I was instantly smitten - *"It's so hard lovin' you, but I don't wanna let you go. Little darlin' I need you, Little darlin' I love you. Little darlin' I want you. Little darlin' I've got to have you.........'* and to this day, it is still my all-time favourite.

Once I returned home, my first stop was a local record shop, where low and behold, they had a Marvin Gaye's Greatest Hits album. *'Could you play me track 4 on side two please?'* I asked the assistant and a minute later it was as if I was back in Blackpool. *'Yes. I'll have that thanks'.*

That record shop, well it was one that had a record department amongst the televisions and washing machines, became a regular haunt on a Saturday. I lived in a small town fifteen miles from this particular shop and yes, it was a small town, as the local prostitute was still a virgin, while the town fire brigade was a ten year old bed-wetter and by then the shop which had catered for the record buying public had given up selling the bits of plastic, hence having to make the thirty mile round trip.

Discovering 'Blues and Soul' magazine made my trips to the record shop even more regular. The magazine was something else that came about by pure chance. One afternoon, I went into one of the local newsagents simply to see a girl who worked there and while she was serving someone else, I noticed on the counter a magazine entitled 'Blues and Soul'. Picked it up, gave her the money, *'see you sometime'* and off I went.

This was one of the early issues of the magazine and it was read from cover to cover and a regular order was soon placed. It also opened up a whole new world for obtaining records and finding out what was being released.

Moving back to Blackpool, the DJ at the Casino Club was Garry Wilde, who I got to know quite well and who had a small kiosk just down from the Winter Gardens, where he would sell cigarettes and surprisingly northern soul records. Apparently, this kiosk was also frequented by a young Ian Levine.

Gary was always happy to talk about the music and I believe he was one of the first importers of soul records into the UK. I didn't buy any of his records, but remember buying a few from a record shop a hundred yards or so away, just down from the side entrance of the Winter Gardens. I can also remember finding in another of those record cum washing machine cum television selling shops, a Polydor LP which contained Edwin's *SOS* and *Headline News* and also *I Spy for the FBI* by Jamo Thomas.

A few years later, a market, a short walk from the Mecca building also produced a good variety of sounds on American labels including *A Love Reputation* and *Have More Time* amongst others.

The Mecca was obviously known about, but this was pre-Levine/Curtis, although 'the music' could still be heard, albeit not in the same excellent format as the Casino at the Pleasure Beach. However, in latter years, once the Highland Room became established, the escalator and the short walk along the corridor would be taken.

Football was, however, my first love and most of the spare cash went on travelling around the countryside watching my beloved United and also buying old programmes and other pieces of memorabilia. However, through the pages of 'Blues and Soul', I learnt that I could combine both music and football.

A journey south in those now distant days meant leaving home on the Friday night, sleeping in a station waiting room at Preston Station and then on to Manchester. There was no hurry to get out of Old Trafford at full time and back to the city centre, as the Wheel didn't open until eleven.

First stop was Victoria Station to reclaim the holdall from the left luggage locker, followed by a quick wash and change in the toilets, who cared for street cred in those days?

With the Wheels late opening, there were always a few hours to pass and more often than not, it was a quiet drink in one or two pubs in the city centre. On occasions, the Ritz would produce a pre-Wheel buzz; something that was required from time to time if United failed to deliver.

Early Sunday morning, it was back to Victoria Station to catch the train home, but more often than not, plain clothed police would pounce and ask where you had been. Mention the Wheel and they were through your bag to see what they could find.

I am still surprised that I did not end up in Glasgow or Inverness, as most of the journey was past asleep!

By the time Wigan Casino came around, the music had taken a back seat and it was United on a Saturday and play for a local side on the Sunday, then marriage and a family took over, although I still went to United, while the records and magazines gathered dust in the loft.

On Sunday, however, in Carlisle's branch of HMV, I bumped into a lad from town, (I had by now moved the fifteen miles), who I knew to say hello to, whilst also knowing that he was into 'the music'.

"*Do you still like the music then?*" I asked. "*Yes*" came the reply. A meeting and an answer that re-opened the door to the world of Northern Soul.

I'll pop round with a couple of CD's soon became a regular occurrence and as I didn't play my records anymore, it was suggested that I trade them in for CD's. Being away from the music, I hadn't even bothered to buy any, but up to the loft I went and after listing them, or at least most of them, as I decided to keep some, I took them down to Manchester and traded them in.

Magazines and books were then bought, as I had a lot of catching up to do, although I knew it was an impossible feat to do so completely. The internet and Sky radio channels were there to be accessed with new sounds, at least to my ears, to be discovered and enjoyed.

Through Jeff, my new soul mate, I discovered that there were soul nights in Carlisle, but how would I feel about attending such a thing after so long away?

"*Yes, let's go*" said my wife, so off we went and surprisingly, it felt as if I had never been away. The sounds were those that I had listened and danced to years before.

The CD collection increased, an ipod was purchased and the journeys to and from Old Trafford were to become enjoyable even if United lost.

The door to the new world of Northern Soul opened even further when Jeff decided to start soul nights in Dumfries and they would enable me to make the odd return behind the decks. "*Playing CD's at a Soul Night*" I can hear the purist shout, but who cares? If I can play Kim Weston's excellent *You Can Do It* and fill the floor with no one concerned about the format, only wanting to dance, then that it fine by me.

Northern Soul is to be enjoyed in any format and who has the given right to say what is right and what is wrong. Blackpool Weekenders are now a regular date on the calendar and I enjoy the music more than ever. Yes, I regret never having visited Wigan Casino, but I am also glad that I didn't give up United for the music, as I would not have started writing and having seen my books on countless stores around the country and in top ten best sellers' charts, there are no regrets.

I still have flyers and a membership card from the Wheel, a membership card from the Blackpool Casino where it all began. I have spoken to numerous United greats, whilst I can now also say that I have met legends from my other love in the form of Edwin Starr, Mary Wilson, Martha Reeves and Duke Fakir.

Having been travelling south to watch United since the late sixties, and having missed only one weekend home game in the past twenty-three years, one day, I will say that's it. However, the beat, the wailing saxophone and the female backing chorus will linger on forever.

Keep the Faith.
Iain McCartney (Author)

21. A young Soul Rebel's story. **Perry Neech**

I can honestly say that I have no real idea about what has been in the pop charts for the last few years. There isn't really many a song in the pop charts nowadays that I feel has real 'soul' in it, which is why I choose to listen to this type of music. When I say 'soul' I mean actual passion and emotion in the music and lyrics. I have only been around the scene for a short while but I feel happy to be part of something like this, and I love the fact that although becoming more popular, it is still quite underground. People in the scene, including myself, are in it for the love of the music and dancing whereas other more popular scenes are all about how much money you have and material things you can show off, here you show off what new moves you have learned or a song you have discovered and if not you just enjoy the music and people generally leave you to it. Not to deter from the fact that people in the scene around my age like to go out and have a good drink that is also part of it, but I know definitely for myself it is also that whilst having a good drink, you do not have to worry about confrontation. There is no aggression in the music so there is no real aggression in the people (well so far as I know but as I have said I am still, compared too many others, quite new to the scene).

Something else I like about the scene, and it would seem a little more popular now with the younger crowd although it has always been around in the soul scene, is that people like to dress smart to go out to soul nights. I personally think it is important to want to look smart as it's not often thought about nowadays within the younger generation and once the older generation aren't around anymore, we are going to be the ones who have to uphold this past trend.

What also comes with this culture are the venues the all-nighters are held in. Generally outside of London, the venues are usually old buildings that have been looked after for many years and the floors kept in fantastic condition for dancing. It's so nice to have a good dance floor rather than a sticky, glass covered slab of concrete, unfortunately there isn't many venues in London, that are used, that have a good dance floor which is a massive shame as the DJ's in London play great music and hold real good nights, "Sweet & Deadly" and "Pork & Beans" are a couple of nights that I go to in London that are great nights. That is why I am enjoying the film I am involved in at the moment,

because it is a venue in London that has a good floor and the place is a working man's club so it also brings back good memories from when I was a kid. It also sells cheaper drinks. London is expensive. Recently I went to a rare soul all-nighter in Wolverhampton, it was the first time I had been to a night dedicated to just rare soul music. It was a fantastic night and I heard some amazing music, in fact one song in particular I would say is one of my favourites. *I'm A Lonely Man* by The Dynamics an absolutely fantastic piece of music, so much emotion in the song and extremely strong vocals, you really feel for the person singing. As I said before you rarely hear music like this anymore where you become totally involved and feel exactly what the person singing is feeling. It took me a couple of weeks to find this song, and I asked a few different DJ's during this time everyone tried to help me find it, a good friendly crowd of people all wanting to hear good music. When I finally found out who it was, ironically it was from the DJ who played the song at Wolverhampton I bumped in to him at another night in Stoke. Another song which is one of my favourites is *The Night* by Frankie Valli. Although many people in the scene would say it is an oldie and that it has probably been over played, I can guarantee when that bass line starts everyone gets a move on and shuffles to the dance floor. It is another song where the vocals are outstanding, harmonies and all, which most people know seen as it's a Frankie Valli song. What I love about this music and probably all music from this time is that it was all live music with real musicians, no computer generated music that is made nowadays. I find it extremely hard to appreciate any music that you create without actually being a decent musician.
Perry Neech

22. Scootering Magazine Journalist **Mark Sargaent** tells a story.

Looking back at my formative years when I was a teenager is unnerving, some of the things that were 'normal'. Discovering girls, clothes, beer, fags football and music all within a few months of each other. Okay, football wise I'd been indoctrinated into supporting my local team, Oxford United, from almost the off by my Dad, as I became a teenager, I'd go with other lads and get involved in both home and, more so, away day excursions. Adopted or tolerated by the local Skinheads and sSuedeheads who had at least 3 years on me, I learnt to ride scooters - Lambretta's, and would bunk off school on Wednesdays to 'work' on a market stall. Not just any market stall, this one offered Levi jeans and sta -prest, Ben Sherman, Brutus and Jaytex button down collar shirts as well as Harrington Jackets and Crombie style coats. A handy way of earning a few quid as well as getting a huge discount on all the clobber on offer. Eventually my school had enough of my antics, which resulted in expulsion a few months before I was 14.

As for the music, in the very early 70's it was Trojan Reggae, Stax, Atlantic and Tamla Motown, there was a youth club in Oxford City centre, The Catacombs. It was there that I made my debut as a DJ, for me the soul sides just shaded it, especially as it was soul that the girls seemed to prefer.

Early 1972 I had my first encounter with what would become known as Northern Soul, a car full of us had been to an away match in the Midlands, on the way back, at the suggestion/insistence of Coco a Suedehead from Bicester, who went to the The Golden Torch, we stopped off in Wolverhampton at a place called The Catacombs. I'd have been 14 at the time, I was full of alcohol and pharmaceuticals, and can't remember much about that particular experience, apart from it was hot, dark and the music seemed to be absolutely brilliant. Mind you I was trying out all my best chat up lines, which for once failed every time.

Saturday nights, football away days excepted, were often spent at Dunstable's California Ballrooms. Bit of a trek from Oxford, but even with a midnight finish, most nights at the Cali' were excellent. There was always a live act in the main room, invariably an American Soul outfit or act, I saw Arthur Conley, Ben E King, KC and The Sunshine Band, George and Gwen McRae, The first 'Philly Busters ' tour package, Edwin Starr, The Four Tops, The Temptations and many more. Downstairs was The Devils Den, where resident DJ Brother Louie served up the hottest new import 45's. Working in what, for a short time, was Oxford's cutting edge menswear outlet, Stag Shop; every day the music on the in house 8-track was Soul. Baggies, both pleated and hi-waisted as well as bowling shirts, leather bomber jackets and 3/4 length coats were first available off the shelf from there. I'd occasionally browse through the assistant manager's copy of Blues and Soul Magazine, when Black Music Magazine came out he'd buy that too. Tony Cumming's first Northern Soul special, starting off with Eddie Foster's spirit visiting the underground UK scene had quite an appeal. Russell Acott's, a music shop that stocked a massive amount of soul music in the upstairs record emporium, both old and brand new imports, proved to be very helpful. In the Black Music magazine feature was a 'playlist' from the scene's past, the Northern soul scene sounded interesting, naively I tentatively enquired if any of the records were still available. On British release, from stock, among my acquisitions were: Bobby Sheen *Dr.Love*, The Poets *She Blew a Good Thing*, Bobby Hebb *Love, Love, Love*.

Fellow Oxford United supporter, Graham Hilsdon, dropped into Stag Shop late September 1973, there was a coach trip to Wigan Casino arranged for early October, was I interested. You bet I was, via working in the shop I spread the word, and all the seats were snapped up rather quickly. Membership arrived, a blue one, which I still have today, it was a few weeks after the Casino's first anniversary that I made my first trip to an all-nighter. A defining night in my life, as once I took my first look off the balcony at the packed dance floor below, I was hooked. Even though the windscreen on the coach shattered on the way back to Oxford, I wasn't put off. Clichéd though it may be, my first visit to The Casino was a life shaping moment.

Excursions to The Casino were every four to six weeks, some of my earliest original 45 purchases included Gwen and Ray *Build Your House (On A Strong Foundation)*, Christine Cooper *Heartaches Away My Boy* and Williams and Watson *Too Late*. While visits to Russell Acott turned up lots of gems, a chap called Brian who worked there on Saturday's had been buying Tamla Motown for years, which led to some nice UK items joining my collection. Cream of which was Kim Weston *I'm Still Loving You* Tamla Motown TMG 511 white demo, for a large brandy!

I'd changed jobs, by now I was working as Bar Manager in Oxford's then top nightclub, Scamps, - classic uptown, late night, meat market part of the Star group who had a whole complex of premises close to Blackpool's North Pier, as well as a chain of clubs across the UK. Work commitments, as in 2.30-3am finish 6 nights a week didn't allow more than one monthly night off required to travel north for 3 hours to The Casino. Train, hitching, the Portsmouth coach, minibus trips, car convoys, got to The Casino many different ways. John 'Kojak' Harvey with his Inter City Soul Club, a kind a travelling soul road show, was quite active at the time, blagged myself a DJ slot at the Oxford alldayers, which were invariably on a Sunday, ICSC also started holding all-nighters in Yate near Bristol. A 50-mile drive. I attended most of the Yate 'niters, under Kojak, then Dinks under the Southern Soul Club banner, and finally Mick MacAvoy, who post Yate held several 'niters at a hotel in Swanage. Yate nights lights would go on in Scamps, and from nowhere seemingly, a horde of people in wide trousers (or flared skirts females, most the time!) eyes as wide as their strides & chewing gum frantically invaded. Collecting, washing and restocking the bar, while I cashed up the last till. Off to Yate within 10minutes, driven down by the then Scamps resident DJ Nigel, who had a transit with benches, fitted each side. DJ Nigel did venture in occasionally, though being a bit of a charmer, he usually took a (different) girl each time, & while we were in for the duration, he was getting better aquatinted. For one night only!

Also during the Yate era I went to most of the Bisley Pavilion all-nighters, while in Abingdon, the Youth centre wanted to raise funds for all weather 5 –a side footy pitches. They oversaw monthly all-nighters, and occasional alldayers, towards the end of the two years or so there were a few funk/jazz funk alldayers too. As well as Northern Soul, I was also into the funk and (soul inclined) disco tunes too. Very occasionally taking a trip to the Lacy Lady, The Goldmine, and later the Rio Didcot, where I guested as warm up DJ a few times. Saturday lunchtime session at Scamps, Oxford was 100% new imports and promo only British (pre-) releases that was my baby for the few years it ran, people coming in from a 30-40 mile radius of Oxford every week. Mind you at that time Oxford had some excellent clothes shops as well as Russell Acott, who had the latest US imports arrive every Saturday morning. The Jazz Funk allayers in Reading (I guested at the one where the Jazz-Funk room & Northern Soul room changed rooms, Jazz Funk in the main room for the first time. At the previous Reading alldayer, Chris Hill led a conga into the main room & put Magic Fly on the decks; Cockney Mick took it off and snapped the 12" in half! Purley, Alexander Palace, the first Caister, Southgate Royalty were all happenings I went to, plus DJ'ing on Sunday nights in the New Inn Cowley Road, Oxford.

During the golden era, I only made it to Blackpool Mecca a handful of times, Cleethorpes Pier and St Ives were others I visited even less. Abingdon all-nighters, although the venue was strange, some christened it the goldfish bowl, though plenty of rare originals changed hands there for very pocket friendly amounts. Wigan never disappointed, Bisley was always fun, and Yate was excellent. The card schools & backgammon as the sun filtered through the curtains to a backdrop (!) of top quality rare Soul, I'd go as far as to say that Yate at its peak laid down the blueprint for the Stafford style of sounds. After I had changed jobs from working at Scamps, a typical Yate excursion went something like this. Meet up in Abingdon, several cars would head off together to Newbury, descending on a pub called the Anchor, (or the Ship), which the local Soul fraternity had stocked the jukebox with Northern Soul 'reissues'. When Yate was on, it was a magnet to most travelling west; then, en masse we'd head off towards Yate, pausing for a while at Leigh Delamere services, meeting others Yate bound.

1978 I acquired a Lambretta GP125, within 12months there was a sizeable number travelling by scooter to the early 6T's rhythm 'n' soul nites as well as early RSG bashes in Hemel Hempstead. All-nighter wise over the next few years, Peterborough, Stafford, Chesterfield, 100 club, Leighton Buzzard and later Bradford Queen's Hall. I was getting regular DJ work at the RSG & Bradford 'niters as well as guest spots elsewhere.

Workwise, I had gone back to electrical engineering, a 5-day week, 39 then 37 hours, freed up more leisure time. As well as regularly going to rare Soul happenings, I was also doing the national scooter rallies, competing in scooter sport events, as well as during 9 months of the year, still going to most of Oxford United's games. Wembley '86 was the pinnacle of the yellows achievements, in the then old first division and league cup winners, now it's Oxford's 3rd season in the bottom division of the football league.

Although I'd always swapped and sold 45's, it was during the 80's that, like many other Soulies, that I pruned many classic, 60's style Northern Soul discs from my collection. Having a cosmopolitan taste in Soul, many went in swaps for, or to fund the purchase of rare 70's & 80's items. Canal Tavern was a superb Soul night with Rod Dearlove at the helm, a real collector's soulmine too, the quality of music played there was ultra-high.

I'd been asked to contribute to a brand new scooter magazine, British Scooter Scene, which became Scooter Scene, then eventually merging with Scootering. Marriage broke up; I was freelancing for the local paper as well as one or two other publications, so I took redundancy from the factory. Venues such as the Hacienda, Manchester & the Ministry of Sound were visited a few times after I'd been to a few early raves, similar to the rare soul scene, but, when you've found your own brand of champagne, others may be similar without actually pressing all your buttons I found. Bizarrely I ended up promoting live music, with work commitments, the Soul end of things went on the back burner for a few years, only getting to occasional functions on odd occasions. Although, one of the venues I worked for via my suggestion introduced a night named 'Retro', format being classic Soul & Funk from the 60's to mid 80's, which proved to be unbelievably popular. Gave me a smug satisfaction introducing tunes like Carol Anderson's *Sad Girl*, James Fountain *Seven Day Lover*, Glenda McCleod *No Stranger to Love* to a whole new audience.

Once you get bitten by the Rare Soul bug, you stay infected, and there is no cure, Metropolitan Soul Club started to hold all-nighters at The Rocket in North London, excellent venue, some superb obscurities, shame about the Northern Scene's politics! I DJ'ed at a couple of the warm up sessions across Holloway road, and had a guest spot (both main room and Modern room) at one of the 'niters. Also I guested at Togetherness weekender in Fleetwood, nr.

Blackpool Since around that time I have been buying, selling and trading rare soul records. There's still a handful I'm looking for, IF the price or deal is right. In recent years I've guested at Bisley, both main and modern room's as well as Talk of the South, RSG and Aylesbury soul club nights. Over the years I've amassed over 10,000 45's, and 12,000 12" and albums on vinyl, not to mention CD's, the vast majority of which are soul records. Even now I can't resist ferreting through second hand vinyl wherever I encounter any! Still collecting, still enjoying (in the main) and still when I can, getting to various Soul nights and 'niters, more years later than I prefer to admit to.
Mark Sarge Sargent

23. A 90's Brit popper and what happened next by **Rob Parker**

It's 1994 and I'm a fresh-faced 15 year old dressed in my finest Brit-pop garb: a uniform of needle cords and Adidas Sambas. I've blown my meagre paperboy's wages on a ticket to see The Charlatans at the Brixton Academy, my first real gig. Already overawed by the scale of the venue and the electric atmosphere, the band take to the stage and set my pulse racing. It's not Tim Burgess' laid-back drawl and loping, onstage-presence which captures my attention, however. No, it's keyboardist Rob Collins' Hammond organ sound, driving and insistent, which beats my ears into submission and has me transfixed. A couple of songs in and I'm completely hooked, dizzy and seduced by that distinctive, high-octane sound. Yet another Hammond casualty...

Back at home, I consult my teenage Bibles, Melody Maker and the NME, and discover, to my pleasure, that it is possible to trace a mini-modernist family tree from the bands The Charlatans cite as their influences. Groups such as Makin' Time and The Prisoners show up on my radar for the first time and start to open up a whole new world of musical possibilities.

Fast-forward a couple of years, and I become a Blow Up Club regular, freshly relocated from the Britpop Mecca of Camden's backstreets to Soho's infamous Wag Club, a venue soaked in its own brand of musical history. It was Blow Up which helped to really kick-start my appreciation of the 'scene'. Who wouldn't be seduced by the sight of London modernists dressed in their sharpest gear cutting a dash on the dance floor to tunes such as Ray Charles' *I Don't Need No Doctor* and Benny Spellman's *Fortune Teller*? My ears were opened to the finest quality 60s R&B, Northern Soul and Motown, and I couldn't get enough. A trip to Adam of London on Portobello Road saw me fitted with a three-button, tonic suit, blowing my savings in the process, but now at least I looked the part.

There was one crucial thing missing, however: wheels, and two of them. By now I was a student living off economy beans and 16p noodles, but I had my priorities straight: my first scooter, a white PX 125 disc model, purchased on finance and customised (or rather, bastardised, in retrospect) in a Mod-by-numbers garb of lights and Union Jacks. It became my ticket into the local scooter club, allowing me to meet and mix with other like-minded members whom I now count as close friends.

The August Bank Holiday weekend of 2002 sees me, my PX 125 and several scooter club pals riding down to the Isle of Wight Scooter Rally. Setting off late, a decision is taken to spend the night at a camp site en route in Arundel. Arriving in the town, we waste no time in getting down to the serious business of sampling the local real ale. Hours later, we merrily fall out of the pub with full stomachs and empty wallets, but soon come to regret our indulgence as the heavens open, sending us dashing to clumsily set up our tents in the driving rain. At 6.30am, word goes round that campers who haven't checked in the night before will be asked to pay the next day. With all our money lining the pub's tills, we decide to make a quick getaway and, rain-battered and hung over, try to dismantle our tents as swiftly and silently as possible. We reach our parked scooters and, to avoid attracting attention, attempt to push them through the quagmire to the nearest exit, all the while desperately trying to stifle fits of laughter. Mud-spattered, we reach the gates, make a quick head count and start up our scooters. Behind us, the camp site owner, alerted by the sound of our engines, arrives at the gates, fist shaking, just in time to see us speed off into the distance.

Rob Parker

24. Bags, Spins and Soul memories from **Will Vincent Hunt**

There's plenty been spoken and written about the history of the British soul scene, so despite decades of personal research, I won't try and recap with my own inaccuracies with who did what, where and when. This is purely a few snippets of my own experience, as I tried to personally recreate how it was, in the early 70s, in amongst an ever changing scene.

I've been a Skinhead since about Easter 1982, some years after the originals, but being born in 70's Sunderland gave me little choice. From musical beginnings, in Ska and Reggae (given a small helping hand by me and me brother Bob pinching me mam's collection of Blue Beat and Island 45's), apart from a few catchy Motown & Stax tunes, I hadn't shown a lot if interest in Soul, until I started attending Mod clubs in Newcastle. This was a relatively underground scene, mostly full of teenagers, but many with a passion for tailor-made suits, scooters and original 60's gems; mixed with a back drop of Soul, R&B, Motown and Ska, in a slightly cider-fuelled haze.

There was a great buzz, queuing outside of Mod all-niters, slyly checking the details on each other's clothes, eager to get on that dance-floor. I'd save my pocket money and dinner money (oh, how I was a hungry teenager!) to spend as much as possible on clothes and nights out. We'd scour second hand shops for original items and get the local tailor to do alteration work on old two tone suits (my pocket money certainly didn't extend to "bespoke"!) and sitting for hours sewing on cuff buttons and turning up trousers. I bought a pair of leather soled wingtip brogues from a shop in Hendon (best part of twenty quid – a lot of dinners missed), a pale imitation of the Cordovan lovelies I have now but I thought they looked the business at the time. If you shopped around Newcastle you could still get basket weave loafers, buckle riders and Hawkins Moon-hop 11 holers, and the charity shops were over flowing with Jaytex shirts and sheepskins for ten bob. I no longer fit into a 14" neck but I still wear most of the shoes I bought back then.

We'd often head off of a weekend, crammed into one of the older lad's cars, off to some grim town in Yorkshire or Lancs for a pure soul niter. I will never forget six of us squeezed into a beat up Ford Fiesta (I'd love to say Ford Anglia, but it was 1986!), none-stop soul in the cassette player, destination The Twisted Wheel in Manchester – still at the original Whitworth Street venue (as it is today). It was the club's monthly night off from Rocky's queers club (a slightly disturbing and amusing fact for a naïve 15 year old). The venue had changed little since its hallowed late 60's days (from what I'd been told). No massive dance-floor like many clubs of the time, but a few smaller rooms in a dingy basement – not a pretty sight. But the atmosphere was intense, and as the night went on, the sweat rained down from the low slung ceilings. My only regret from the night was getting ready at home thinking that a good choice of footwear would be my new riders which I'd previously hammered about 40 segs into each sole. A shiny wooden floor smeared with beer, sweat and talc didn't often agree with a full set of Blakeys, if ye wanted to risk more than a (Harlem) shuffle. I remember some old bloke (probably in his early-thirties) shaking my hand and chuckling summet to his mate like 'ahh - look at the little Skinhead'. I did look very young for my years back then! The strange thing is, even now at niters 20-odd years later, I look around and I'm still one of the youngest there.

I'd often head off to Keale with a mate Little Micky, niter bag over me shoulder with a small towel and a bottle of Brut, long before we had our own transport, walking miles to the station, a coach to Manchester, bus to Stoke, another bus to Keale and a walk through the campus. Must have been almost a full day's travel either way. After a quick change in the toilets, we'd endure what seemed like marathon dance sessions, then scab a lift into Stoke and spend hours on buses long after the excitement had all worn off. Always back for more though as the music, friends, atmosphere all made it worth-while.

Spins There's always been a manoeuvre on the dance-floor that ye can do, or ye can't ...... and that's spin.This first became apparent at our regular Tuesday night spot, The Wreck; I watched as two old soul boys had a spin-off against each other to Jnr Walker's Tune up (still probably my favourite Motown tune).

Always a tryer, I've been spinning for years, mostly unsuccessfully. For me (and I'm sure plenty of others, there's that moment when you carry off what seems like a perfect spin and an air of smug satisfaction washes over you, leaving a grin lasting at least 'til the end of the record. Then there's the other 90% of times when you spin off like a top across the floor, banging into people along the way (its often a good job the Soul dance-floor etiquette allows such misdemeanours without a fight breaking out as it often would elsewhere).

My 'worst spin of all time' has to be in the soul room on the Isle of Wight, some years back when I went into a massive spin, through what seemed to be a black hole in space and time. I landed flat on me back, looked up and all I saw was nothing. Everyone had gone; the thumping beat had disappeared and I was staring at a dark ceiling. For a moment I was totally confused. Had I been asleep? Had the do finished and I was on my own, still on the dance-floor? Then a big door swung open and large bouncer figure held out his hand, frowning with distain. Apparently, I'd spun across the floor, through some double doors, into another room, so by the time I landed the doors had swung closed, shutting out any evidence of where I was supposed to be.

So I am genuinely jealous of those you see on the floor, spinning effortlessly for what seems forever. Cap doffed.

Oxford bags Clothes have always been a big part of being a Skinhead for me. A recreation of the original styles with an attention to detail and authenticity. From the work boots, rolled up Levis and braces look that came out of 60's Mod, through the check Bennies, toniks, Crombie's and beyond, I've always been, what can only be described as obsessed, recreating looks from the whole era, through to Suedehead, Smoothie & Soul Boy. As trousers started to get wider in 1971-72, straight leg Levi sta-press evolved to parallels, waistbands thickened and Oxford bags (or Birmingham or Brummie bags) emerged. A million variations on a theme came and went, but the bags were common place in the Soul clubs of the north, like The Torch, Catacombs and later onto Wigan.

Now I know I was in nappies when all this was going on, but I've had me fair share of parallels over the years. 2, 3, 4, 5 button waistbands, multiple pockets, crown flaps, leg pockets, buttons galore and sometimes enough fabric to sail a ship. In the true spirit of youthful one-up-man-ship, "biggest is best" often prevailed (as it did, at times with biggest sideboards, most mirrors on your Lambretta, most ticket pockets or cuff buttons on yer suit etc etc.). I was at a scooter rally, late one night, arguing with an old mate, Dosser about who had the biggest pair of oxford bags. I had some 18 pocket, high waisted 32 inchers at the time (bought in Aflecks on me way to Keale), so confidently argued my point. So we agreed that when we met up next, we'd settle the score. I'd heard through the grapevine a few weeks later that he'd been to the tailor and had a pair of 36 inch parallels knocked up especially.

With no time to see a tailor myself, and never wanting to be outdone, what choice did I have? So off to the fabric shop at the weekend to get some supplies. Having never made a pair of trousers before, it was a little daunting, so asked the advice of the shopkeeper. I picked out some suitable black cloth ..."*I'm making a pair of trousers and need some help*" I said. So we went through outside leg measurements etc. "*They'll be quite wide - about 40 inches at the bottom*" I continued. "*No problem*" she muttered as she measured it out. "*And there'll be a few pockets*" ... bit more fabric ... "*and some buttons – 72, so give me 80 just in case*". The woman never raised a smile the whole time. So, with me mother's 60s Jones sewing machine, I set to work, with tailor's chalk and optimism. My first attempt of a waist-band and fly wasn't too professional, but after a re-think and what must have been every night for a fortnight, beavering away like Rumplestiltskin, they were done. It was Bridlington Scooter rally ('89 I think), and it was one of those moments when I walked into a very crowded pub, the place went silent and everyone looked round with gasps of horror and amusement. Me mate turned up in his newly crafted strides but they were no match for my home made efforts - 16 button waistband, 22 pockets, 72 buttons and 42 inch parallel legs were enough to win any prize. I still wear them now, but I've since learnt how there's a trick to getting down stairs without falling down them and how to piss in the gents without filling up ye turn-ups.

While I'm on about bags, I found an old 70's tailored pair once with about 48 petal flaps, too many buttons to count and a good 40 inch straight leg. I took them away with me to a soul week in the Canaries. First night on, I then noticed that the zip catch was bust and it wouldn't stay up. So I carefully safety pinned them from the inside, then off to the do. My first trip to the toilet meant fiddling on with my safety pin for ten minutes, a rigmarole I knew couldn't continue. Next time in, I realised that the trousers were so baggie, I could roll up the leg and simply piss out of one side. This did get me a few funny looks, later when there were no spare cubicles.

It will be a sad shame when the original crowd finally hang up there favourite leather soles and the scene disappears. There are a few youngsters around, which is refreshing to see – not just nightclub tourists, but genuine Soul fans, often leaving me green with envy as they handstand and fly around with the exuberance of youth firmly on their side. But the core has always (in my time) been the old crowd who were there at The Casino and beyond. Hopefully by the time it disappears, I'll be too old to backdrop (is there such an age?!) and will have banked enough memories to bow out gracefully.

After 20 odd years of niters and Soul dos, I've met a lot of good friends; chewed a lot of Wrigley's; lost a lot of weight (I think 9lb in one night was my record); ruined a few pairs of shoes (I danced the leather sole clean of a pair of Solatios one night, leaving me trying to dance on an insole and a few nails); talked a lot of rubbish (and listened to a lot more); split a few pairs of trousers; showed off (and been showed up); danced in the isles while Junior Walker wandered, blowing his sax, amongst the appreciative crowd; suffered various minor injuries; I've grabbed a couple of hours kip after a long night of dancing, before riding me Lambretta home, bleary eyed and dehydrated (mind you, that was about 2 years ago); I've danced to records that made my hair tingle, made me laugh, made me cry.

But for now, I'm still dressing like its 40 years ago, still riding Lambrettas and still making the most of the thriving scene that eases the opportunity to never grow up. All in all I'm pleased and proud to have played my part in what has to be the coolest underground music scene in existence. Long may it continue?

Will Hunt Vincent

26. A mods point of view from **Mark Smith**.

Mods speed back: The first time I can consciously recall hearing anything about Mods was during a mid 70's edition of BBC1's then flagship early evening news and current affairs show 'Nationwide'. Why anchor Mike Barratt's niche item on Mods and Rockers struck a chord with this fairly ordinary Home Counties boy, I couldn't say. Nevertheless, despite briefly labouring under the naïve and unfortunate misconception that Mods and Rockers were actually 'Mods'n'Rockers' and two parts of the same whole, the term, the idea, the word 'Mod' began to slowly resonate with me.

Not long after this unsolicited brush with the Mod ideal, teatime titillation arrived in the form of Bill Grundy and The Sex Pistols. A couple of well-placed live TV 'fucks', 'shits' and 'bastards' giving further impetus to the head of steam already built up by The Pistols and their acolytes. The raw heat and light generated provided a timely focal point for a certain youthful minority disinclined to fall into line with the generally banal, mainstream rock, pop and fashion then on offer.

Punk's totemic shock tactics notwithstanding, there were other credible street styles around. Bowie boys, Soul boys, re-stoked Skinhead embers et al, all circled in wary orbit. But by summer '77 the main factions had begun to polarise into two distinct camps, Punk and 'New wave'.

Then my nascent Mod leanings received a nudge via the seven inch singles rack in Woolworth's. Released in the July, it was the front cover of second single 'All around the World' by vanguard new wave act The Jam that initially caught my attention. A proud, hardboiled, no nonsense image and attitude emanated from the three stage suited protagonist's, backed up, I soon found out, by a distilled, aggressive, contemporary R&B based sound. Casting around for some early teenage form, instinct lent me towards the sounds and styles of this up and coming band.

Meanwhile, much captive time was spent as a supremely reluctant attendee of a brutish and spiteful all boys secondary modern. Relieving the tedium at this blot on the landscape were the sole two other boys my age sharing the same loose, unformed Modish daydreams. Through the rest of '77 and into '78, an increasing number of pointers came our way. The music papers in particular ran a number of features on the original Mods from which we gleaned big hints on the necessary manners and mores. We heard about scooter rallies in exotic, far flung locations like Southend. Tales of an un-dead Northern Mod scene (though in the photographs we saw, they looked to us like moustachioed renegades from the Crimean war, in their greatcoats and flared trousers) filtered through. Inspirational, Paul Weller fizzed across the piece. Radio's 1 and Luxembourg crackled out medium wave 'revive 45's' and 'golden oldies'. 'Best of' albums by the likes of Georgie Fame, Otis Redding, The Kinks and The Small Faces were knocked out on budget labels.

Part time jobs freed up a little money, generally enough for ten fags and the train fare to London. By now three had become a half dozen or so and we would gravitate towards Soho and the King's Road. Mostly we would just meander around the West End. Sometimes, depending on cash flow, one or another of us would buy a record, an item of clothing, stump up a round of teas in a caff, or take a punt on an esoteric sounding film and go to the pictures.

Our take on the mod perspective however, was never destined to be a straight re-run of the 60's. The economy was tanking, the winter of discontent in full flow, the incumbent Labour government about to breathe its last breath. Around the corner lay Margaret Thatcher and an unemployment abyss. Initially taught in imperials and my first pocket money paid in shillings, I was about to leave school at 15, unqualified, and enter a landscape of metric decline. Part of a peculiarly hybrid age group, left by an accident of birth uneasily traversing the optimistic yin of the 60's and pessimistic yang of the 70's, it was small wonder I suppose, that some of us chose to pick the pocket of the past.

These downbeat circumstances and a meagre budget meant that bespoke mohair suits and handmade basket weave shoes were not about to be on our page anytime soon, so thrift shops, dress agencies, and baby boomers wardrobes were plundered, and from these we attempted sartorial homage to the original spirits. For myself, at this point I favoured the Ivy League look, American import second hand clothing store 'Flip' being from where I actually bought such clothes, John Simons Ivy shop from where I aspired to buy such clothes. Meanwhile, on the home front, small town friction prevailed.

My then hometown, an hour South East of central London, was, for a teenager looking for a get out of jail card, something of a paradox. Staid, uninspiring, and possessed of a deathly stillness on a winter's Sunday afternoon, it was nevertheless de rigueur to run the gauntlet of the didecois, squaddies, Skinheads, Bikers and general malcontents who teemed in and out of the numerous pubs on a Friday and Saturday night. As budding Mods, we had been no more or less likely for a share of this boisterous recreational violence than anyone else and were tolerated as novice drinkers in certain backstreet boozers. This would shortly change.

Curiously, another crowd, more scooter oriented, (these lads had a year or two on us and lived in the surrounding villages) had developed in virtual isolation to our town based, non-mobile small gang. Our paths began to cross somewhat, but most, (though not quite all) were, as is often the way of things in such age based hierarchical situations, cold and aloof, and for the most part we never did hit it off. Ironically, in the longer term this enmity would leave them as peripheral players in our burgeoning Mod scene.

Over the next half year or so, three formative occurrences marked my mental card. The Observer magazine led with 'Mods Speed Back', a tip of the cap to the mod renaissance by now well under way in Southern England. To me, this article and the accompanying shots of Mods from Southend Scooter Club proved something was happening in the here and now and we weren't just manning the battlements of castles in the air. Next came the estimable Richard Barnes book 'Mods!' which gave me the hard copy means to look to the past to look to the future, and then finally, the cinematic release of Quadrophenia.

Not quite the tour de force it perhaps could have been, the film of Quadrophenia, taken in context, was and remains a decent piece of work. Sitting in the Granada on that 1979 Sunday, Mods on one side, Bikers on the other, and unfortunate neutrals in the middling crossfire (verbal and otherwise), there can't have been a single person present who thought the film would be venerated thirty plus years down the line. For us, the unforeseen fallout from our raucous, smoky, main screen afternoon's entertainment rapidly became clear. Viewed by our peer's pre-Quadrophenia as semi-secretive, slightly fogeyish youth cult outsiders, post Quadrophenia, any notion we ourselves may have had of stand alone non-engagement with the madding crowd were quickly dispelled. Mods became the madding crowd.

Up to this point a sparse coterie of likeminded friends and associates, events now cannoned past us. Our scene, such as it was, quickly diluted and mushroomed into headline news and staple fodder for every other high street Jack and Jill. Whilst this made for even more lively and interesting weekend town centre jousting, one couldn't be too precious. The silver lining of this populism was social. Everybody wanted a piece of the action so pubs, private parties, nightclubs and live bands, (some bandwaggoners, some not), all wanted in. We'd been all dressed up for a while, now we had somewhere to go.

Small but constant dramas came and went. Violence was endemic but most of our close circle also went to football so either partook, (with varying degrees of enthusiasm) or had the nous to get out of a tight spot. Spontaneous exuberance, word of mouth, flyers, fanzines and the New Musical Express all served us perfectly well in the constant pursuit of thrills and spills. A series of Saturday night gigs held in the ballroom at the end of Hastings pier featuring many of the up and coming Mod bands of the day were a must. London remained a perennial favourite for gigs, and as out of towners we were not hidebound by the adversarial north of the river/south of the river divide, so nowhere was out of bounds, (suffice to say ignorance was bliss and we sailed pretty close to the wind on that front). Bank Holiday runs were back on the agenda and much anticipated. Our general headquarters, slack night fall-back position, and safe house hideaway, complete with gated courtyard for scooters (by now we all had wheels) and an upstairs function room, was a typically homely working class pub set amongst tightly packed Victorian two up two downs, one of a plethora of such public houses, many, including this one, now late and much lamented.

A year down the line, a seventeen year old me sat with a cold beer on a hot Cayman Islands beach wondering what my Mod mates were up to. An earlier decision to join the navy had at the time seemed a good way out of a likely difficult and humdrum future. When, in the thick of the second Mod era the moment came, it didn't seem the smartest of moves anymore. Either way, I did my best to put my misgivings to one side and went off to sea.

Although not a completely absent friend, over the next few years my trips back became less frequent. After the high water mark of 1980 it was intriguing, on my visits home, to see how the scenes core Mod element had unravelled and splintered. A fleeting Indian summer of Psychedelia died an almost instant death, and then scooter rallies became the pre-eminent place to be seen. Inevitably the dress code down shifted to suit. Jeans, boots, a button down shirt and an MA1 became the order of the day. Musically, most of the '79 bands had withered on the vine, leaving Soul and Reggae nights to come to the fore. Girls, drugs and travel variously played their part.

Pretty soon, dissatisfaction with the stylistic nadir of the 'scooter boy' phase set in and led, for some of us, to something of an amalgam of styles. Football fans, gadabouts, and at heart Mods, a hybrid look encompassing the 80's terrace fashion vogue and 60's street Mod look developed. Slightly down the line the 'back to the land' ethos of the Pheonix Society caused a slight stir. But in truth, by 1985, when I left the navy, the ties that bound had loosened on us as friends, never mind 'Mods' or whatever it was that we saw ourselves as. People were getting married, buying houses, moving on.

The inelegantly monikered '1979 Mod Revival' has been harshly judged in many a critique, including by some on the 'preserved in aspic' wing of the Mod fraternity itself. What is often overlooked is that there was a small but ongoing, revitalised Mod scene two years and more prior to the film release of Quadrophenia. What there was not was any general interest in the 60's outside of these strange creatures who wanted 1978 to be 1964. In part at least, these imperfect 70's Mods acted as a benign Trojan horse for the

subsequent revisionist explosion of all things 1960's, the reverberations of which, for the betterment of all of us, echo on long and loud.
Mark Smith.

27. **Val Weedons** account of being a young Mod in the heart of swinging London in the mid-60's.

Val was born in Lewisham, South London in 1950 and was the youngest of five children. In 1963 Val and her family moved to Bromley in Kent. Like lots of other teenagers Val became a huge fan of The Beatles and it was this that sparked her interest in fashion and music. The Beatles were associated with the Mod movement because of their sharp suits and they set a trend with their fashionable haircuts. Her siblings John, Ray, June and Erik, all had their own record collections. Eldest brother John played guitar and for a brief period was in a skiffle band. But it was Val's brother Erik, who was the closest in age to Val that had the most influence introducing her to Blues music. Included in Erik's record collection were artists such as Muddy Waters, John Lee Hooker and The Rolling Stones.

In 1964 Val moved to Chesterfield in the North of England with her mother and father, sister June and brother Erik. Eldest brother John got married and stayed in London and Ray joined the Merchant Navy and set off around the world. Val's father worked for the accounts section of the GPO (part of the Royal Mail) and had been transferred to Chesterfield with his job. The family found themselves living on a housing estate just outside the town centre, which had been constructed especially for those workers being relocated there from London. This caused some resentment with local residents. And as Chesterfield was a small town Val had noticed there was a definite north/south divide. Val added "*The housing estate was still being built when we moved to our house and local gangs of youth would invade some of the building sites at the weekend, spraying graffiti on the newly plastered walls, saying "Go Home Londoners".* "*Kids at school would make fun of my south London accent. But I couldn't understand them at first either!*" Val used to go to small Blues clubs in the town centre with her brother Erik until she found her own circle of friends. Most of them associated themselves with the Mod movement and Val got more involved with this scene because of her passion for fashion and music.

The town's main live music venue was the "Chesterfield Ballroom" and this is where Val saw her first live bands such as The Pretty Things, Them and the

Mod band The Small Faces. Val was at an age where her parents struggled to keep control of her. "*I was very rebellious and there was a lot of conflict with my parents*" Val tells me.

In some ways that's why being a Mod was important to Val. It made her feel good and that she "belonged" to something that her parents and her other siblings weren't part of.

Most Saturdays Val would hop on a bus to Sheffield which was about 12 miles away from Chesterfield. It had a much bigger shopping centre so it's where Val got most of her clothes and where the Mod scene was thriving. There were a number of Mod clubs, but Val was never able to get into them because she looked so young. A lot of the music she listened to at this time was mainly bands coming out of the North playing the "Mersey sound". Bands like The Beatles obviously, but other bands such as The Searchers, Gerry and The Pacemakers, Freddie and The Dreamers.

It was when the Small Faces came to perform at the Chesterfield Ballroom that Val started to feel homesick for London. After the show Val hung around at the Stage Door until the band left the venue and walked back to their car with them. Val explains "*I asked if I could hold Steve's hand and he was really sweet and said I could. I was so excited and told them how great it was to hear a London accent! As I waved them off in their chauffeur driven car I was really sad and so wanted to get back to London. My brother Erik was also unhappy and even ran away from home briefly after a row with my parents about it all. Our parents gave in and we moved back to a terraced house in Torridon Road in Catford.*"

Val quit school when they moved back to London. She had no qualifications but her father found her a job training to be a typist in a Stock Broker's office in the City. A job which Val describes as "*the most boring job ever*"

"*I hated it so much and my boss was really horrid to me!*" So Val would "bunk off" work and go over to Carnaby Street where The Small Faces management and fan club offices were located. Pauline Corcoran had just been taken on as The Small Faces Fan Club Secretary and she and Val became great friends. Pauline begged Don Arden's step son Ricky, who was the Office Manager, to take Val on when it was mentioned she needed an assistant. So Pauline recommended Val because she had already been helping out! "*I got offered the job of "Office Junior" but only if I promised never to pester the band (Steve, Ronnie, Kenney and Jimmy) I was offered £6 a week, which was a drop of about ten bob, but I didn't tell my parents of the reduction in case they objected. As long as I still paid them £3 a week for my "keep" they never questioned it!*"

Val's role was to get everyone's coffee in the morning from one of the coffee bars around the corner from the Carnaby Street office, take the cheques to the bank and sort the mail out and generally run errands.

"*The one thing they wouldn't let me do at that time was answer the switchboard because they thought my south London accent was too common!*"

The office hours were 10am to 6pm, which were the usual hours for people working in the music and entertainment industry. It was very handy as it helped with the partying lifestyle that Val became accustomed to. Val says she would finish work and most nights go straight out to a club with Pauline, often staying at her flat in Wembley where Pauline lived with her mum and two brothers. Of course she got to see The Small Faces a lot during this time.

We got to meet lots of bands and I started going out with the drummer from a band called The Lonely Ones and they were connected to the same booking agency as The Small Faces. But they went to work abroad and although my boyfriend asked me to go with him, my parents blocked it as they thought I was too young. This made Val realise she wanted more independence and soon after she left home and got a bedsit in Notting Hill where a lot of people she knew from the music industry were living.

Through one of the musicians wives she became friends with another young girl called Jeannie from Guernsey and they partied a lot, frequenting all the hot and hip spots of the day like 'The Bag O'Nails' and 'Speakeasy' and a host of basement clubs, like 'Tiles' in Oxford Street and others that were part of the London scene in the 60's. Val was at one of the clubs on the night Jimi Hendrix turned up and jammed.

I asked Val some questions on the fashions of that period. Val described many of her hats she'd had, especially those big sixties chick floppy rimmed ones. She also had a reputation for favouring trousers over skirts and described to me her 'pride and joy' bell bottom jeans that she had and customised by adding small bells on the bottom. "*we would do things like this to our clothes*" Val explained "*it was creating our own little trade mark, we would also sew black and white circles onto our tee shirts, we were trying to be different*". They would try to replicate what they saw in the magazines and especially what the fellas in the bands were wearing. Silk scarves were also a favourite along with round toed, square heeled shoes with a strap that she could only get from a dance shop. Val also described her haircuts as being short "*to copy the guys*" and yet on occasion she would sometimes wear an Alice band that had a hair extension attachment. She told me she was not a Biba or Granny Takes a Trip type of girl, but preferred the high street shops like Chelsea Girl and Top Shop or similar chain stores, plus the big department stores like C & A.

Clothes were an important part of Val's growing up and she had the lifestyle to show them off and had a cracking job to boot. Val told me of how Kenney had told her about his first encounter with Ronnie Lane. It was a pub in east London that Kenney had been gigging with the house band. One of the bar staff was Stan Lane, Ronnie's brother. He told Kenney how his brother was trying to put a band together. The following week Ronnie walked in the pub, dressed in a sharp suit and super starched collar. So when Ronnie moved his head from side to side his shirt would stand still "*Kenney said it looked so funny, but it was because Ronnie was so skinny and small*" The two of them hit it off straight away and then they met up with Steve Marriott and Jimmy Winston. The rest is history as they say. The Small Faces were renowned for being Mods and Don Arden had set up accounts in all the Carnaby Street stores.

By now Val had also befriended two of the agents from Galaxy entertainment, Sue and Tony, who took her under their wing because she was only sixteen. "*Their office was just along the corridor from mine and I used to hang out there a lot*".

Sue and Tony used to organise all the tours for bands, including the Small Faces. Val says "I *would sometimes stay with Sue, who lived in Surrey, when there were any music industry events, such as the launch of Small Faces singles. It would often involve a very late night and Sue didn't like the idea of me making my way back home on my own. She was very protective, so I used to stay with her overnight and we would travel back to the office together the next morning. I went to work with Galaxy who moved offices to Denmark Street when the Small Faces left Don Arden. Galaxy took on a number of other high profile bands such as Amen Corner and The Move.*"

Val says that Don Arden was a good boss to work for, "*He was a larger than life character and could be scary sitting behind his large desk. He was firm but good*".

Don used to take the office girls out to one of the pubs in Carnaby St for liquid lunches, although Val was never allowed to go because she was so young. Val did however recollect a fantastic story when one day whilst in the office Don called her into his office to help decide what should be The Small Faces next single to release. Steve Marriott was in the office too and it appeared Don and Steve was at loggerheads over the best out of two recordings they had to release as a single. Knowing that Val was a huge Small Faces fan, Don played the songs and asked Val what she thought. "*I was *really embarrassed and sat on this chair terrified. I couldn't make up my mind at first. I remember one was an instrumental, which I really liked, and the other a ballad type song. Can't remember which songs they were now, but I do remember when the single was released they hadn't chosen the one I suggested!"*

Val described to me with great detail and fondness what it was like working for Don Arden and being in that office. She told me about the people she met whilst in the job, how Steve Marriott *"was a real laugh"*, also her short stint as girlfriend to Jimmy Winston (as mentioned in Ian McLagan's book 'All the Rage'), Val also kept in contact with Jimmy after he left the Small Faces and saw his many other bands like Winston's Fumbs and Jimmy Winston and his Reflections, and then his acting career in 'Hair'. Val also recalled feeling a bit sorry for Jimmy and the way he was treated after being sacked from The Small Faces. She would help Jimmy promote his band Winston Fumbs by getting an ink stamp with the bands name on it and go around some of the tube stations stamping their name on the walls practically covering Tottenham Court Rd!

Val showed me her scrap book of The Small Faces (some pictures Val has given permission to include in this book). The scrap book is priceless with cuttings and jottings from a 16 year old girl (that's how old she was when working in that office alongside The Small Faces and Arden's other acts of the period). The scrap book has several autographs from The Small Faces, a photograph of Val in the audience at a Small Faces gig during the Radio England 1966 tour at the Lewisham Odeon (Aug 12th 1966). Val remembers her favourite blue and white double breasted suit getting torn at the gig. There are also original copies of The Small Faces newsletters that Pauline use to compile and Val's job was to take them to the printers in Wardour St.

It was fascinating to hear some of the stories attached to the Galaxy period when they moved offices to Denmark Street and what it was like to work with bands like Amen Corner and The Move. In more recent times Val admits to using the name Galaxy Entertainments as a banner to work under helping to promote a number of Mod bands and the Small Faces tribute band The Small Fakers. After leaving Galaxy Entertainments back in 1968, Val had a few other office jobs until 1973 when she left work to have her first child.

Thanks to the internet, in 2005 Val made contact with Small Faces fans again and reconnected with Pauline Corcoran, whom she'd lost contact with when they both got married and had families. Val started attending Small Faces conventions and in 2007 she led a campaign to get a commemorative plaque put up outside the old offices in Carnaby Street in honour of Don

Arden and all the members of the Small Faces. The unveiling took place on September 4th and was attended by Kenney Jones, Jimmy Winston and Don Arden's son David (Sharon Osbourne's brother). Don Arden had died earlier that year.

Spending the time that I did with Val and hearing first hand accounts of being a teenager in the 60's, working in Carnaby St and meeting and working with the Small Faces and so on was a real unique pleasure. Getting to look at a teenage girls scrap book of the hippest band in the 60's was great and to get a female account of being a mod even better. Very grateful cheers Val
Val Weedon interview

28. **Eddie Piller**, founder of Acid Jazz records gives tells his story.

I discovered Soul music through the same route as so many other teenagers in the early 80' through the Mod Revival...You remember us; the kids in the parkas that turned up at the Wigan Casino in '79 asking for *Green Onions*! Often vilified in the books about Northern Soul, it is said that we didn't belong, that we actually spoilt 'the vibe'.

Now I've been going to Soul do's for over 30 years and I have always found this attitude prevalent, even today. The incumbents regard the scene as 'theirs' and any new blood coming in only dilutes the 'sacred' community of the few remaining warriors that carried the original torch, quite literally, at Blackpool, The Casino, The Twisted Wheel and er...The Torch. It's absolute bollocks, of course, because the Mod revival quite literally saved the Northern Soul scene. Had it not been for us, Northern Soul would be just another forgotten dance-led craze like Go Go, Disco or even Jazz Funk. Mod gave it a second life.

I and many like me never went to The Casino or The Highland Rooms, but we got into the Soul scene through a kind of Mod osmosis. You know the thing: '79 was a time of bands; The Who, Small Faces, and The Kinks, or even The Jam, Secret Affair and The Purple Hearts – and in the South, thousands of youths declared themselves Mod because that's what they regarded themselves as. Separate from the Punks, who were often their elder brothers, and regardless of what they understood of the original Mods: We did it to belong.

Quadrophenia blew the scene up nationally and the Mod revival spread to the north. Revival bands, like The Cherry Boys from Liverpool (who featured Chris Sharrock, of latter day Oasis fame), The Killermeters from Huddersfield and The Gents from Warrington, sprang up to cater for the Northern Mod revival, which was slightly different from the scene in the South as it still had an element of Northern Soul in the background.

After a while, the music began to bore. After all, how many times you can listen to *My Generation* before it becomes a cliché. Even in '79, mods began to look further afield. *Green Onions*, sure, that bugbear of the original Wiganites, proved that horizons were expanding. At the end of the year the booming mod revival propelled the record into the top 10; far higher than Booker T. reached when *Green Onions* was released in the '60s. Soon, DJ's began to appear on the bill at The Marquee club, between bands. The first was an original '60s mod called Jerry Floyd who managed Long Tall Shorty. He was the first to play Soul records in London, as far as we knew anyway. Sure, there were tiny clubs littered around the capital (well more like pubs and social clubs) that played Nolan Porter's *If I Could Only Be Sure* or some other lost sixties gem to an ever decreasing bunch of enthusiasts, but theirs was a separate world from ours. They looked different, were at least ten years older, and viewed the encroaching Mod scene with borderline contempt.

There were exceptions, of course. Randy Cozens was one: A legendary 'Hard Mod', the type that sociologists now cite as providing the template for the original Skinhead, back in '67. Randy had stuck with Mod virtually on his own. His love of Maxine Brown, Nella Dodds and Ernestine Anderson drove him to berate those sixteen year old 'tickets' that wandered around Soho in parkas jumping up and down to The Jam. He wrote letter after letter to the music papers of the day, Sounds, NME and Melody Maker, who printed them as a kind of mod lament. *"Reject this way of life and search out the true path, the path of your mod forefathers: Soul and Italian tailoring."*

Being a Mod was very hard in 1979. There was no internet, no microscopic dissection of what was or what might have been. Instead there was the hard reality of choosing a way of life outside the mainstream. No-one told us what to do or wear, we just did it and although we often got it wrong, we searched. The magic unveiled itself to us gradually. Nothing was given to us on a plate and often it was a hard lesson.

The word Northern wasn't used in London back in '79 or '80. We didn't have a clue what it was, where it was, or what it meant. Randy's persistence eventually paid off though, and in August of '79 Sounds printed Randy's top 100 Mod tunes as the original Mod chart (97 soul tracks, 2 ska, and a fake, to stop anyone claiming they had all 100). This was a whole new thing for us burgeoning Mods, and people dipped into the list to add some classic sides to their ever growing collections. Randy's chart didn't have too much effect though, because at the time Mod in London was going through a very 'swinging' sixties phase; LSD, paisley, Psychedelia and the Nuggets album (even Weller wore paisley on the cover of Strange Town). Clubs like The Groovy Cellar and Alice In Wonderland were the places to be seen, and clothes shops like the Regal and Kensington market stalls dictated the style pace.

Soul gradually seeped into our consciousness, but only gradually. Randy and Ady Croasdell set up the 6Ts soul club, originally in Belsize Park and later at The Saracen's Head in Covent Garden. At the time, I was, like many other clued-up Mod teenagers, checking out the live Soul sounds of Mod and Mod-influenced bands like The Step, Small Hours and the Q Tips. These were at the forefront of a new-soul sound, based on the Stax and Atlantic rhythms of the mid '60's. Now this was a specialist off-shoot of the Md revival, and only really appreciated by maybe a hundred or so people. But for the first time, 'mod-soul' faces were recognised as we all ended up going to the same gigs a couple of times a week. People like Nick the Comb and the Welling crew, or maybe Ivor Jones and the lads from Ealing. It was still Mod but taking on a different slant. It was only natural that two girls on this 'scene within a scene', Charlotte and a beautiful Suedehead called Claire should invite all of us down to a gig at their local pub in Belsize Park, and the 6Ts legend was born.

It was a weird place, not that many Mods at all. Some Skinheads and Rude Boys, some Northerners with flares and tank tops, and some straight-down-the-line 'normal' people made it an interesting experience. We honestly weren't used to mixing with normal people at the time and especially not Skinheads as London was a violent place for young Mods and we were extremely tribal by necessity. The music, though, was out of this world, and many of the tracks were chosen from Randy's original Mod Top 100, excepting the fake of course.

It was only a while before this new sound started to spread around the London Mod scene. Simply called Soul, new clubs started up...Tony Class and Andy Ruw in South London and...but I'm starting to run ahead of myself.

So how did I really get the soul bug?

Again it was a coincidence, but on this occasion it was most definitely a Mod coincidence. I'd had a scooter since '79 and by the middle of 1980 I was the proud owner of an extremely dysfunctional GP175. Now people who know scooters understand that a Lambretta, especially a re-bore with a big carburettor, is the least likely vehicle to be chosen as the ride of choice for a motorcycle messenger.

I met another Mod lad on Tottenham Court Road station platform. As was so common at the time we fell into conversation and it turned out he'd been to the same gig as me. I can't remember who, possibly The Purple Hearts. Whichever band it was, we'd been at The Notre Dame Hall off Leicester Square, a wonderful old ballroom run by nuns and home to regular Mod gigs in '79 and '80. As we were talking he let slip that he worked in the Labour Exchange in Wardour Street. My ears pricked up as I'd recently left college and walked out on a business management course in order to find employment in the music industry. I'd always wanted to work in music. My mother ran The Small Faces fan club in the sixties and hustling in Tin Pan Alley sounded like just the thing for me. Only it hadn't proved easy. Jacquie Curblishley, wife of Bill, manager of The Who, whom I'd known since I was a kid helped me with a few interviews at Polydor and MCA, but I hadn't got far. One tip she had told me, though, was that the music industry - then still based in Soho - advertised its junior jobs in the Wardour Street Labour Exchange...

I offered to buy my new found friend a pint in The Ship, next to The Marquee and a real 'industry' hang-out, and begged him to keep an eye out for any 'runner' jobs that came up in the 'business'. I heard nothing for a couple of months but true to his word, when something did arrive, I got the nod before the card was displayed on the wall. Consequently, I got the first interview for a small Indie label a week before anyone else had even seen the ad.

Based in Pall Mall and called Avatar, they had an impressive address. I was relatively pleased at the opportunity as I'd come across the label before; a Mod revival band from Essex called Sta Prest had released a single called *School Days* on the label six months previously (a single that now sells for upwards of £150). This knowledge left me in good stead at the interview as it appeared that I'd actually done my homework and prepared for it by listening to the available material. The boss, a genial bearded guy decked out in classic late '70's playboy gear (medallion, linen shirt undone three buttons down, kick-out trousers, and an obligatory hairy chest) was called Jon Brewer, and he told me they were looking for a committed and enthusiastic messenger with their own two wheeled transport. "*Did I have a bike?*" "*Yes,*" I replied and was immediately handed the job. My mate told me he'd never put the card up on the wall, and later Brewer asked if I knew why no-one else had applied for the job...."*er....dunno boss.*" Best fiver I ever spent!

It was much more interesting than it sounded. The label had a roster which boasted Stones guitarist Mick Taylor, and personal heroes Georgie Fame and Todd Rundgren. One release I remember fondly was *Two Pints of Lager and A Packet Crisps Please* by Max Splodge (who I later roadied for when he was in The Angelic Upstarts), and we also had the publishing to *Baker Street*, which was one of the biggest hits of the '70s, and ensured that the cash rolled in. The staff were either relics of the mid '70s industry heyday, new coming-men, or gorgeous Swedish blondes. This was most certainly the place for me.

It didn't start well. The Lambretta was a disaster on the short, stop-start journeys, never starting unless it was coaxed into action with a fifty yard jump-start sprint and clutch drop. I suffered weeks of torment at the hands of my two department heads, Geoff Thorne, the press officer, and Pete Chalcraft, a bearded super-heavy metal fan who was the A & R manager. They were constantly giving me non-existent packages to be delivered just around the corner, and admitted years later that they'd only done it to watch me, from the third floor window, panting up and down in the rain wearing a parka outside St James's Palace, where even the bear-skinned guards had a giggle.

Things changed for the better in the autumn of 1980. "*Do you have a real driving licence and can you drive a car?*" Jon Brewer asked. I answered in the affirmative and was told, in a kind of surprised grunt, that "*You've just been promoted to the promotions department. In a couple of months you'll be taking Edwin Starr on a tour of some northern clubs. You like soul music don't you? Good. It's called the Ric Tic tour, promoted by Chris King, and there's a whole load of singers on the road...*"

It turned out that we'd picked up the latest Edwin Starr album from the States and this was his big promo tour. Now I'd never been up North, certainly not to a Northern Soul night club, and the prospect both appalled and excited me. Brewer told me to brush up on the history of Detroit Soul so I wouldn't embarrass myself in the radio stations. My specific job was to take Edwin, and occasionally JJ Barnes, from their hotel to radio station interviews, and to get them back to the venue in time for the gig.

I didn't really want to go on my own, so after hustling DJ's Ian Clark and Tony Rounce for some background on Ric Tic, Golden World and Tamla, I persuaded Ray Margetson (who ran the highly successful Patriotic mod fanzine) to come with me. Avatar's largess didn't extend to hotels for the promotions kid, so I was faced with a sleeping bag in the back of the hire car...I didn't mind though and thought I could write about the experience in my own fanzine, which was called Extraordinary Sensations – and had just started a special soul section, written by the afore mentioned DJ, Ian Clark

We followed the Ric Tic tour and it truly opened our eyes. So much so to the extent that in the following spring Ray and myself started our own Soul night at a working-man's club in Ilford. Within a month we were full and cast the net further afield. We found the Regency Suite in Chadwell Heath. It was part of the Essex Jazz-Funk triangle that included the Lacy Lady and Zero Six, Jazz-Funk legend Froggy was the weekend resident, and the manager, obviously sceptical of a night playing sixties Soul, offered us a Monday. We didn't care what night of the week it was. We knew that the Essex mod scene was massive and literally, had nowhere to go to hear the new soul sound that we'd heard on the Ric Tic tour and were keen to play.

Sure, there were regular gigs that mixed soul in with more regular Mod sounds. They were mainly based in south London and run by Andy Ruw and a much more streetwise Tony Class...but, and it was a big but...they weren't specifically specialist Mod-Soul nights. Our Mondays were soon attracting upwards of 400 people a week with a hundred scooters in the car park. The Monday night scene grew and soon the guvnor offered us the Friday as well. This was also a success and we hosted guests like Peter 'Soul Cellar' Young and Capital radio's Gary Crowley. Word spread and soon the BBC arrived to film a documentary. The Mod revival had truly disappeared and Perry Haines, their style consultant was amazed at this totally underground scene that could attract punters from as far afield as Southampton and Peterborough every week, twice a week...The East London and Essex Mod scene reached a peak in late '81 and '82. Southend soon became a regular Saturday night trip, following the Essex Soulboy tradition of heading to the coast for the weekend (they had Zero 6 and TOTS and we had Scamps and Chesters with Chad and Del). But the Regency grew so fast that we soon hired the Ilford Palais for our first Mod alldayer. I was actually too young to sign the hire papers, as I was still 17, so my dad, who shared the name Edward, stepped in. In an attempt to distance ourselves from the whole rip-off Mod environment, we named the promotions company MIND and recruited Tony Matthews and Dean Port to help us sort it out....The Palais sold out and there began the rollercoaster ride of the next few years. But that's a different story.

Eddie Piller (Acid Jazz Records)

29. Northern Soul, it's not all grim up north! by **Simon Stevenson**

I grew up in Blackpool, born 1966, so inevitably Northern Soul became part of me and my friends life, from attending the local Church Youth Clubs, denomination didn't matter then and doesn't to me now either. Starting off local, St Paul's on Whitegate Drive was the first place I heard Northern Soul and Motown. It was not the sort of music my parents entertained. My dad referred to it as 'jungle music', when jungle hit the scene in the '80's I played him some and he had to agree Northern Soul had musical merit. We soon found our way to St Cuthbert's Youth Club; they had a nice hall with what I recall of as being a good dance-floor. All forms of current music were played, guessing the year would have been about 1978-80. There I met lads who were several years older and already regulars at Wigan. Then I could do all the moves, front and box splits, and Olympic circles (forward and backwards) but couldn't spin. It was around this time that I was although officially too young to get in, but using my brothers birth certificate, 2 years my senior, that I got into the under 18's discos at the Norbreck Castle and little did I know how important it would be in the scene, The Highland Room at The Mecca. It was at the Highland Room when I first realised I was a good dancer because in the Northern Soul sets there would be up to about 20-30 dancers surrounded by an appreciative audience. Here we really showed off, the age range was from me 14 to guys in their 20's that would come there before going off to Wigan or elsewhere. One day I saw a lad called China, jump up in the air and touch his toes (like Leroy in the opening credits of the TV show Fame). Egotistical little shit I was/am - *'I can do that and go one better'*. Up I went, made contact with my toes and wallop, straight down into box-splits. There were yelps of sympathetic pain from the audience but it was no problem for me, I just drew my legs back together into a vertical position finished with a high kick. This became my move. My mum wasn't that impressed that every time I came home from dancing I had blood all over my socks from skinning my ankles on the floor. Ahhh well.

The first record I brought was: Gerri Granger *I Go To Pieces* / Reparata & The Delrons *Panic* / James & Bobby Purify *Shake A Tail Feather* (UK Casino Classics CC3) original 3 track UK 7" vinyl single with the Wigan Casino Fifth Anniversary Souvenir Edition paper sleeve released in 1978. I still have it, as I do the full set. Over the next few years I built a collection of about 400 singles.

Time moves on, beer and dope are discovered and Northern Soul gave way to Roy Harper and Hawkwind. I still had my records buried in a wardrobe at my dads in Blackpool and always thought one day, they're going to be worth money, never realising that many were bootlegs - BUGGER!!! When I eventually got round to buying Manship's price guides I was blown away, *Stranger In My Arms, That's No Way To Treat A Girl*, several Okeh classics, Mirwood, all the great labels except Shrine, all the high value ones were bootlegs, all except *Oh Happy Days* by Flame N King And The Bold Ones. Which I flogged to Sean Chapman with a load of other records for my expenses of going to a Northampton Weekender, considerably less than the £300 it's now on his site for (I just checked), probably not my copy after a few years.

I still have lots of great tunes to sell, a lot of 70's kind of Blackpool sounds I got from Ian Levine a few years ago now. I tart a box around with me to many events, come up and say hi and have a look-see.

The clock on the wall spins like a Soulboy on whizz to show the passage of years, we're now late 2007. A guy at work has been listening to Mark Lamar on the radio that played some, and introduced, tracks as Northern Soul. These tunes impressed my colleague who in a warped train of consciousness linked that because I'm from up t'north therefore I must know about Northern Soul. 'Well', say I, 'As it happens.........' I knew the 100 Club did all-nighters but had no idea how huge the scene had become. After a few days searching on the internet I discovered that there was stuff on all over the place. The next one being a Soul In The City do at a club on Watling St behind St Paul's Cathedral. I went. I tried to dance, a bit clumsily at first but by the end of that night my legs remembered what to do and I was recreating the walk I did way back when. A brief but fabulous club for my renewed love was at The Castle, backroom of a pub at Tooting Broadway, S. London. I was soon going all over the place, Bidds and King's Hall in Stoke, 100 Club, the fabulous Bisley Pavilion, Twisted Wheel, Northampton Weekender loads of small do's all over the South, now having attended every weekender at Blackpool Tower, Whitby, etc. Yet to do Skeggie or Prestatyn but we'll get there eventually.

Mentioning Blackpool Tower reminds me of an occasion in the 80's when as teenagers we'd nick into the Tower when it was raining sometimes. One day I had my early model Sony Walkman with me playing Northern Soul. So I stepped onto the Tower Ballroom and danced to myself for a few minutes until one of the security guys chased me off with the words that have stayed with me since. *'Oi you, get off there, you can't dance on there!'* What else is it for? Now I'm there, spinning like a top in my Spencer's bags, best dancing shoes, pulling high kicks, handstands, jumps, etc, oh yeah, and occasionally landing on my arse but so what. I love it. I hope you do too.

I'm very fortunate that I can listen to music while at work and have found a fabulous internet radio station on www.live365.com just search on Northern Soul it's provided free by someone called Dave from Manchester. Thanks to him I've now played classic Soul to many colleagues some of who know what it its others just like the tunes. Cheers Dave, whoever you are.

Of course I must not to forget to mention and thank all the really great, fabulous and some beautiful people I've met over the last few years. I'm crap at remembering names but you all seem to be able to remember when and where we met previously. Cheers to the great friends I have made and to all those I've yet to meet.

There's just one thing I don't understand - why do some guys drink so much they can barely stand up let alone dance. I've even seen one geezer fall asleep stood up with a pint of lager in his hand which went all over the dance floor. You can't be having a good time, and more worrying are you driving home, knackered from some all-nighter - scary.
The little fat guy with long hair who spins like a Dervish
Simon Stevenson

30. **Nicky Porter**, Skinhead girl

It all began in a leafy outer suburb of London. The year was 1977. I remember the day like it was yesterday. I had taken the bus to a salon in Hounslow as my usual hairdresser had refused to cut my long auburn hair off! I had asked for a boyish cut, the stylist called it the "Elfin" look, and basically it was a crop. My parents returned from their holiday in France. The reaction was not good. I can't remember how many weeks it took my Dad to look at me. My mother, to this day, blames Johnny Rotten. Punk had arrived.

We became creative, painting shirts with "*God save the Queen*" and hunting Oxfam shops for granny style clothing to go with our old school blazers. We altered our jeans so they became drain-pipes and teamed them with plastic sandals or winkle pickers. I started listening to live music following friend's bands "The Dials" and "The Wardens".

Around this time we all went to the Winning Post in Whitton. It was 8th June 1977. Three sharply dressed young punks came on stage. Awkwardly, the lead singer introduced the band, "*Good evening, we are The Jam*" followed by "*123*" and the most exciting raw sound I had ever heard. We followed them to several gigs after that, The Nashville Rooms, Hammersmith Odeon and Bracknell sports centre to name a few. Little did I realise then that, nearly 35years later, I would still be listening to Weller's music and loving it. Punk and New Wave had hit the streets. Weekends were spent on buses and the tube searching obscure bands in London pubs, 999,The Rezillos, Milk, Buzzcocks, Penetration, Generation X, The Clash and X Ray Spex to name a few. I was lucky to be at the Top of The Pops studio when X Ray Spex performed and I saw myself on the tele when it was screened on the 18th May '78.

When we weren't trawling London we gathered at the Walton Hop disco, hoping for a sighting of local boy Jimmy Pursey and his band Sham 69. Jonathan King was the D.J. One night my mates dared me to dance on the stage in a competition. I was thrilled to win Jonathans latest single, even more so to be judged by Jimmy and Parsons (guitarist). Luckily, I wasn't invited back to one of Jonathan's parties!

On Friday 5th May we attended the Coronation Hall in Kingston Upon Thames to see Sham 69 play. It was to be a memorable night. A small group of trouble makers spilled into the streets after a tense gig. Plea's from Jimmy to calm down had fallen on deaf ears. That night the route from the hall to the train station was a dangerous one to be on. The small disruptive group became more aggressive and destructive as they ran through the streets, kicking out at vehicles and anything or anyone that got in their way. In the pouring rain the sound of crashing glass and sirens echoed out. Dozens of pairs of jeans were being looted, single shoes lay in the puddles in the road promptly driven over by the buses and police vans. My favourite jeans store had been emptied.

Elmbridge Council barred the band from performing at its halls. It didn't stop them playing many more times, even America, with the final gig (1979) ending in the usual violence at Middlesex Poly. It was about this time that Two-Tone had taken off. The Nashville Rooms on the corner of the Cromwell Road at West Kensington was a popular place. I think the first time I saw The Specials was here in June '79. It cost £1 to get in! It was a great venue, a large room adjacent to the pub and it was here that I saw Madness. 1979 was the year of change for me. My parents and sister, who shared my love of music, left for America for a year and I became an Art student in Epsom.

The music movements were developing. Where once you found Mods, Punks and Skin bands on the same line-up, now they were diverging. I was listening to more Reggae and Ska and original sounds from around the late 60's.I began to collect rare vinyl imports from Jamaica guided by the old hippy on his stall in Kingston market, Trojan, Pama and Treasure Isle were some favourite labels.

My obsession with charity shops and flea markets became a refined search for original 'sta-prest', Ben Sherman's and Brutus. I found my Crombie in an Oxfam in Epsom High Street. It was a deep dark navy almost black and a perfect fit. Kingston station had a 'gentleman's- outfitters' that sold red tab Levis. The original shrink to fit. I remember sitting in the bath until my legs had gone blue, from the dye not the cold! We altered the length of our jeans with a minimal turn-up, 1/4 inch, displaying the pale inner denim and the red and white selvedge edge. The shop was popular with the Teddy Boys and Rockabillies and had many coloured drape-coats on the rails. Alongside the suede creepers they stocked Frank Wright shoes, loafers, brogues and smooths. I had a pair of these loafers in black with tassles. I wore oxblood monkey boots in the day at college. When we got dressed up for a night out I preferred my highly polished penny loafers, also oxblood red. I always bought the same make. They were expensive but worth it from The Natural Shoe Store on the Kings Road. They were an American make, Bass, with a stitched leather sole. They were a more feminine loafer and perfect with a tonic jacket and skirt. We'd always add metal blakeys to the heel. I also continued to search Kensington Market. In the punk days when we were looking for something a bit different we came here. I became the proud owner of many checked shirts, all original Ben Shermans, some Brutus. A good friend , Belinda later sourced, I think from one of the vintage markets, white ribbed tights with a keyhole detail down the outside of the leg. I think we were the only ones to wear them on the scene.

It was when I went to Art School that I made some new friends that shared my passion for clothes and music of this style, one of whose sister had been an original skinhead in '69. She kindly gave me her original petrol blue and gold tonic jacket, it had been hand made for her. This fed my obsession and soon I owned 4 or 5 tonic jackets and coats, all slightly different but with the all important detailing of the fabric covered tiny buttons. I inherited tie and hat pins from my Grandma, my favourite was a butterfly which was a popular theme in the late 60s early 70s.I also had a good selection of silk hankies for the top pocket, perfectly folded to 3 points and occasionally a paisley scarf to finish off the look.

I moved in to a flat with Sharon a fellow art student. She shared my love of this era and of Northern Soul. Together we had an amazing record collection. I continued to see my old mates and at weekends we met at Feltham Football Club. Skins and Punks mixed well here and often a live band played. If not, local boy Tony Curtis would DJ playing a great mix of Ska, Reggae and Punk. Other times we would take the train to Clapham Junction walking through a dodgy estate to The York Tavern. Skinheads from all over London and further would meet here. It was one of the few pubs where we could all meet up and were accepted, enjoying a drink and listening to our music. It was a popular place, quickly filling up and spilling onto the streets.

We continued to shop at the second hand markets. There were quite a few in the Kings Road, Chelsea, and it had always been a good place to meet new faces. It was here on a Saturday in 1981 that Sharon and Andrea (my sister who had returned from America) and I were stopped and asked about our "look". We were dressed alike in our Levis and checked shirts and closely cropped hair. On August 29th we found ourselves in Woman magazine. It was a feature titled Street Life and included the various youth cults. We had been photographed and labelled "Skinheads". According to them we listened to Oi and hung about street corners and football matches, how wrong they were.

Bank Holidays were spent on long train journeys to various seaside destinations. Often on arrival, because of our "look", we would be put straight back on a train for London by the police. The Skinhead revival sadly was getting a bad reputation.

My four years at Art School had come to an end. I moved back to my parents home in Sunbury and got a job at Normansfield Hospital, the start of a career, I hoped, in Art Therapy. Around this time my sister had a new boyfriend with a Lambretta. Not long after we joined him on 2 wheels. Our newly acquired Vespa's took us to fresh venues and we began to enjoy a scene free from the racism and violence that was growing in other areas.

On a Wednesday I would occasionally go to a club in Kingston, at the back of the old Bentalls store, for a night of Soul and Ska. The Sheperds Bush Hotel was popular on a Sunday night at Sneakers, the club run by Paul Hallam, a local boy from our home town of Sunbury. It was here that I met Mr Extraordinary Sensations and was promptly nicknamed "Suedehead"! My barber in Epsom had always given me a scissor cut, probably the equivalent of a no.4 with a carefully layered longer fringe and neck. Now it had grown into an authentic feather cut brushed off the forehead to one side. I dressed accordingly adding a paisley Ben Sherman, tank tops and a fairisle yolk neck jumper to my wardrobe, always worn with one of my tonic jackets.

Sneakers and The Phoenix became regular fixtures. The mod scene was full on, always somewhere to go with new clubs popping up all over and bands to like Makin' Time and The Untouchables to go and see. Scooter rallies took us to the coast and the Isle of Wight for long weekends away. Back in London we would meet for cappuccinos in Carnaby Street by day before deciding which club to go to that evening. Sometimes we would travel to North London to meet up with the Camden Stylists. They too shared my obsession with authenticity and tonic and a love of ska. It was here in Camden at Dingwalls that we danced the night away to Desmond Dekker. That was around '84/'85.

Now all these years later I still have my prized record collection and listening to the old sounds still makes me smile. I sold my wardrobe, in a weak moment, to my old friend Belinda keeping my favourite green and gold tonic coat. I still wear Levis. I have a better scooter now, thanks to my husband, a fully restored Lambretta LI 150 Silver Special. I live a quieter life and on a sunny day can be seen out riding in New Zealand, remembering the good old days.

Nicky Porter (formerly Locking)

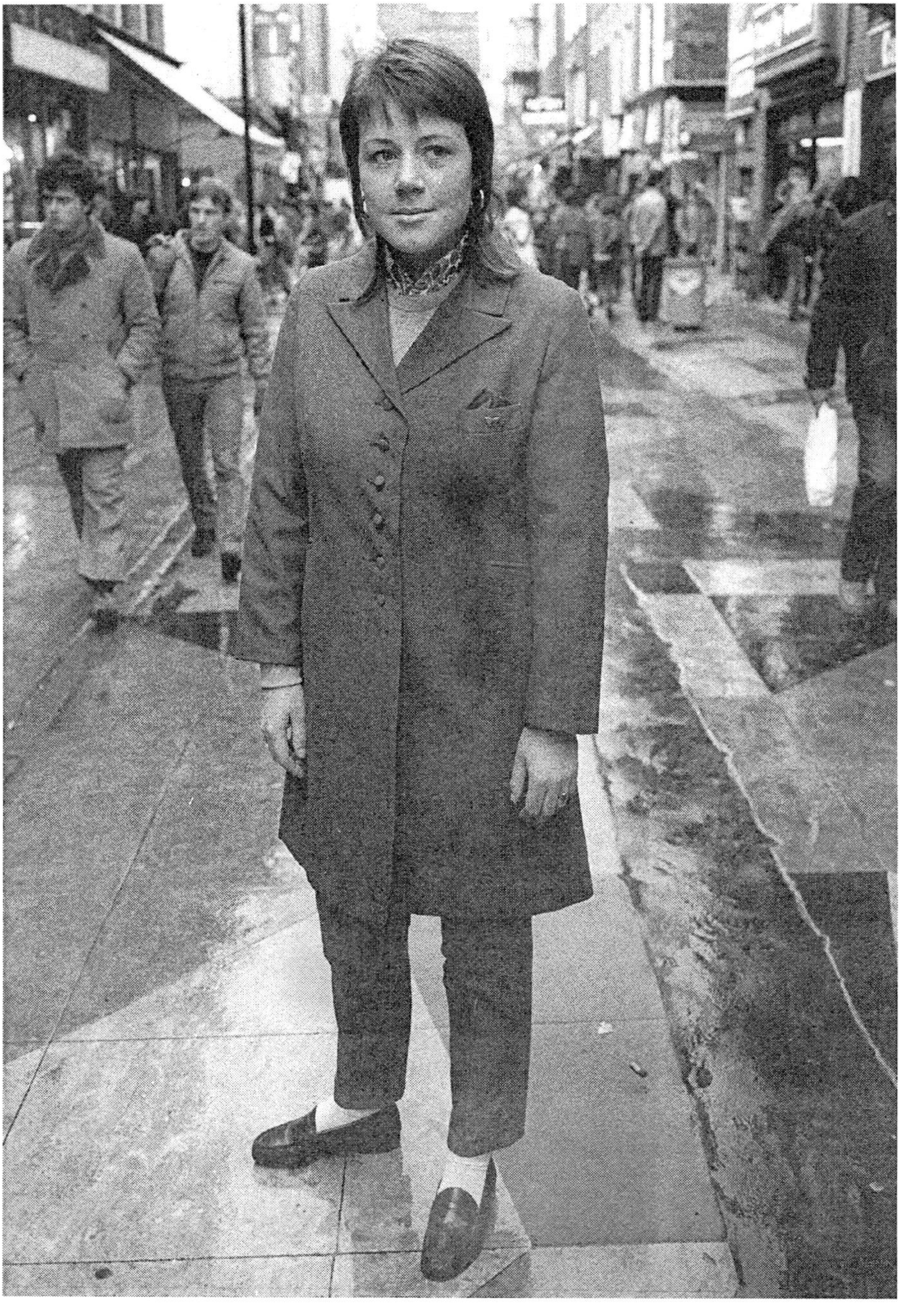

31. **Stuart Deabill**, 80's Chelsea Casual and co-writer of "Thick As Thieves – a collection of memories of The Jam".

Summer 1982, just left school and although I'd seen the odd person in expensive sportswear attire, it never hit me till the day a few of us went up to Ruislip Lido where some of the other kids from my West London outpost, Northolt, were going for a row with some rocker/psychobilly types.

As I got off the bus, amongst the Adidas Kagoules/T-shirts and Levis which most of us were sporting was this fella I vaguely knew from school. He looked resplendent in a Navy /Red/White Cashmere Diamond Pringle, and what I later found out were faded Lois Jeans and Light Blue Adidas Gazelles.

I couldn't take my eyes of the jumper though. I never imagined something that possibly Bernard Gallagher, Nick Faldo or even Ronnie Corbett would wear could ever rock my world. The kid was even first in for the tear up so he became a cult hero in my eyes in an instant.

That was my introduction into the world of Casual as it later became known. I badgered my mum and dad something rotten for something similar. I'd already got a pair of Farah's to go with my new Adidas Hawaii's but the jumper was another world.

Even back then it was 70 to 80 quid, but on holiday in Bournemouth we went into this big department store and there was Pringle's in the August sale. Happy Days.

With some birthday dough and the old man finally relenting with his wallet, I managed to purchase a plain light blue V Neck. That buzz of putting that jumper on with the Farah's and Hawaii's made me feel I was unique, special and I walked round the chalet park that night feeling untouchable. By the time the football season started, I realised quickly that I was just one of many who had the road to Damascus (Or Stuart's, W12) over the summer and all my mates had got on board.

As Chelsea were struggling in the second division at the time, the away days to Rotherham and Leeds became fashion parades not only to show the away fans the way forward dress-wise (the arrogance of being young and from London) but also to show each other who had the latest items.

It became far more important than the game itself as we were shocking on the pitch. That October, I started work on the dreaded Youth Opportunity Scheme at £25 a week, and after bunging my mum some money, was left with 15 notes.

As things were out of my league, you had to spend wisely. It helped that the local golf shops got broken into on a regular basis but a Fila BJ Matchday track top was out of the question.

Then I started buying and selling records amongst other things so that helped to keep the wardrobe fresh. As 1982 went into 1983, the label of a certain curly-haired tennis player who was a bit touched wore Sergio Tacchini. It became a massive part of my young life. I'd started to become a regular in Stuart's and my namesake would always drop a fiver off the retail price for me whilst giving me a sneak preview into what was coming in next week.

I bought a White Tracksuit with a waffle type material, which became the most impressive item in my wardrobe. The name of the exact Trackie escapes me but wearing that to Marcia Baillie's 18th party in Harrow Cricket Club I felt that good, I knew I would be batting the women into extra cover with a shitty stick. Especially as my hair was at the right length for me to flick out of my eye for added drama.

That was until my Phil Nolan pulled the bottoms down when I was holding two pints, in front of the whole gaff.

Never again did I wear the bottoms out.

As Chelsea had saved themselves from relegation at Bolton, where I had managed to spill coffee on my new beige Diamond Lyle And Scott Jumper on the train, making me feel like a tramp for the rest of the day, we all looked forward to the new season as Bates and Johnny Neal had pulled out some decent players and on the opening day, we smashed Derby 5-0.

When I looked around me in the West Stand Benches that afternoon it seemed like every kid was wearing a label of some sort, apart from the few muggy boneheads still wearing MA1 jackets and DM's.

I'd bought some Lois Cords and split the hem to give them extra width over my new brand Diadora Borg Elite. The kangaroo leather made them feel like you were wearing gloves. Very handy if you had to avoid the police baton when needed (Newcastle springs to mind) or see off a mob at Euston.

Also the ubiquitous Kickers boot (or Noddy Boot) became a staple on the trotter front. The piece in The Face magazine that summer gave us the name Casual and it stuck. And Chelsea were fucking Casual.

We had the swagger that the clothes gave you the confidence to carry as we strode purposely around alien streets (do you want fruit in that bowl son?). We had the team that also had the swagger in abundance on the pitch for the first time since the early 70s and the fans turned out in droves at cities and towns such as Sheffield, Manchester, Blackburn and Derby.

No one came near us that season on the pitch, on the terraces and on the clobber front. I loved every second of that season, getting back in the local to give it large after an arduous train journey home from some hick town and people asking you how much the Fila Mohair Jumper you was styling was. (Though when my best mate bought an identical jumper I nearly cried, such was the individualist in us true dressers. He never did it again). The strive to be part of something but to be wearing something that no one else had was an unbelievably heady time to be young and alive. Chelsea got promoted as champions and the first game of the new season was Arsenal away. We had the whole Clock End and to me it was the defining moment of being a teenage Chelsea Casual. 15,000 crammed into that end alone and most of those golden faces were under 25 and wearing Armani to YSL.

When Kerry Dixon smashed one in the top corner, the whole end with scores amongst scores of Wedge haircuts, Lacoste and Fila Polo shirts and Fiorucci jeaned kids going absolutely barmy stays with me. (We drew 1-1).

As the season went on the clothes got more garish and colourful and I remember an ill-thought out outfit of an overhead Leather 3 coloured patchwork jacket, pink Pringle polo and Canary yellow cords worn with grey Trimm Trabs. No wonder the old man thought I was on the turn.

As the 80s progressed, the style sort of left me (though I was still sporting Adidas Trainers and Lacoste) as I started getting involved in bands. Then in 1990, a certain Massimo Osti came into my life and carried me back in, but that's another story.

Always wondered what happened to the kid in the Cashmere Pringle...
Stuart Deabill

32. **Dan Derlin** discovers The Jam.

Thinking back it must have been a Thursday night. It was early March 1979. The usual suspects had congregated around Ozzies house. His big brother Bangor was out for the night and Ozzie had free reign. In we trooped. The TV was turned on 7.30 and we were now passing judgment on the latest tunes being played and performed on Top Of The Pops.

The usual suspects were Ozzie, Fatty (Ian Chorner), Paul Savage and myself. I was 14 at the time and 15 in July of that year. The programme was passing us by with a minor highlight here and there. Then a band came on with their latest offering. My ears pricked up. The band looked different and they now had my full attention. The chit chat and murmur and usual piss take in the room stopped as we all tuned into the song being played.

The song was *Strange Town* by The Jam. We couldn't stop talking about them. I actually tried to find out everything I could about this band and the cool lead singer. A seed had been sown. Punks, Skins, Rockabilly etc never really grabbed me and I found myself turning towards a movement that kept cropping up in conversation.

Later that year Quadrophenia was released and although an 18 I managed to get into the local cinema. It was double billed with Scum, a right win double. The dye was cast, the final cog had fallen, and it was to be Mod for me.

My friends and I all took it on hook line and sinker. We lived, worked and played a Mod life style, or at least a version of it. Happy days. I still own a Lambretta and socialize with most of my old mates and still lean towards a Mod style in a dress sense much to my wife's disdain at times.....I wouldn't change a thing
Danny Derlin

33. From author **Pete McKenna** 'Once upon a Soul'

Blackpool 72-73 and the whole worlds a disco. Apprentice bricklaying at the time freezing my bollocks off building the Crest Motel, Preston five days a week with blokes I had nothing in common with. Three day weeks, strikes, power cuts - what the fucks going on? Weekends on the disco merry go round on the piss pulling birds, scrapping with the hordes of grockles from pub to club to prom and back. Jingle bells jingle bells jingle all the way and all that bollocks. How can life be so crap for somebody so young. Searching for a way out, something different to do but when and where. It can't come quick enough, that I do know.

Starting to notice Lambrettas and Vespas everywhere and mates I know driving them, sheepskins, Levis and Doc Martens. Looks like a well cool scene to get into and I feel an escape from Tinseltown is on the cards at last. A few weeks later and I'm in with them, The Okeh Scooter Crew with a brand new bog standard Lambretta GP125 courtesy of John Halls HP scheme. A discerning bunch of lads who don't suffer fools gladly, lads who go about their business different from the rest. A few weeks down the line and AFR539L is looking the business of a chair. Black paintwork, chrome side panels, crash bars, Bermuda backrest, Square Eight spot lamps with a 175cc barrel and piston fitted to give her some clout and sounding sweet. Great days out driving where we wanted to go in a squadron, sunshine, chrome mirror shades and no crash helmets to spoil the image.

Driving up to Cleveleys one Saturday night, walking into Gallopers and I immediately discover the music to fit the scene I'm now a part of. The one and only Pete Haigh behind the decks playing this music they call northern soul, a track by Jerry Williams call *If You Ask Me* and I'm instantly hooked, rooted to the spot, listening to it. The vocals, the beat, the rhythm, like nothing I've ever heard before and I needed to hear more and fortunately didn't have to look too hard.

Unforgettable nights in The Peacock Room and Blackpool Casino with Bob Blackwood and the inimitable Baz Stanton - RIP gone but not forgotten - behind the decks. Great teachers to all the new students of Northern Soul. Sat nights up in Blackpool Meccas Highland Room with Ian Levine and the legendary Colin Curtis in charge of the music. So many people packed into such a small place, the passion and energy was unbeatable, meeting like minded Soulies from all parts of the country there for one reason; Northern Soul, and what a reason, what a scene as I finally waved goodbye to Tinseltown banality forever more. Rumours circulating around the scene of an old ballroom in Wigan with an all night license playing Northern Soul. Sounds too good to be true but what if?

Sunday soul sessions in Scoeys on Victoria Street reading a poster advertising a coach trip to Wigan Casino, places going fast and postal applications for membership accompanied by a stamped addressed envelope. Booked there and then and a week later, my memberships dropped through the letter box and *I'm On My Way*. All-nighter bags, towels, Brut, booze and Wrigleys wondering what will be waiting at the end of the line. An hour or so later, we're parked up outside this shabby

Victorian ballroom that had seen better days but you can't judge a book by the cover can you. Crowds of Soulies standing around waiting for the witching hour, evil glares from a couple of stern looking Skins "*What the fuck are you lot doing here*" the same kind of looks we'd be giving strangers to the scene a few months later.

Walking into The Beachcomber for the first time, a narrow black tunnel lined with speeding eyes and not a pleasant sensation by any means. Into the main room that served as a garage in days gone by, a concrete lined hole with a DJ spinning sounds to dancing Soulies while others sat around in groups, tea, coffee and Bovrils waiting for the main event. Seen nothing like it before, basic, rough but there was a great atmosphere - the lull before the storm kind of thing - and then we're outside in the queue crushed up tight, the Tuxedo doormen pulling in the animals two by two and we're in memberships at the ready up the stairs and the double doors leading to the main hall full of expectation at what we were going to find.

The Devonnes *Pick Up My Toys* was playing as we pushed open the thick plastic doors and walked into an unbelievable nocturnal world. A large dark hall packed full of Soulies from all parts of the country, an ultra violet strip light hanging above the dance floor emitting a ghostly glow on the dancers below. People shuffling effortlessly from side to side, balanced and poised to perfection, stripped to the waist, baggies and leather soles shoes, spinning, back dropping, kicking and clapping, everyone doing their own thing but together in a unrehearsed choreography of dancing I'd never seen before breathing in the smell of hundreds of bodies mixed with a hundred different deodorants. Breathtaking just watching the action from the wings, and up on the balcony, dealers buying and selling soul gems. My first taste of a Wigan Casino all-nighter knowing I'd be back for more.

A few weeks down the line and my first chemical romance with black bombers, Filon, Blueys, Green and clears, Midnight Runners and Amphet powder tasting like cat piss - UGHH - but needs must. Energy pumping through me rapid as I joined the army of glaring eyes and bodies soaked in sweat. Staying in all week on the comedown paying back what I'd borrowed from my body and then the weekend, always the weekend to look forward too. Cars, vans, trains and coaches arranged for the lift over making sure everyone had a place whether were skint of not. Soulies in railway carriages dancing to portable cassettes on the last train to Wigan. Trying to keep warm in my mates Rover Coupe huddled around the heater waiting for the doors to open. Charnock Richard Motorway Services meeting up with mates from all over the place. Handfuls of gear in exchange for a few crumpled notes and change and off into the night once more. Freezing cold nights wandering a round Wigan, crowds dancing in the fish market warming up for the big one and always the coppers keeping their beady eyes open for people to bust. People clustered around and parked up in cars dealing gear, a nod, a handshake, a brief chat, a rummage through an inside pocket and sorted for the night. "Cheers mate. See you next week. Have a good one".

Hot sweaty nights greeted by ice cold mornings, walking back to the station crowded together in the waiting room freezing to death - "*where's the fucking train then?*" - exhausted, dreaming of a nice hot brew and a warm bed to crash into and the next weekend. Searching for Soul, Saturday mornings, scooters parked up outside Sandy Mountains Symphonia record shop on Cookson Street. Inside packed out with sheepskins and Martens demanding records for their collections. Hundreds of singles lying around all over the place in some kind of orderly chaos and the learned Sandy standing there smiling, the font of all soul knowledge there to lend a hand. "*If you can't remember the title or the artist, just sing it or hum it and I'll find it for you*". Job done, bagged up and back home dying to put it on the stereo and practise a few moves before the big one. And Preston bus station, a young guy who knew a thing or two about northern operating from a small stall, picking up Temptations *Calling My Name* and *Super love* a few ahead of the crowd.

Why do all good things have to come to an end? The shock as the realisation kicked in that Wigan Casino had burned down, driving over to see for ourselves if the rumours were true and indeed they were. Just a smoking shell of unforgettable memories lay before our eyes parked up on the car park wondering what we were going to do next. Lou Pride, Dean Parrish, Dean Courtney, Phillip Mitchell, Rita Da Costa, Don Covay, Major Lance, Paul Anka, Williams and Watson, Johnny Bragg, Joe Hicks, NF Porter, Freddie Chavez, Judy Street, Christine Cooper, Brenda Holloway, Jimmy Radcliffe, Jimmy James, Case Of Thyme, Mirwood Strings, Al Wilson, Frank Wilson. I could go on forever along with the memories, mistakes and regrets of a time and place in my life I am unable to forget so I'll leave you with the words of the immortal Tobi Legend. *Time Will Pass You By* and doesn't it just. Keep The Faith

because at certain times in a persons life. Faith is all we have left and believe me, I know all about that only too well.
Pete McKenna

34. **Geoff Blythe**, an original Dexy

Back in the mid 70's, first time on the road, blowing tenor on stage with Geno Washington, The Ram Jam Band, jamming. Loving my immersion into Soul after coming from a Jazz Fusion back ground and a two month stint counting screws and bolts in a car parts factory in Tysely, Birmingham. We'd just walked on stage , in a huge, half full Bingo hall, to a bunch of Ena Sharples glaring at us. Total silence, until one of the hairnets yells out to her cronies,"*Ya can tell them's on drugs, can't ya'.*

We played all kinds of places from cool clubs to the Scampi and Chips circuit in the Welsh holiday towns. The horn section was two tenors, a great sound. I always thought that adding a trombone would have made it perfect. The band used to travel around, with the gear, in a big box van, trying to see where we were through a haze of smoke. Our chauffer was a Portuguese bloke who kept talking about his "*preek*", while side swiping parked cars (it was a really wide box van). Geno used to travel with his wife, 'Frenchy', and her two papillon dogs in their Volvo.

Long story short, Geno ends up returning to his native America (suppose he had enough scampi), to reinvent himself in LA with a bunch of Hawaiian shirted, guitar playing surfer looking dudes. That left me back in 'Brum', on the dole looking for something to do. I eventually saw an ad in the local rag, looking to form a 'new wave 'soul band. Main influence, coincidently, Geno Washington. I made the call and next day met the 2 Kevin's (Rowland and Archer), and Dexys Midnight Runners was formed (although of course, we did not have the name yet).

Influences were the likes of Sam and Dave, Wilson Pickett, Jimmy Johnson And The Bandwagon, Chairman Of The Board, etc. Most stuff was original but we would cover a few songs, including a Northern Soul fave by Chuck Woods, *Seven Days Are Too Long*.

I had the job of designing the horn sound. I decided to keep the section to 2 saxes and "Big Jim" Paterson on the trombone, losing the trumpet we had toyed with for awhile. I thought this gave us more "Stax" sounding horns. Funny enough, as Stax Records was out of Memphis ,TN, that brand of soul is known as 'Southern Soul' in the States.

We rehearsed anywhere we didn't have to pay for. From garages to squats and even the local arts centre. When not doing that, we spent our time discussing strategy over multiple cups of tea (and when we could afford it bacon butties) in a greasy spoon cafe on Broad St., or ' bunking' trains to London to get things going there.

Eventually, three of us (Rowland, Archer and myself) were signed by EMI. With the rest of the crew in tow we recorded *Searching for The Young Soul Rebels*, which is now considered a classic. When I got word that the single *Geno* was the #1 hit in the UK I didn't dare go to the pub to celebrate as I only had enough in my pocket for one pint. I knew I would be expected to buy a round or two. We toured as much as we could in the UK, Europe and Ireland, including playing Belfast during the height of 'The Troubles' when few, if any British bands dared to do so.

Funny thing one time returning from Ireland to the small Welsh ferry port of Fishguard. We were a bunch of rough looking donkey jacketed wooley hatted 'fellas', and were pulled out of our Transit van by two very nervous security guards, a young kid and an old codger, and the only ones there. They went through the van and found our instruments. The old guy asks "*You a band?*" and we say "*yeah*" and he was wiping the sweat off his brow, looking like he was having a heart attack, gasping "*Why the hell didn't you just tell me that in the first place?*"

Interesting time then, post punk, The Specials were breaking big with the Ska thing, our first tour was with them, replacing Madness who had dropped out. There was a Mod revival, a Skinhead movement and, oh yeah , the start of the New Romantic synthesizer snooze fest. The Mods and Skins didn't mix so well, as I witnessed at one of our gigs in Glasgow watching a Skin wearing some poor Mods outerwear while torching it with a Zippo yelling " *Eh Jimmy, someone's set fire to me Parka*".

We were, I thought on a roll then, with visions of where we would be taking our Soul inspired music in the future. My dreams came crashing down however when Rowland told me that I should learn to play the fiddle, and Big Jim the cello. My reaction of course, drop dead, this is a Soul outfit. The beginning of the end, yes, of the original, and to my mind the only version of Dexy's Midnight Runners that deserved to carry the name.

With the majority of us wanting to continue down the road on which we had started, the band split and we formed The Bureau, with Archie Brown as our new frontman. Signed to WEA, we made a great album, spawning a hit (*Only For Sheep*) in Australia. I think it was probably the title that sold it in Oz. We toured America and the UK with The Pretenders, but the band fizzled like a wet roman candle after a regime change at Warners, where, as often happens in record companies, the baby got thrown out with the bathwater.

Lots of water under the bridge since then, including hooking back up with Big Jim for various projects, including the T.K.O horns, recording *Punch The Clock* and touring for a year with Elvis Costello, and another short lived EMI band, "The Neighbourhood" which was a George Clinton inspired funky "thang'.

After that I moved to New York where my main thing for years was playing with the Celtic rock band 'Black 47'. Also, it was nice to do a Bureau reunion to celebrate Warners re-release of the album, but efforts to take it further were not forthcoming due to lack of commitment from various members.

Funny how things go in circles though. Back again working with Big Jim and Archie on our new stuff, being released under the name GI Blythe. Sounding amazing, first three songs already charting on internet radio , and me loving having brought this thing firmly into the twenty first century. Come a long way from the old Dexy's, but you'll still be able to cut your Northern Soul moves to this stuff more to come

Geoff 'JB' Blythe (Dexy's Midnight Runner)

35. A day out at Brighton with **Paul Crittenden**

Brighton at the weekend and I have just failed my test. Bollocks! I'll take my girlfriend on the back anyway. 1984 and one of my first seaside excursions by scooter. It's Friday, work finished and my time is spent peeling the stick-on L plates from the front and rear of my new white Vespa. My thoughts turn to the old fart of an examiner at the test station. What the fuck did he know about my ability to ride a scooter? A quick phone call to my mate 'Peanut', to check he was insured and that he agreed to me assuming his name for the weekend. Great! What a clever little bastard. Seventeen years old and I had everything covered. Having picked my girlfriend up and perched her on the back, we made our way on the A Roads from Maidstone down to Brighton. An uneventful journey which took all of 2 hours including fag breaks. On nearing Brighton we started to ride with fellow scooterists and I simply forgot about being illegal.

The sun was shining. I was in my element. What more could I ask for sun, sea, scooters and a girl to keep me warm. Suddenly a police road block flagged us in to check documents and scoots. Time to assume my mates identity and blag my way out of this situation. After half an hour in the police station my plan was turning sour. The police were suspicious after contacting my mate's insurance company and finding that he was not covered Bollocks! To top it all they phoned my mates Dad who was asked to describe his son. Surprise, surprise I didn't look nothing like him. A stout looking police officer with a face like thunder stared straight at me and said "*Is there anything you want to tell me*" Still thinking I had got away with it I said "*No*", and he took me outside the station. There I found my girlfriend being offered a lift on the back of a cut-down matt black wreck of a scoot with some drugged up nutter driving it. Hesitantly I agreed to let her go the short way to the rally site with him. As I was led back into the police station all I heard was her screaming in the distance, hanging on for dear life on his broken back rest. Bollocks! Things now started to get nasty, and I started getting pushed over, tripped and generally abused for lying to a police officer.

Three hours later I emerged, definitely not going to use that scam again, with 4 points on my license and a £100 fine. Riding solo the short way to the rally, I cursed my mate for letting me think he had insurance. I had even taken the little shit on the back of my scoot to work for 3 years because he said he had past his test. The Bastard! Finally I reached the rally which lay just outside Brighton. Piss taking aside, I enjoyed a superb rally. Very Mod with great sounds, all set in the courtyard of an old castle. Completely wasted on drink we stumbled into Brighton to find a B&B for the night. Every time we asked for a room we were looked up and down and turned away. Finally we found a hotel which said we could stay, but the room had only just been decorated. Grateful, we paid our money and fell into a deep sleep.

We woke next morning only to find the room had no toilet. I stumbled to the door only to find it completely stuck tight with wet paint. Fucking great! After pissing in the sink we kicked the door enough for the Hotel manager to force the door open and let us out. Out in the fresh air we finally found my scooter and not trusting the police and the roadblocks outside town, put my girlfriend on a bus for the journey home. I found some friends to ride home with, and set off thinking nothing else could happen. Heading out on the A27 from Brighton we caught up with an old White Transit van. We indicated to overtake and all of sudden the doors flung open and rocks, bricks and all sorts of crap started being thrown from the inside by some local wankers. I threw the scooter to the right to avoid a particularly large rock and mounted the central reservation and flew across the opposing carriageway narrowly missing oncoming traffic. I skidded to a stop having half killed myself with my mates pissing themselves laughing. Ha "Fucking Ha! I limped home back to Maidstone and soon forgot all the shit, my mind buzzing in anticipation of the next rally.

Two weeks later, I and a few mates were on the way to a rally in Margate. My newly sprayed Lambretta TV175, purring beneath me, and my girlfriend riding her newly purchased Vespa 50 Special. This was an organised mod-rally with the entertainment being in the local pubs. Upon arriving we searched for a B&B close to the seafront and locked our scooter up around the back of the premises. Showered and dressed we made our way down the hill into town, with a few other scooterist's warning us about the local Skinheads. It was a dark night and while passing a rough looking pub, the doors flung open. A parka clad man started running across the road towards us followed by a gang of Skinheads. I turned to stop and help this Mod, thinking he was being chased .As he got closer he took a running swing at my head with he's fist and knocked me to the ground. Bollocks! I wasn't prepared for Skinheads in parkas! After taking a good kicking, I got up and ran to regroup with my mates. My only clothes for the weekend tattered and torn, I sat nursing my wounds in a pub on the seafront. We then made our way to one of the pubs with entertainment and had a great evening, pissed and happy I stumbled back to the B & B' and fell into bed.

My mate looked out of the window to check the scoots and shouted across "*Your scooter's been nicked*". Shit this weekend just gets better and better. Wandering the streets, pissed at two o'clock in the morning looking for a dark Green Lambretta is not my idea of fun. Reporting the theft to the police I succumbed to the fact that I would not see my prized scoot again. The following morning I hitched a lift back to Maidstone on the back of my mate leaving my girlfriend to find her own way home on her 50 Special.

I now look back and laugh at these early rallies. Nearly 25 years later and I'm still on 10" wheels. I may be older and slightly wiser, but i still get a buzz riding my scooter....
Paul Crittenden

36. A young drummer, **Russ Baxter** who drummed his way into a Secret Affair

My first memory of discovering music that really blew me away was at Grammar School way back in 1982. A friend of mine, who was much more 'with it' than me, gave me a BASF tape one day. On one side, he explained, was Madness and on the other side was a band called Secret Affair. I still don't remember why he did this but he must have thought that I needed educating or something. I took this tape home and listened to side A – *Complete*

Madness. I have to say that I listened patiently but it did nothing for me – I think I thought that it was a bit too fun. Side B was a different matter. *Business As Usual* by Secret Affair really knocked me for six – I couldn't believe my ears. I played it constantly – until the tape did that thing's that tapes do and you can only try and fix them with a biro.

Trying to copy what these guys wore was extremely difficult. The best that I could do was to try adapt my school uniform as best I could. My tie was turned around to be thin all the way down. Next was the addition of a gold and black Secret Affair badge (to be worn to and from school – but not during – I'd never get away with that). My hair was made to look as Mod as humanly possible. The last stop was to do something about my flared school trousers. I had a word with my Mum - who was a whizz with the sewing machine. Things did not go according to plan however – she took the trousers in from the knee. My first day with my new look saw me looking less like the Ace Face – and more like a member of the Canadian Mounted Police.

Russ Baxter

37. 80's Scooter boy **Jason Yeandle**

Seeing photos of my Mothers 150 Sportique when I was 6, listening to her Tamla Motown records & cassettes, my sister starting secondary school and bringing home early Jam 45's, her friends, her party, all the Mods turning up on their small-frames, starting secondary school with an obsession for all things Mod, scooters, The Jam, Tamla Motown, The Who, seeing Quadrophinia for the first time when I was 11, trips to Carnaby street, Shellys shoes, Trench coats, Bowling shoes, Boating Blazers, Sta-press trousers, Fred Perry T-shirts, cycling shirts, Desert boots, getting all dressed up just to hang about with my mates, trips into town on a Saturday and trying to avoid the Skinheads, getting even more obsessed with music, riding round the woods on a Ll125, paying a tenner for it then leaving at the friends house, Paul Weller splitting The Jam, feeling like I'd lost a close friend, gutted when their gig at Canterbury University got cancelled, getting into mid 80's Indie and alternative and leaving Mod behind, noticing the Scooter-Boys around town, combining my love of scooters, Soul, Indie, New Wave and getting into the scootering scene, Northern and 60's Soul nights at the Stour Centre Ashford, trying to track down the records and then taking them to school discos so my

mates and me had our dance-floor time, King Kurt, Ra-Ra skirts and slam-dancing, my 16th birthday and on the road with my PK50, seeing The Stranglers at Folkestone Leas-cliff hall with my best mate, 2 grams of whizz and lump of puff then trying to kip at the ferry terminal, getting kicked out and ending up getting a lift back to Lenham with a bunch of complete strangers, rushing through my woodwork exam to get ready to leave for the Margate Rally in '86, camping on a bit of wastland, pissed, stoned and whizzing listening to my mate calling out "*I want my dawn chorus*" to the bird in the tent opposite, going to gigs every weekend with my best mate, planning and getting ready for the Isle of Wight rally in '86, 8 hours solid riding on our 50's, getting searched before getting on the ferry and panicking with a few grams of whizz taped under my petrol tank, the buzz riding off and watching the swarms of scooters as far as the eye could see, Edwin Starr live, throwing up in my own lid, watching with disbelief the riot and not liking it, riding 8 hours solid in the pissing rain with a soaking wet lid that stank of sick, Great Yarmouth and tales of things getting darker and moody in scootering, getting rid of my PK50 and part exchanging it for a P125, The Tangerine Dream, Margate '87, seizing the engine and overtaking a car on my arse, breaking my ankle on a trampoline, buying a vespa 90 cut-down for £30, getting my mate to ride it whilst I rode pillion with my leg in plaster, riding it to work, getting pulled over and the copper just laughed and cautioned me, said he felt sorry for me, hearing more tales of aggro at rallies and deciding I'd had enough, concentrating all my time to music, records, gigs and mind altering substances...... the love of scooters, Soul music and style have and always will be a part of me, now onto my next chapter of scootering..............
Jason Yeandle

38. **Pete McKenna** memories

Watching Blackpool at Bloomfield Road as a kid and always with my old man whether I liked it or not. Blokes everywhere marching to the ground - clanking turnstiles - stewards in orange coats - standing there freezing my bollocks off stood with my old man and his cronies, tangerine and white scarves, rosettes and wooden rattles everywhere and not a woman in sight - managers in primitive dug outs watching their teams, them and the players getting abuse from the crowd venting their feelings on the slightest mistake made - "*pass the fucking ball you dead leg, pass the fucking ball will you*" half time breathers and snacks, crisps, meat and potato pies, coca cola, tea, coffee, hot Bovril - bogs unfit for human use - take a deep breath and dive in to do what you have to do, the overwhelming stench of hundreds of blokes piss blended together - back in the ground for the second half "*Come on the pool*" Jimmy Armfield, Ray Charnley, Peter Hutchinson, Alan Suddick, Alan Ball, Alan Skirton, Glynn James, Hugh "Chopper" McPhee and the immortal Sir Harry Thompson in goal who had a talent of making hard work of the simplest chances and vice versa - great days, great players one and all.

"Sea - sea - sea siders" came the chant from the Spion Kop, a vast open space of concrete and steel barriers, home to the Blackpool mob - The Rammy, the hardest bunch of lunatic supporters a team could ever wish for - terrace wars every match, the away mob on one side, the Rammy on the other and in between, the thin blue line of cops trying to maintain law and order by keeping the warring factions apart - no fuckin chance - my attention drawn to the Spion Kop every game listening to the chanting, watching the aggro - the old man unimpressed clipping me round the head - "*Watch the bloody game you daft sod*" - "*Yeah alright dad*" - but the seeds had already been sewn and were growing inside me rapid, a desperate need to be on the Kop with the Rammy getting into the action - fuck standing with the old bastards every game.

Meeting up with great mates prior to the match, coffee bars and cafes, waiting for the arrival of the away fans train at North station, Skinheads and Suedeheads, Levis, Wranglers, Lee Riders, Ben Sherman's, Fred Perry's, Slazenger's, hobnails, monkey boots, Bombardiers and the classic Doc Marten stitch up - eight or ten hole in black or red polished up to fuck ready for the afternoons fun and games, the only boots to be seen in - Cappucinos, bacon sarnies, jukeboxes packed full of ska, reggae, Stax, Motown, Atlantic and the new stomping beat music northern soul, Italian Lambretta's and Vespa's all parked up in a row looking the business, old cultures blending in with new and the faith just keeps on keeping on - "*Hey up lads, here they come - Your gonna get your fuckin heads kicked in - your going home by fucking ambulance - Sea - sea - sea siders*" and so on and so on.

The buzz building up as we join the tail end of the column of away fans, tension fizzing crackling in the air, through the town centre down to Bloomfield Road and back again, shop windows smashed, people running everywhere, getting stuck in, the cops all over town in their Panda cars and Transit vans nicking everyone and anyone, Blackpool fans mixed in with the enemy en route to the cop shop to be charged - "*Tough fuckin luck lads, we'll see you when the pigs let you out*" - down to the ground across the vast Mecca car-park, the perfect battlefield, and onto the Kop for more of the same, packed out with Blackpool and the away fans, the overstretched thin blue line linking arms in the sway, always the sway, half an hour to kick off and the chanting starts, lads standing in the rook on steel girders taking the piss the mad fuckers. Then the fun begins, aggro in the air, faces pointing laughing, fuck off and wanking gestures all over the place, the cops bracing themselves for the onslaught, bricks, bottles, sharpened up pennies raining down from the heavens - the lads on the front line getting stuck in, all of us packed in tight, fists and boots, - "*Here we go here we go here we go - Gab gab gabble - ha ha ha ha*" - ooohhh altogether oohhh altogether oohhh altogether the cops steaming in dragging lads out from the crowd, cops getting kicked and punched, helmets flying all over the place - "*Who's that fella in the funny black hat, copper is his name*".

Welcome to the 70's, the age of mass hooligan wars before the firms got smaller, more streamlined and organised, chaos and mayhem on the streets of every city and town in our green and pleasant land, away days on trains, all the lads in high spirits, amphetamines and Tennents, looking forward to a good days aggro, the buzz of getting lost on foreign soil, everyone getting stuck in - "*Sea sea sea siders sea sea sea siders*" - notable moments, too many to mention, Millwall on the telly a week before they come to Blackpool and we're ready for Harry The Dog and the rest of his lads - Chelsea in town, mass battles on the Kop, a big black lad with one arm leading them, bottles and bricks coming in thick and fast, after the match, hunting them before they caught the train back to London - Wolverhampton in town and loads of the fuckers, a mixture of Skins and Bikers in German helmets, black driving gloves and Trilby hats, a hard days work and talk about pleased when they fucked off back to Wolverhampton - a night match with Celtic and the jocks invade the cop in an orgy of drunken violence, whisky bottles thrown everywhere, the fuckers pissing all over the place - West Ham on the Kop, Prince Of Wales check Harrington's and flat caps - "*I'm forever blowing bubbles, pretty bubbles in the air*" - that's the problem with bubbles, they burst easy, steaming into the fuckers, Martens and hot

Bovril in their faces, not so pretty now you cockney fuckers - Bolton at Blackpool, and Kevin Olsen a sea sider stabbed to death in the bogs, all of us locked in for hours while cops took statements - *"Get a move on you fuckers, we need to get our dancing shoes on and get to Wigan Casino"* - the arch rivals Preston PNE scum, mass battles in Ashton Park, setting fire to their end, pitch invasions, always guaranteed a great day out when we play Preston home and away.

Oh oh, FA Cup draw and it's Man Utd at Bloomfield Road and the infamous Red Army at it's worst as Blackpool braces itself for the onslaught, shopkeepers, hotel owners boarding up windows, a week to before the match and they start arriving, ready for the big day, Doc Martens, red and white scarves, Skins and Suedeheads everywhere, weird baggy jeans called Skinners - *"Fuck me, hundreds of the fuckers and they still keep coming"* - the cops of maximum security alert, sirens going off all over town as the Red Army start to enjoy themselves, battling with the cops, rioting in pubs helping themselves to free beer, up and down the Prom and the cops are on the run, smashing up the Laughing Man on the pleasure beach, journalists lobbed over the sea wall, cars and vans trashed - *"Utd fans we are here, shag your women and drink your beer, oh oh oh oh oh oh"*. A week of unimaginable seaside anarchy as the big day arrives and Utd take over the Kop in glorious sunshine, 2 - 1 Man U the winners courtesy of Best and Law and the whole town breathes a huge sigh of relief as the Red Army make their way back to Manchester - *"Goodbye Blackpool goodbye. We'll see you again we don't know when, goodbye Blackpool goodbye"*.

Caught the Utd bug big time, walking into Old Trafford for the first time standing with the thousands of Reds on the mighty Stretford End, a different buzz altogether, watching Best, Kidd, Law Charlton, Stepney, Morgan, Fitzpatrick, looking out to the Utd fans on the Scoreboard End where the agro kicked off - *"Come on Scoreboard, come on Scoreboard"*.

The away team scores first and there's a breathless hush in the ground, the Stretford Enders walking to the Scoreboard End humming the death march as the away fans prepared for the inevitable. "The Belfast Boy", the one and only George Best dancing and dribbling his way to immortality, Beatles, Oasis and Pele all rolled into one, too many goals to mention. One in particular, Tottenham at Old Trafford, George lobs the ball from the penalty area straight into the net, arms raised to the adoring crowd, Chivers with his new sideburns gets a pen facing the Scoreboard, the ground erupting in a tidal wave of noise - *"Chivers is a werewolf*" - ball over the bar and Utd the winners, night match against Chelsea leaving Chopper Harris on his arse, passed two or three more and then it's Best versus Bonetti and there's only one winner there as George dribbles the ball into the Chelsea net, end of.

Memorable times flitting between the Stret and Scoreboard End in the baking sunlight, stripped to the waist, red braces, Levis and Doc Martens, Liverpool home and away the dirty Scouse bastards, Munich 58 banners and Shankly Is Dead, always a good day out when we get Liverpool, Wolves on the Scoreboard and the Bikers are out in force again, somebody gets thrown off the bridge outside the ground and the countless times away fans locked in for their own safety until Utd get bored of waiting and piss off to the pub, Salford Reds the hardcore and Cockney Reds too, hundreds of them, many sporting serrated cut here tattoos around their necks, Skinheads, Boneheads, Suedeheads all in the man mental Red Army mix. Stoke City away and a mass battle on the bridge close to their ground, trapped in the middle, a bloke selling hot-dogs and hamburgers from his stall trying to pack up and get out of the way rapid, away at Leicester for the FA Cup, battles breaking out all over the place, the Red Army on the wooden Kop stomping up and down as Utd go through, four of us lost in the city centre after the match, kicked to fuck, me hiding in a carpet shop thinking I'm going to die as a horde of Utd fans arrive in time like International Rescue and it's goodbye Leicester until the next time.

Back at Old Trafford and the famous West Ham Inter City Firm have come to pay us a visit, locked in a special pen on the Scoreboard End, showered with pies, tea and coffee all of the fuckers sitting there quiet as mice as the chant echoes all around the ground - "*Where's your famous ICF*" - Leicester at home and their goalie gets a dart in the head thrown from the Scoreboard and it's the beginning of the end, massive public outcry as the government takes action by forcing Man Utd to erect a steel cage all around the ground to keep the animals in and so the good times are over, the Northern Soul beat and Wigan Casino starting to take their toll on me so it's one or the other, can't do everything and I need the all-nighters more than football. Great days, great mates, so many unforgettable moments and memories but a man's gotta do what a man's gotta do, time to move on, love it, leave it and move onto the next buzz. Game over.

Pete McKenna

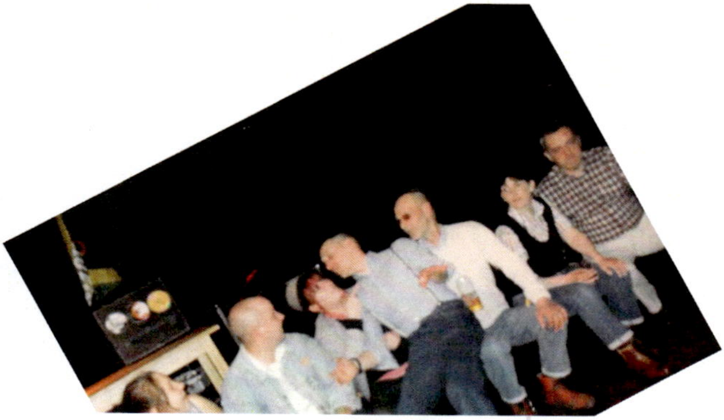

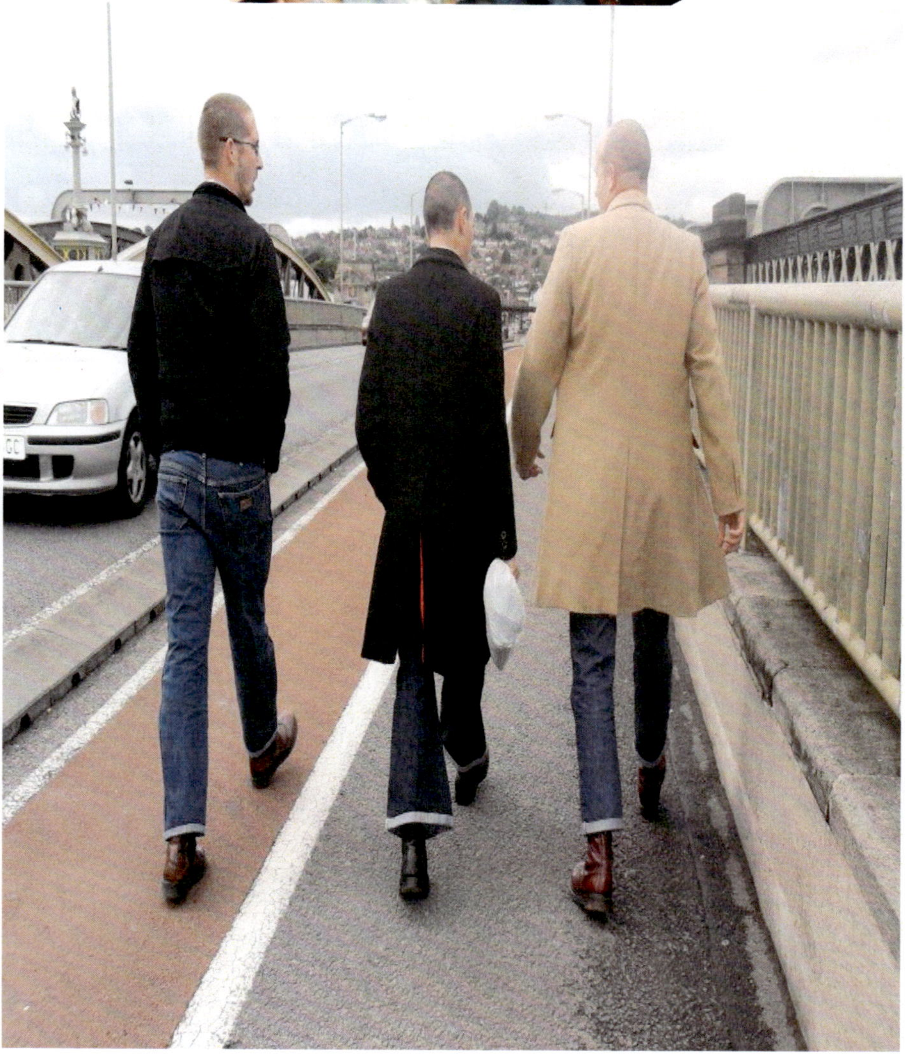

39. Another young Soul Rebel, Essex Soul lover **Jay Hall**

So let's start with the basis. My name is Jay Hall I come from Essex and was born March 1991. So compared to most people on the Northern Soul scene I am relatively new due to the fact that I am younger and did not come across Northern Soul music until I was 16 in 2007. But with in this short period of time I have heard a lot of great music and met a lot of great people and along with meeting a lot of great people you create a lot of great memories. So here are a few of them memories and my life of Northern Soul.
 So as I previously mentioned I am a relatively new Soulie and I am pretty new to the whole scene. The weird thing is though I still remember every Northern Soul do I go to and the people I meet. I can still remember the first time I heard the music properly. I was a arrogant sixteen year old walking into my dads house and I was like what is this music I had never heard it before and my dad turned into the typical old school dad and was like "*son this is Northern Soul I used to listen to this music when I was your age.*" So after a while of listening to it I thought to myself this music is not half bad. Being truthful it was a bit different to the drum and bass I was used to listening to on my local council estate were I was hanging around making a menace of my self. So after that day of being at my dads I found out that there was a scooter club that used to meet at the pub at the end of my road.
 So after attending a couple of their meetings they had an end of season do a couple of bands and DJ's playing Tamla Motown and Northern Soul. I thought to myself I might as well get a ticket every one else is going but when I got there I was amazed to find out that it had its own style of dancing to go with the music. After that night I decided to do a bit of research on it so out came the laptop goggle on I started trawling through the thousands of results and I admit I did not know how big the whole Northern Soul scene was finding out about Wigan Casino, The Twisted Wheel and The Blackpool Mecca so after that I thought to my self this seems like a really great scene but by this time I was already involved in the scooter scene so I was learning the main stream northern like Frank Wilson *Do I Love You* and Al Wilson *The Snake* and just general tracks like that.
 It was not until 2008 that I actually attended my first proper Northern Soul do and I still remember it clearly it was the 16th of February and the headline DJ was Dave Evison. It was a great night I just wish I knew how to dance a bit better then from that night on I kind of made a decision in my head that the only music for me now was Northern Soul. So I got a few CD's and started

listening to it more and more now I have a I pod and phone full of Northern Soul after that I discovered vinyl so round to me old mans, nicked all of his from the eighties then up into my mums attic and took all of her Motown records but I can safely say I left all of the Abba and Blondie ones up there. Now the problem is my wages come in and then they go straight back out again to people who I do not know due to the fact that I am straight on eBay looking for a bargain but the trouble is I can never find a bargain I always find the ones that make me skint. I do believe it is to my sisters dismay that since I have come across Northern Soul they have to tell me to turn my music down but it seems my parents and sisters have switched roles because my parents let me play my music just that little bit louder now.

As I mentioned earlier I couldn't really dance and before I discovered Northern Soul the only dancing I done was at family parties and school discos if you can count that as dancing. So I thought to myself if I am getting into this music and going to do's I have got to learn how to dance to the music. So relentlessly I went to my dad and asked for his help in my quest to learn the dance so he showed me the basic side back forward footwork. With what he showed me I went off and practiced for hours jus to get my footwork to a reasonable standard. Then I watched different videos on you tube of various dancers to get different floor work moves and techniques. So off I went again practicing for hours on end with me mum thinking I am going to come through the living room ceiling but I just started off with the basic backdrops then side splits and progressed from there now I am creating my own floor-work moves saying that I have suffered the pain of many bruised knees and bent fingers but they all seem worth it now I can dance reasonably well.

What Northern Soul has done for me?

Northern Soul has done a lot for me over the past few years in a way it has helped me get on the straight and narrow since I have got onto the scene I have got away from the life I was living hanging around on the streets and local estates causing trouble smoking drugs thinking we were untouchable hard men but truth is we were far from that just little boys. With Soul music and the scene I have found a whole new life and a whole new lot of people. When they say 'Northern Soul - a way of life' they do truly mean it also it has offered me great opportunities one of them was to be a dancer in a short film called Young Souls by Dean Chalkley and also do a magazine shoot for that but the biggest opportunity is to be a dancer in a feature length film ironically called 'Northern Soul - the film' it is being directed by a wonderful lady called Elaine Constantine and this is her dream project due to the fact she was born and raised in Manchester and has listened and danced to the music her whole life so the film has the influence of that and are dance teacher Paul Sadot who is making sure we are in the dance style of Wigan and so forth it is jus a over all joy to work with the guys and cast.

Some of my favourite songs have great memories of and nights I have been to I could probably name a good sixty or seventy songs but I don't think you would want to read all of that so here is a few of my favourite tracks in no particular order Judy Street *What*, Roy Hamilton *Cracking Up Over You*, The Jades *I'm Where It's At*, The Holidays *Making Up Time*, World Column *So Is The Sun*, Bobby Kline *Say Something Nice To Me* and last but not least Tobi Legend *Time Will Pass You By*. Some people will disagree with me on my choices but I do not have a favourite record if it makes the hairs on the back of my neck stand up it's a great song and plus I'm still newish to the scene so still have a lot of records and artist to discover.

Some of the soul dos I have been to!!

I have been to quite a few different venues such as the 6ts all-nighters at the 100 club and Crossfire. Shooting Star - this is only a small venue but all you hear is great records all night I have been to a couple of do's at the Kursaul in Southend-On-Sea one of these nights had Russ Winstanly and Ian Dewhurst as the DJ's for the night I attend a little Soul club in my home town which I attended quite a lot and have played a few sets at called the KTF soul club Saks in Southend and Capons which has now shut down the best nights I have been to is probably is the nights that Elaine Constantine has organised for the film. The whole atmosphere for the night is just unreal everybody having a laugh with each other all the dancers helping each other perfect moves and the dance floor with mostly young Soul dancers on it which is a rare sight and the DJ's so if you see a night for Elaine Constantine that she is putting on make sure you are there I would also like to get up north to Kings Hall and some of the midlands events because as most people know it's a different sound all over the country.

Jay Hall

40. Another interview with original soul boy **Pete McKenna**

Pete first went to an all-nighter at The Wigan Casino when it had only been open a few months but news of the club had reached them back in their own town of Blackpool. The coach parked up outside The Casino. Pete and his three mates were full of anticipation and excitement. Pete recalls looking out of the coach window where he caught the eye of two Skinheads who gave

Pete 'the look'. This was not a look aggression or anger but more of *'who are you'? Are you here to fuck up our club*?' Pete tells me that several years later when the 'vulture cultures' started arriving at the club around 1978 that he found himself giving them 'the look'.

The four lads were not new to the Soul scene, they had been attending the Northern Soul events at The Highland Rooms at the Mecca in Blackpool for the past two years. But the Casino was different. I spent a weekend with Pete where we attended one of the Kent soul club nights, had a few beers and over the weekend I conducted interviews with Pete in an attempt to find out more about his books 'Nightshift' and 'Who The Hells Frank Wilson' and learn something about one mans personal experiences of his time on the Northern Soul scene that begun in the early 1970's and took him to many clubs, introduced him to many people and many of thiose enduring 45rpm soul records that he has come to love.

So I kicked off the interview by asking Pete about some of the dress codes and fashions at the Casino over the years. He began by telling me about the Fiberg trousers, these were big waisted and varied in flared bottom, up to 24" sometimes. They would also have a 1" turn up, *"always a 1" turn up for some reason"* says Pete. Fred Perry was a main stay throughout the Casino years along with Slazenger jumpers. Pete recalls with fondness the faded wrangler denim shirts and bagatell shirts too. Sheep skin coats, great in the winter months and great for the scooter or 'chair' riders. And for the girl's long leather coats and floaty skirts that would flare up when they danced looking fantastic. There was also a time when berets (with patches sawn on to them) were worn by both genders (although Pete says he steered away from that look!).

The footwear was always Brogues. There was a period in the last years when bowling shoes were worn too. Pete was a regular wearer of the Timpson royals and Adidas Samba's. There was also a period when the Dunlop Green Flash was in vogue too. Pete also recalls the Como shoes from Italy being worn. Interestingly Pete told me that he never saw talcum powder be sprayed on the floor to help them dance. Brutus and Ben Sherman shirts were there for the duration of the club too. The stereo typical look that the world media portrayed around the 1978/79 period of vests, patches, Spencer bags and Brogues was also there, but was by no means the typical look of the average soulie at the casino.

I asked Pete if the '79 Mod look had any influence on the club. He said no.

The club was not invaded by the smart set, suit wearing Mods. That Mod look was separate. I've always been curious over the fashion questions. I then asked if the '76 punk explosion had any impact on the soul scene. Pete's response was yes, but only because the casino held punk nights. And often the soul boys would have to armour themselves with big brooms and sweep and tidy up after the punks had gone.

I ask Pete about the atmosphere inside the Casino. Again much has been written about this and it helps those of us that did not attend the club to catch a glimpse and get a sense of the club and that era of Northern Soul. But Pete does confirm the chaos getting into the club, the queues, the car park dealings, the toilets, the sweat dripping from the balcony onto the couple of thousand soulies dancing. He goes onto to tell me about the provinces. He means the Blackpool corner, the Burnley area and other groups (sometimes the Wheel Heads, these were from the old Twisted Wheel club, shut down many years before the Casino opened its doors) that would travel from around the country. Pete says he made good friends from all over because of the Saturday nights at Wigan.

Pete tells me of the drug culture in the club, the use of speed (black bombers, dexy's etc). An area of contention it seems that has been denied by some involved in the club and openly admitted by others. Again, Pete just tells me of his experience of the Casino. Pete goes on to tell me that people would sneak in cider. Not massive amounts, just enough to takes swigs of to help the pills go down. He does acknowledge that due to the no alcohol being sold on the premises this contributed to the fact that the club never seemed to have any violence. In Pete's opinion 80% of the males at the club were footy goers, hooligans of the 70's even and Pete says *"but at one minute past midnight soul became the family"*.

Pete told me of a friend who has several tape cassette recordings from the Casino. There's loads of general chatter and in the background the songs being played can be heard. I ask Pete about the reason for the tape recorder. He told me they would record bits of songs they liked that were being played then take the tapes to record shops and record dealers, play them the tape and ask the if they knew or had the song. Pete says *"there were so many songs coming through"*. He also mentions Mr M's at this point saying that *"many tunes were broke in that room"*. Pete also describes Mr M's a little saying it was like a mini version of the main room. I've only seen one photograph of Mr M's and I've not seen a great deal written about it but Pete states it was the room

for the Northern Soul purist really "*100 mile fast stompers*" he informs. Pete also talks endearingly about all the casino DJ's Searling, Ellis and Russ Winstanleys contribution to the Wigan Casino Soul scene.
Soul boy interview

41. Influential Mod DJ **Paul Hallam**, who started one of the biggest Mod clubs of the '80s; Sneakers early mod days

I had been a mod for over 8 months and was coming along quite nicely. Obviously I hadn't been to many clubs or gigs (my mother wouldn't let me) but, I had a collection of Kinks, Who and Small Faces albums to add to my older collection of Beatles and Stones and somebody had taped me Motown's 20 Mod Classics so I was practically a face.
My 16th birthday was looming and along with all the usual perks, sex without consent and being able to buy cigarettes (even though I didn't smoke, come to think of it I didn't have a girlfriend either) I was eligible to drive a 50cc vehicle of her majestys roads.
My father had long been a motorcycle obsessive. He had raced them in the fifties and worked and owned a shop selling the aforementioned two wheeled monsters long before I was born. My childhood holidays revolved around trips to Brands Hatch and then later the Isle of Man for the TT races. Although 8 months into my love affair with Modernism I believed that I knew everything there was to know on the subject, I still hadn't been won over the chosen form of transport for these clean living specimens.... The Scooter. All my friends at school told tales of how they would be getting a vespa 50 complete with leopard skin seat and mirrors for there birthdays later on in the year.
I would be the first to reach the magical age of consent and I knew that even if I had wanted a Vespa or Lambretta my father would laugh and me and direct me towards something Japanese.
He tolerated my Modness, ("*I'm sure he's gay*" he would explain to my mum "*but we'll soon knock all of this aftershave business out of him*"). I reached 15 years and 11 months and nothing had been said. Then one sunny afternoon during the school holidays I sat listening with intent in my front room to *My Generation* the album. Wow life didn't get any better and my mum had ordered me a black Fred Perry from her clubbook. Thoughts of smokey nightclubs playing 60s sounds filled my adolescent head. I would be a Face, I would have a tailor made suit, a pair of loafers not from freeman hardy and willis and my record collection would include ALL the Who albums (only up to

68 obviously). My thoughts were disturbed by a beige transit entering our drive.

It was driven by one of my fathers work force, Woody a jolly chap whose dad made films and as a result was able to never having to have a proper job in his first 23 years of life. I saw him out the window put on my hush puppies and went to see why he was visiting us when it was obvious dad was at work.

On the back of the pickup sat a gleaming white Yahama DT 50. "*Gis a hand getting this down mate*" he requested and I opened the garage door as he wheeled it in. Hmmm whats all that about? Still with thoughts of Townshends windmill guitaring in my head I thought no more of it and offered him a cup of tea.

"*So this is your birthday present from your dad then*"????

A confused horror overtook me. It was OK not to have a scooter at 16, I could always pretend I preferred to ride my push bike complete with audio tape player on the back rack blaring out badly taped classics but.... a trials motorbike.

How was I ever going to explain that?

I made the tea for the deliverer of the said motorbike and went back to the front room to contemplate the injustices of teenage years.

Its not that I didn't want a motorbike, I'd be able to ride it to school before anybody else had a licence, I could go places that my 5 geared bicycle would never take me but.... I couldn't let any of the Mods ever know about this.

6.30 came and my father returned home from work. He mentioned nothing about the Yamaha had his tea (Bacon and chips I believe) and went off into the garage. I returned to the front room and put on some headphones. Within minutes my mum entered the room and informed me that I was needed in the garage.

Ooooh I know whats coming next. I couldn't be seen to be ungrateful so I combed my hair, applied some lacquer just in case anybody was to see me on my walk through the garden and went off to receive the 'jubilant news of my present'.

"*Well son, what do you think of this?*" asked Dad sitting on my new mode of transport.

"*It's great dad, really, really great*".

"*Obviously you can't ride it 'til your birthday but me and some of the lads are going out over the army range for a riding session next week. It's off road so you'll be able to come along and get used to riding it*".

Oh joy.

"*Obviously first you'll need some proper gear*". What did he mean proper gear? I had hush puppies and a 3 button suit jacket bought from the Cancer Research shop at the local shops.

"*It's the motorcycle show next week son so as part of your present we can both go along and get you some boots waterproofs and a decent leather jacket*".

My ears were ringing. It was bad enough riding a Japanese modern trials bike b.b.b..ut boots and a leather jacket. This was going too far.

The following week came along oh too soon and off we went on our annual father and son day out together. The Earls Court motorcyle show. It followed the same pattern as every other year. We'd drive up early in the morning to avoid rush hour, get into the show early and then I'd hang around for hours while dad spoke to approximately 54 different people about subjects ranging from weren't Aerials the best bike ever made in 50s Britain to how the recession was affecting sales of bikes this year (even though its not maggies fault its the bloody labour government before hand who are responsible for this..)

A pair of boots were purchased. Luckily dad didn't think it was worth spending too much on these as Id probably grow a bit more in the next year and for my 17th birthday I could get a really good pair of bikers boots. Groan.

The waterproofs were next. Belstaff with the complimentary tin of wax. "Dont forget boy you have to spread this on your trousers at least once a month".

The wax smelt and stuck to my hand like grease. This was all some kind of sick joke. Oh but hang on over there. Its a Vespa stand. Perhaps we can just go past it and.... not a chance, Mick from Suzuki in Croydon appeared and dad wanted to show off his only son and explain how Id be a biker within weeks. Fantastic.

I had one last hope, a local Mod lad had acquired from a charity shop a Moleskin coat, it was sort of like leather and was very very mod. Perhaps I could persuade my all knowing parent that this would be better than a padded safe leather jacket that would spare my limbs should I fall off. But no. "*That's a girls jacket son that wont do you any good if you come off doing a hundred miles an hour*".

"*Dad my bike goes 28 with the wind behind it*".

"*Aah but son next September you'll be 17 and then you can pass your test and get a bigger bike. Who knows within two years you'll be able to buy a 500cc beast or bigger. That's it I'm buying a car as soon as I can*".

I tried to invent a pathetic story about being allergic to leather and how I sweated whenever i went near the material. Dad looked at me concerned. Luckily before he could expand on his theory that I must definitely be gay Frank who ran the BSA owners club appeared and suggested they had a beer and talk about a whole box of original never before used 1950s small end bearings that somebody had found in a shed in Somerset.

I stood and listened. It was rivetting stuff. Time was running out. Dad would never stay passed 4.00 and sit in traffic. Perhaps I could go off to the toilet and take as long as possible thus ensuring there was no time to purchase the offending item of clothing. I make my escape. I could pretend i was lost, perhaps just walk passed the vespa stand and look at what was on offer?

It worked 15 minutes later I reappeared.

"*Where on earth have you been*"?

"*Sorry dad I got lost*".

"*Spose youve been eyeing up the naughty models on the Kawasaki stand*".

"*Er yes yes thats right I was looking at the nude models*".

Great he wont bully me about being gay anymore.

"*Well we've got no time to buy you a leather jacket now son. A bikers jackets not something you can just pick off a peg and walk away with. It's like a wife it's with you for life. In fact it's more durable, more comfortable and longer lasting than a wife*", he chuckled to himself.

"*Does that mean I dont get a leather jacket today then*", I asked hopefully.

"*No thats right son, instead ive bought you, and only cos its your 16th birthday and I dont want you to think im spoiling you........A............. Belstaff wax jacket to go with your trousers. Be sure to wax it every....*"

"*Yes I get the message dad*".

It wasn't good but it was an improvement. At least now if I was spotted out and about people would just think I was an apprentice traffic cop instead of a biker in mods clothing. Well not even that a biker in bikers clothing with a Fred Perry under my waxen clothes.

The future year turned out to be far less worse than expected. At first dad would check me every day to make sure I was wearing the appropriate clothing before letting me leave for school. I did get abused and teased for my choice of transport but everybody elses birthday came and went and none of them got scooters either.

There's no point they explained a Vespa 50s rubbish. "*I'm waiting 'til my next birthday then I can get a Lambretta TV 175 with lights mirrors and all things Mod that come with it*".

After a while my daily inspections relaxed and after a while I got used to leaving the house a safe motorcyclist only to change into my hush puppies and boating blazer 100 yards around the corner. I was a Mod on a motorbike but it didn't matter I was mobile.

As the next September approached a change appeared in my ever so straight laced ever so biker orientated dad. He watched me sitting with my headphones on (now listening to the exotic side of mod such as Stax and Northern Soul) staring longingly at the pictures of scooters that filled Richard Barne's 'Mods' book. He said nothing but observed.

Almost a year to the day that the DT50 had arrived in my house, my father came home with a different present. This time a red Vespa 100.

"Well son I guess you'll never be a biker. But you can still wear your Belstaff waxed clothes on this thing. If you come off doing a 100 miles an hour you'll......"
Paul Hallam

42. Young Skinhead **Tom Edwards**

Saturday, eyes open and I feel rough, me delhi going round like a washing machine, (should have remembered the ole rule, early start Saturday stay in Friday!)

Walking the long way to the paper shop trying to clear my head, back for a shower, next thing me blower is going and I realise I am meant to be in Barnhurst.

Bowling down the road knowing I look the business, proper sharp. Burgundy Bass Weejan Tasselled Loafers, red socks, a pair of 505 Levis quarter inch turn ups and a crease stitched in, white Farah Polo 5 buttons down the front with a buttoned down collar, a Latties woven Gabicci cardigan topped of with a dark blue Aquascutum Mac.

I got a cup of tea and a pasty, not sure whether to eat it or bin it. Found out the chaps have headed to a pub at the ground so I prepare meself, I know what's coming as I walk in 2 hours late *"here's the tart, alright darling you late coz you was getting ready, get the sweetheart a drink"*

Good turn out today, a lot of smart faces. Gucci Loafers, Armani Jeans, Burberry Macs, old Adidas, Barbour jackets noticing a bit of tweed creeping in. A couple of the old Skins, polished boots, pressed Jeans, shirts and MA Jackets. Then I twig one of the boys in a red Pringle polo and I'm glad as I almost wore the same top, I mean mines blue but there ain't nothing worse than standing there next to each other in the same top.

Pint down me, I start to feel alright so I head of to the ground and get a bite to eat. The game goes ok 1-1 draw with 5 minutes to go and the word goes round that they wanna pop so we start to mob up but as we get down the road the law are all over us and them, we get pushed in the pub and quite glad coz me clobber was way to smart for rucking. (what a tart)! After an hour or so and a few pints im heading to me drum aint staying out today, better things up West. Home to get a bit of kip, don't last long me blower aint stopping, food then getting ready. With a pair of light blue Burlington socks that match me shirt and handkerchief in my breast pocket.

The shirt is a 3 finger button down collar with full sewn in pleat in the back and double cuffed with mother of Pearl cufflinks with a matching pin holding the handkerchief in place, I've gone for the 3 points hanky today. Both bespoke by Garry McCarthy.

The whistle is dark blue made by George Threadneedleman off the Walworth Road. The strides have got a 3 quarter inch split up the outside of the leg with frog-mouth pockets and belt hoops holding the black leather belt by Crombie. Jacket has one ticket pocket with a single 10 inch vent up the back, three clothed buttons at the front and 5 matching on the sleeves. Inside lining is electric blue with two pockets and 2 razor pockets. Rhythms black and polished like mirrors and a khaki green Crombie overcoat with a dark green velvet collar bespoke. Paisley scarf courtesy of George.

On the train to Charing Cross and meeting up in The Bell and Compass. By the time I arrive a few chaps are already there half hour later there's around 15 of us. All smart, 12 suited up and the others wearing Loafers, Sta-Prest and a good bit of knit wear. Good mixture of Crombies, sheepskins and Macs. Were looking mustard and on the move, it's a great buzz being mobbed up, all smart and stomping through the West End. We head up through Leicester Square to the Imperial then onto O'Neils in Carnaby Street, over to Little Portland Street and in The Social. Set The Tone tonight and as I look about I know its gonna be a good night. Comfortably busy with Skins, Mods and a couple of Rude Boys for good measure. Just seems everyone is *really* smart tonight with no tourists this place normally has a habit of filling up with them. I'm looking around and everyone is dancing, bunnying on, drinking and having a good crack.

There's only 45 minutes till closing so I crack on to get some grub before heading back along Oxford Street. Bit of a touch no queue and I'm straight in to The 100 club. Result! Set the Tone and Northern Soul at The 100 club all in one night what a rare occurrence. As I walk in a few of the boys are at the bar getting served so no waiting around - another touch!

After a while of dancing I get a tap on the shoulder and a dicky bird in me ear, "*look lively son*". We start mobbing up and looking across the club at 3 smart looking fellas were looking about to see if there are more of them in the club (the funny thing is there are 9 of us with 6 different teams amongst us) but we don't know these blokes faces and word comes back they are Northern. Everyones racking their brain of who was playing in London today. As were doing this they start heading towards us, the geezer in the middle was in a pair of Gazelles and his Jeans were just like the pair I had on earlier in the day, nice turn ups and the crease stitched in but these were 511's Fred Perry and the reason I can remember what he wore was coz he had a beautiful Monkey Jacket on.

So he gets close and were thinking here we go and he just sticks his German out and says "*hello*". He came over to talk about the Whistles. Turned out he never did away games but did today as he wanted to go to The 100 Club. We ended up having a proper giraffe with them. They was into their clobber as much as a few of us are.

Next thing I know I've been booted in the leg, I jump up and realise I've proper mugged myself off I've sat down and dropped off in The 100 club! Mug! The two in front of me are wetting themselves laughing , one of them had a motor round the back doubles so we head up the stairs and the sun s just starting to come up. Oxford Street is funny at this time, not quiet but not busy. We jump in the motor southbound to Blackheath cuppa tea before I get home. 8 hours time I should be in me local for me Roast and a Sunday session. Back in the motor and all were banging on about is what were gonna wear later, luckily I got me two and throws ready. I'm gonna be in dark brown Suede Bass Loafers, beige Ralph Lauren socks, Light blue Farah slacks (think I was having a blue weekend) and a Reborto Carlo top Beige like the socks with dark brown suede around the collar and breast pockets. Sheepskin over the top. It then dawns on me I never did find out wear the Monkey Jacket come from? Fair play I like to keep some things close.

People seem to think I have a clothing addiction.................I can't see why?
Tom Edwards

43. **Mark Seargent** reminisces about a Saturday afternoon ritual

Territorial instincts are one of the many primal urges in most if not all Englishmen, no matter how much the PC and new male brigade claim otherwise these days. It's ingrained in our very being dating back to prehistoric times, law of the wild being survival of the fittest, which is how the human species evolved, by being fitter if not physically certainly mentally than other species, to become the dominant force on planet earth. Pseudo intellectualising apart, young males do enjoy a bit of a scrap in their early years, and some enjoy the adrenaline rush so much it stays with them for years. Don't ask me how or why football became renowned for confrontations between rival factions, during the latter 60's and 70's, with many of the Skinhead culture attending home and away games, some groups following opposing teams traded insults, threats and occasionally traded punches before, during and after football games across the length and breadth of the UK.

As Skinheads transmorphed into Suedeheads, which themselves evolved into Smoothies, incidents at football matches didn't necessarily increase, they did however get a lot of coverage from tabloids as well as television. Whoever decided it would 'shame' those involved into desisting made a really bad call, as it had an adverse effect as to what was desired. Instead, every terrace tearaway had an eye on his latest exploits topping what had been reported on previously. Added to which a series of fictional novels by Richard Allen, with titles such as Skinhead, Suedehead, Smoothies, Skinhead Girls, became low rent instructional manuals for wannabes who wanted to part of an underground movement.

Oxford United's Manor Ground in Headington had only been hosting league football since the early 60's, as Headington United the club had quite a reputation as non league FA Cup giant killers before replacing Accrington Stanley. Followers of visiting teams mistakenly assumed that as Oxford is Internationally renowned as seat of learning that it is all "OK Yah". Facts are a million miles from that, Cambridge would never have become a University City if it hadn't been for the town and gown riots, which started at the Swindlestock Tavern in the 11 hundreds. Some scholars couldn't face the constant and continual conflict between academics and the townspeople and headed off to found Cambridge University. During the 50's and 60's Oxford was a manufacturing centre, one of the motor cities of the UK, cars were made in Oxford, indeed they still are today. Needless to say with factories springing up to cope with the ever growing demand for motor cars, the residents of Oxford were in the main of working class stock.

In the early 70's the pre match ritual for some of the various crews from the many estates in and around Oxford, for home games, was to muster at The Black Boy in Old Headington for a couple of cold ones, then at staggered times each estate crew (on a truce for the afternoon at least), would head en masse to the ground, via a series of back allies which led to the Cuckoo Lane end of The Manor Ground. Of course in the early 70's there was no segregation between rival fans, the most vocal of each faction at Oxford were channelled into the London Road end. If there were large amounts of away supporters, at best there would be a line of police separating the rival fans in the London Road end.

1972-73 season was Oxford United's fourth season in League Division 2 (now the Championship), the Suedehead era was moving into the short lived Smoothie extension of the Skinhead sub culture. Late November '72 Oxford were playing Aston Villa for the first time in the League and for the first time at the Manor. Hooking up with my mates at The Black Boy around half past midday, as various crews arrived the word went round that 'Villa had arrived in numbers. Mind you speculative rumours were always part of the match-day experience back then. The beer went down well, Oxford footy songs were belted out, the crew I was with left the pub around 2.15pm, most of us paying junior entrance fees at the Cuckoo Lane turnstiles. We were greeted by a cacophony of noise and a sea of claret and blue in OUR end, there were a handful of Oxford youngsters squished into more or less a small portion of the London Road end. We made our way to OUR end, and joined the younger element, numbers of Oxford fans grew and grew in the London Road end as kick off time approached. By sheer weight of numbers, we had more or less regained half the London Road end with nothing more than insults and gestures being exchanged. By 5 minutes to 3 a double line of police separated the Oxford and Villa factions. A few minor scuffles, more or less 'handbags' went off behind the stand, during the first half and at half time, nothing serious though. Sporting a jumbo collar shirt, with a tank top plus a pair of leather soled boxtops (or Norwegians depended which part of the country you lived at the time), and a pair of Rupert check sta-prest, which was top clobber at the time, my mates any many other Oxford lads were similarly attired, seemed to be rather amusing to the 'Villa. Most of who were still decked out in tonics, crombies and other, then to us, outdated Suedehead gear, of course not so good natured pisstaking was exchanged over the heads of the coppers. 10 minutes before the final whistle the twin line of police exited the stand, presumably to be in position for post match crowd and traffic control. One particularly gobby 'Villa fan had got me a bit wound up, as Hughie Curran smashed in Oxford's second goal making the score 2-0, both sets of fans in the London road end surged towards each other, I was heading for the big mouthed suedehead, he beat me to it by stabbing me in my inner thigh with his brolly. I was knocked slightly off balance by the force of it then carried

forward and into the now retreating Villa hordes by thousands of Oxfords finest. Fists were flying, it was mayhem, the Villa mob although more or less even in numbers, didn't seem to fancy equal odds. Wave after wave of them flooded over the wall and exited up the side of the pitch to the relative safety of the Cuckoo Lane end. Unfortunately for me the Match Of The Day cameras were at the game, earning me a clip round the ear of the old man, and the silent treatment from me mum after they'd seen it on TV. The brolly stab wound wasn't deep or that serious, requiring a clean and one stitch, as for my Rupert's they never recovered. In retrospect maybe it wasn't big or clever, but the rush of defending our end and ousting the invaders is something I've never forgotten. Following that incident at the Manor ground, for many seasons to follow the chant *'You're gonna get what Aston Villa got'* was an often used veiled threat by the Oxford lads. Granted there have been other incidents both prior to that and countless others since, its the satisfaction of standing our ground and defending our end makes that first match against Villa stand out above them.
Sarge

44. Another from **Sarge**

By the summer of 1970, like pretty much every town and city across the UK, Oxford was a hotbed for the relatively new Skinhead subculture. After Mod had ran its course, especially in the South, the more flamboyant clothes obsessed, self styled fashionista transferred allegiances, via Psychedelia, to the American led flower power and hippy uprisings. Other deserters crossing invisible style lines were followers of bands such as The Who, err, who, along with certain bands, had deserted their Mod origins to follow a heavy rock direction more beloved of greasy Bikers. Those with a need and desire to remain looking sharp, sussed and smart with an ear for US Soul sounds and Reggae emanating from Jamaica refined the clean cut look of their older brothers, mixed in a degree of the American Ivy league college boy neatness as well as borrowed from the imported West Indian Rude Boy appearance to evolve into Skinheads. More uniform than their mod predecessors, nonetheless slim fit Ben Sherman, Brutus and Jaytex shirts, Levi sta-prest, highly polished 8 hole cherry red Air wear Dr. Marten boots or clumpy leather soled brogues or loafers, mohair suits and the like, topped off with short cropped hair and clip on braces was an image that was both well presented yet came with an underlying implication of menace. A popular school kids taunt of the time *"Skinhead, skinhead over there, what's it like to have no hair, with bovver boots and braces too, what's it like to be like you?"* was often chanted, from a safe distance, in the direction of anyone with short hair sporting button down collar shirt. If challenged, the mouthy youngsters were already away on their toes. Occasionally you'd make a bit of a show of meting out retribution, though I never tried to hard to catch 'em, rhymes such as the aforemention actually made me smile, as a young teenager it felt like I'd been noticed.

In all honesty I was too young to count as a fully fledged Skinhead in 1970, I lived on an estate where there were at the time few teenagers residing. Unlike across the A40, where there was a huge council estate and an abundance of Skinheads. Aged 13, via a paper round and bunking off school to work at the Wednesday market, (on a stall selling all the right clobber), plus badgering my mum, I'd latched onto the Skinhead look. Through a school pal we started hanging out with the older Skinheads across the A40, tagging along to football, disco's even pubs after being adopted as their mascots. Unlike today, it was so much easier to get served when underage back then, a large helping of self belief and a confident order of what you wanted at the bar usually did the trick. Through hanging out with the older Skin's I learnt how to ride Lammy's and still carry a few scars to prove it too. Oxford until the Mod revival was always a Lambretta City, with not only a branch of Kings in the City, but also a little way down Botley Road, until the mid 70's was Scootique, a shop specialising in Lambretta's. Outside of the football season a summer Saturday usually consisted of sleeping off the nights previous excess', arising mid morning and heading into the city centre, by bus, to meet up with mates and acquaintances outside of the Woolworth store on Cornmarket street. Maybe go round the record shops, clothes shops and the like, buying if you had cash, lifting if you didn't, and of course making arrangements for the all-important Saturday night out.

Following a rather 'productive' Friday night of, along with a few mates, inviting ourselves to a house party, slapping a couple of spotty student types who were supposed to be keeping undesirables out, consuming a sizeable amount of free drink on offer and copping off too I was feeling particularly good. Catching my reflection in shop window as I went in to buy 10 number six tipped en route to the bus-stop, even though I say so myself, I was looking good. Number 4 crop with a razor parting, an Oxford cotton white Ben Sherman with the sleeves folded (not rolled), halfway up my forearms, Ice white Levi Sta -prest with half inch turnups sitting just above my ankles. Which revealed a pair of red socks which perfectly matched the red half inch

wide clip on braces I was sporting. Completing my crisp appearance were a brand new pair of gleaming black Royals (brogues), complete with metal 1/4 heels and wing tips at the front which gave a satisfying click as the wearer swaggered along, plus being a hot sunny day, a pair of Polaroid shades topping of the picture. After getting away with a half fare, I went upstairs and to the back of the bus, passing several females of the species, who giggled and whispered to each other as I sauntered past. Unwrapping a stick of Juicy Fruit gum and slowly and deliberately chewing, then sparking up a Number 6, I felt I was the absolute epitome of cool. Part of the Saturday morning ritual was as the bus heading into the heart of Oxford city centre was to get up and walk down the aisle, without being thrown off balance, as the bus turned right from High Street into Cornmarket, timing it just right that as the last step from the upper deck was descended it coincided with the bus doors opening outside Woolies. On this particular Saturday, there I was, 100% proof, 24 carat Jack the Lad, half swaggering, half slow strutting from the back seat to the stairwell, the hint of a self satisfied smirk ghosting across my face as I passed the girls, then, disaster! With an almighty metallic ping, the right hand side of my clip on braces decided to stop gripping the waistband of my sta-prest, instead rocketing upwards and colliding with the bus roof. Reckon my face matched my socks and braces for quite a while after, an experience best described as the ego deflated. Still the best thing about being a young teenager is mishaps often happen, if they're not noticed by anyone who matters they're just as quickly forgotten. Probably just as well too.
Sarge

45. It was in the mod family. **Michelle Collins**

It was going to be inevitable that I would become a Mod. My parents were original Mods in the early '60s and all I can remember whilst growing up into my teens was listening to the likes of Motown, Stax and 60s R&B bands like The Yardbirds and The Small Faces and of course Ska.

My father was a Ska DJ for a short while in the late '60s and when I was a toddler he used to take me to Lewisham and Deptford on the number 61 bus most weekends to buy all the latest imports from Jamaica and America for his next gig. I remember the black men hanging around the record shops with their amazing afros with giant spliffs dangling on their lips. They always greeted me calling me "their lady" and they would watch me dance inside and outside the record shop. I always left in tears because I never wanted to go home.

In 1973 aged 7 my mother found a Motown label album in a local shop and I pleaded with her to give it to me. That album was the best. I played and played this album until it worn out. Whilst my friends were into Donny Osmond, David Cassidy etc I was into Marvin Gaye and anything Motown. I will always remember my favourite track on that album *I'm Ready For Love* by Martha Reeves WOW that record blew my mind and still does to this very day.

Years went by and during the terrible strikes of the mid-70s with Mr Callaghan being our Prime Minister the general public had had enough and rebelled by making political music called Punk. Not for me though, during this time I was still listening to 60/70s soul, Motown and 60s R&B bands and my friends thought I was weird liking this music and couldn't understand why I would rather go to record fairs to buy classic EP vinyl instead of buying Top Of The Pops chart crap.

In 1977 the world woke up to a group called The Jam. I bought their first album *In the City*. With their mainstream 1960s rock influences I was convinced this band will be huge in the Modworld, the rest is history.

After school we used to go to the local Wimpy bar in Orpington High Street to catch a glimpse of the Mods with their scooters. We scraped together small change in our pockets to buy a lime milkshake each and sit in the Wimpy bar staring in awe at the scooters and being mesmerised by the atmosphere, I was like a little girl watching their favourite pop star on the TV and drooling over the scooters and thinking how smart the boys looked with their blazers, hush puppies and cravats.

A scooter turned up outside the Wimpy bar that belonged to a guy called Jez I hadn't seen before. It was silver Vespa 125 with many mirrors and headlights on the front and I WAS IN LOVE but not with the guy only his scooter. I ascertained Jez came from Orpington who joined the Orpington Panthers Scooter Club. I have to say before I go any further this troubled me at the time as in my opinion the Orpington Panthers were NOT a nice bunch of people, I found them to be extremely menacing who always went around bullying people and being very competitive with other scooter clubs which I thought was pathetic and for this reason I chose not to hang around with the Panthers I didn't want to be seen to be like them and they gave Mods a bad name but nonetheless I had to get to know this guy so I can be seen riding on his scooter.

I racked my brains on how I could get to know this guy and in the end I thought the best way is to just go up to this guy and say hi and see what happens from there. I found out Jez was going to the Civic in Orpington the following Thursday which was the local youth place us Mods used to hang out. Thursday arrived and I put on my best Mod outfit, a crew neck pinafore dress in bright pink and green paisley (thanks to OXFAM) and made sure the night before I stuck sellotape to each curve on my bob haircut so that the curve kept straight all day we called it the Mary Quant look.

When we arrived at the Civic, I started chatting to a few Panthers when all of a sudden Jez arrived wearing a burgundy tonic suit, I was captured by his coolness and I couldn't keep my eyes off him all evening. The evening went really well with lots of dancing and the DJ Andy Ruw kept playing the best of the best and when it was time to go home I knew I couldn't let Jez go without me speaking to him so I managed to find the courage to say *"Alright Jez, may I have a ride with you?"* His mates just burst out laughing and before I knew it the whole of the Civic were laughing at me and taking the piss. Jez's reply was *"fuck off"* and the look on my face said it all, I have never felt so humiliated in my life. I ran out of the Civic and ran all the way home in the rain in tears. A hard lesson was learnt that evening and I didn't go to the Civic for weeks.

Eventually I plucked up the courage to go to the Civic one Thursday with a girl called Sarah Evans who was a regular at the Civic and I became very good friends with her and today we are still in touch. Sarah was very popular and a real cool Mod indeed, fantastic taste in music and dressed so classy. Sarah lived in New Eltham and she introduced me to the SE9 Mods, too many names to list but I was very fond of the SE9 Mods. Hanging about with them in Carnaby Street and catching a train to Brighton, Hastings and Margate on bank holidays was and will always be an enjoyable memory.

The Civic became extremely popular with Mods and the word got around that it was the place to be seen but believe me when I say the Civic was a shit hole but Mods from afar used to turn up every Thursday. The Mods from Eastbourne arrived one Thursday evening and my friend Kelly Shaw and I thought they were a good laugh so we started hanging out with them. They all had peculiar names like Jengus, Stavros and Boffin. One of the Eastbourne Mods called Clive I started dating with. He had a burgundy 50cc Vespa that had seen better days and I fancied him like mad and nobody forgets their first love so they say.

Every other weekend Kelly and I used to train it down to Eastbourne to meet Boffin and Clive or they would drive up to Orpington on their scooters to come and see us. Clive's scooter always broke down at the most inappropriate places. One weekend we broke down outside the Houses of Parliament and the old bill decided to come and have a chat with us. Clive hadn't passed his driving test so therefore we were driving illegally. We just didn't have a clue how we were going to get out of this one but when the copper came up to us and asked for documentation etc he let us off because he was a Mod himself and was on duty that day. We couldn't believe our luck. We managed to get the scooter going but by the time we got to Bromley we broke down again and this time we were rescued by 2 Rockers who saw us stranded and were kind enough to take us home so Clive had to sit on one motorbike and I was on another wearing our Mod gear so imagine the scene, a Mod and Rocker on both motorbikes how crazy is that and when they dropped us off at the end of my road (no way was I going to be seen getting off a motorbike outside my house) Clive and I made a pact that we wouldn't tell anybody what had just happened.

Kelly and I had many laughs down Eastbourne with the Mods. We used to stay in a very old caravan with Kelly's mum who had seen better days but we didn't care because we just wanted to be with the Mods in Eastbourne. It was raining one particular Sunday and we all charged into a local cafe to get out of the rain. After some mucking around and canoodling on the wooden benches, Kelly and I had to get back to the caravan so we ran to the bus stop and I remember waking up 2 days later in hospital. Apparently I had slipped over in my kitten heel shoes (bought in Kensington market) in the rain and knocked myself out. My eyes rolled and the ambulance man thought I was on drugs. I woke up with a bad headache and saw mum and dad sitting there looking extremely worried but relieved. I had to convince my parents that I wasn't on drugs and when the doctor confirmed that I had none in my blood my folks knew I was telling the truth. My holiday was obviously cut short and I tried to telephone Clive but to no avail, he pegged it that day for some known reason I will never know but the following Thursday he turned up at the Civic with another girl on his arm.

If we were not going to visit the Mods in Eastbourne we used to head up to Carnaby Street and Kensington Market to get the best vintage clothing. Sarah and I were the first Mods to buy white boots with flat heels and red velvet lining inside the boot. We wore the boots to the Civic on Thursday evening and the following week all the Modettes were wearing the same boots. That stall in Kensington Market done well out of Sarah and me.

Some Fridays we would catch a train to Charing Cross and head straight for the Le Beat Route Club in Soho. In 1981 the Mod club scene in London was growing and Le Beat Route was definitely the Mod hangout with many bands playing like The Chords and The Purple Hearts.

Then the ILFORD ALLDAYER arrived in 1981. This event was huge with live bands and great DJs playing the best music ever. We all packed on a coach from the Civic to Ilford and I remember the queue being longer than a mile with Mods and scooters everywhere. When the doors opened I will always remember the first record being played *Indeed I Do* and the Northern Soul boys just flew themselves on the dance floor with their high kicks, back flips, scissor jumps it was absolutely amazing.

Being a Mod was all about the music and taking pride in the way you looked. Mods always looked smart and scooters were beautifully painted with a theme close to their owner's hearts. Mod is part of our British culture which we are losing each day but this culture isn't going to go away and will continue for decades.

Thank you for giving me the opportunity to write some of my memories as a Mod and I would like to dedicate this memoire to those who have kept the dream alive all these years and also to my parents who are still Mods today aged 70 and 65 and who have brought me up listening to the best music ever made.

Michelle Collins

46. Rude Boy **Richard Lambert**

I was a Rude Boy between 1981 and 1982, I was 11 years old. I loved Madness and The Beat (as well as Dexy's Midnight Runners and The Jam). I had a pair of Frank Wright loafer's, which I wore with white towelling socks. I was also a member of the Madness 'nutty boys' fan club.

Being a Rude Boy at 11 years of age meant there was a uniform and a look that could be easily copied. I wanted to copy the older boys at School. The 'cool' older kids were all Rude Boy or Mods, the ones that I used to look up to. There wasn't any Rude Boy in the small Kentish village where I grew up and I think this was part of the appeal. My older sister used to take me to a local Church youth club, It was called the Monday Nighters and the 't' in the Nighters on the club sweatshirts was the symbol of the cross. Most of the young people who went to the club listened to Queen or Peter Gabriel. *Bohemian Rhapsody* would often be sung on the minibus to club outings or activities.

School was the place to be a Rude Boy. I had a friend in my class, Ian who was a Mod and we would constantly talk about the clothes and the music. He knew a lot of the older boys at School because he had an older sister. My friendship with Ian, meant that I was acknowledged or tolerated by the older mods and Rude Boys. I remember being tested by an older kid one lunchtime about my Rude Boy credentials, I was asked about my knowledge of the music, I was able to talk about Ska, Two Tone and Blue Beat. I seemed to pass the test and I didn't get the piss taken out of me.

I wore my Frank Wright loafers to school and had a metal quarter tip put into the heal and the thin part of the tie on show, the fat part tucked into my shirt. I didn't have my head shaved but had short hair and a centre parting. I don't think my parents would have allowed me to have a Skinhead or Suedehead. I remember my dad taking me to Huckel's Men's clothes shop in Maidstone to buy my school trousers. I wanted a pair of sta press but my dad bought me some grey woolen flairs. I was devastated, I knew I couldn't go to school wearing a pair of 'Lionels' and was so upset when I got home that my mum sent my dad back out to exchange them and get the ones I wanted. The sta-prest sold in Huckels were made by ziggy's and had an orange 'z' label above the front right trouser pocket.

Huckle's stocked all the gear, sta-press, Fred Perry's, tonic suits, button down shirts and shirts with holes for tie pins, waffle jumpers and cardigans. A trip into town on a Saturday involved going into Huckles to look at clothes, as well as into the record shops to buy cassettes and pin badges. When you bought clothes at Huckles, the plastic bag with the Huckles logo was then used as a School bag. Huckles was the place to buy your clothes, or rather for my parents to buy my clothes. The cheaper alternative was the weekly market, where I got my pair of maroon sta-prest and black waffled v neck. I also had an older cousin, who was a Mod and I used to get his hand me downs. Not bad considering I got a blue Fred Perry V neck jumper, a Tonic jacket and a pair of Dr Martin boots.

Along with wearing the clothes and having an identity at school, there was a genuine love of the music. Madness made being a Rude Boy accessible to younger children. *Baggy Trousers* was a song aimed at school kids. I had *One Step Beyond*, both Specials albums and *Dance Craze* on cassette. My favourite band was The Beat. I used to listen to The Beat's *'Wh'appen'* album and I still do today. The Beat were a political band who wrote songs about racism and growing up in Britain under Mrs Thatcher's Government. They played a sophisticated blend of Jamaican, African, Reggae, Punk and Ska music and sung about promoting unity among black and white young people. The band were from the Midlands, the home of the Specials and the Two Tone record label. The Specials wrote songs about inner city violence and looked like *Gangsters*. The Beat and The Specials made music to make people dance but with a social conscience and message. Whilst I got the music, most of the message went completely over my head. I was too young.

During 1981 and 1982, I went to Vinters Boys High School before taking my 13+ exams and moving onto a Grammar School. At Vinters I was in the same class as Ian. The decision to become a Rude Boy was probably a lot to do with Ian. Ian was a Mod and I didn't want to copy him, so my thinking was, *'well if he's a Mod, I'll be a Rude Boy then'*. Going into the second year at Vinters I no longer considered myself a Rude Boy. It was a short lived attraction. I remember going a School trip to a Museum in London and disappearing off with Ian to Carnaby Street. We both purchased and got on the coach home holding 7 inch copies of Benny Spellman's *Fortune Teller*. From that point on, my love of The Jam, listening to my parents Kinks records and new found interest in Northern Soul, meant a new look and new music to get into. However I didn't switch and become a Mod then and have never considered myself to be a Mod since.

At 41 years old, I am still interested in Mod clothes and Mod music. There is a dress code that I follow and haven't deviated from for the past 30 years. Fred Perry's, desert boots, Dr Martins, button down shirts, Levi's etc. I finally bought a M65 Parka last year when I turned 40. I am also blessed in being a Northern Soul fan, those classic sixties Northern Soul Stompers are surely the best music that's ever been made. Being a Rude Boy for that brief period set me up for a lifelong interest in all things Mod. I am still friends with Ian, who asked me to contribute to this book. When we meet up we still talk about the clothes and the music.

Richard Lambert

47. **Paul Hallam** on an early Mod encounter

Unlike probably every other person writing in this book/article my introduction to mod did not come through Secret Affair or The Jam or even Punk / Quadrophenia.

My world changed in the summer of 1977. I wasn't influenced by Punk, Generation X or The New Hearts or anything like that. The key that opened my door to all things '60s was an advert using clips from silent horror films.

1977 and I had three loves. The boys brigade, Millwall football club who I had recently converted to from the mighty Liverpool FC and old horror movies. BBC 2 must have been showing them late Saturday nights and I was allowed to stay up and watch. I had dabbled with music earlier in the 70s listening to

George Formby, Tommy Steele and film soundtracks rather than the hits of Slade and Bowie like my class mates.

Then one night I lay in bed in nylon pjamas and on TV came an advert for the new Beatles Album – *Live at the Hollywood Bowl*. Obviously there was no live footage of the band to be had so they used old horror clips from 20s and 30s.

From what I can remember it was a screaming girl in a Dracula carriage with *Ticket To Ride* played over the top. *Help* to some monster scene and so on.

I used to watch the TV (pre videos) more and more to watch the clips and found myself loving the music.

My sister was and I guess still is 12 years old than me and had been a Beatles fan from 1963. She was more than happy to lend me the relevant albums along with some early Cliff (her fave), Gerry And The Pacemakers, The Searchers and a Tremeloes single. I was hooked. I left the boys brigade and inherited a guitar that I failed to learn to play. For me it was Beatles all the way but I learned and listened and bought The Stones, The Hollies, Manfred Mann, The Kinks and then some Who.

It was still early 79 and I had yet to see Secret Affair on Top Of The Pops.

Then I did. I was on holiday with my mum and dad in Hayling Island and there they were on Top Of The Pops. I think I was watching to see Buggles who I really believed would be the new biggest band of all time. They sounded good. Almost like the heroes of my record collection. And when I got back home I asked for a copy for my birthday.

Trouble was so did everybody else at my school. And if there was one thing I couldn't agree to be part of it was a fashionable movement. Remember I was the one kid watching *Half A Sixpence* when it was cool to see Slade in *Flame*.

I went back to my Beatles coloured world and started buying up the solo catalogue. I even pretended to like Ringos 1978 disco album.

A year on a my cousin from Wales who was 5 years older with a fantastic record collection moved down to live with my parents for work. He brought with him a massive record collection and an even larger knowledge on all things music.

It was through him I heard my first real Motown – Cooley High soundtrack album, first Ronettes etc – Phil Spector greatest hits tape and so on.

Then in December 1980 disaster struck. Lennon was shot dead and my dream's of a Beatles re-union was shattered.The following week some of the school Mods were heading off to Feltham Football club for a club night. They had asked me previously to tape them Kinks, Beatles, Stones tracks and now they asked me to join them on our first ever trip out. My mum was horrified but I insisted I was going. I borrowed a Fred Perry from a Skinhead at school, worn with a pair of cheap Sta-press and some tassle loafers that bizzarely enough I owned despite having no fashion sense at that stage.

To get to Feltham football club I had to walk 2 miles to the next town Ashford and get a lift in a small lorry with about 20 of the local Mods.

I walked there fearing for my life – the Sunbury Skins were out in force that night. Eventually I made the meet and we waited for the transport. We waited. We waited and we waited.

I was about to go home (and if I had maybe I'd have had a different life with a different wife, different friends and shudders… who knows what I'd be doing now) when the van appeared. I piled in the back. 'Bout 15 of of us. I was probably the youngest and everybody was in parkas or green mac's and stank of cheap aftershave. Nobody spoke much least of all to me.

We got to Feltham football club and went straight in. I was just turned 15. No ID. No questions and I could even get to the bar and buy a drink. At this point I still hadn't read Richard Barnes 'Mods' book so didn't know it wasn't cool to drink John Courage pale ale. A pint of that and then into the dark room that housed the dj/band. I had never seen anybody on ampetamines before in my life so wondered why everybody was chewing like mad and talking to me of all people bout how "*fucking brilliant that fucking last fucking song was MATE*". I even knew of a few songs that were played. Mostly '60s pop and commercial soul but stuff that my cousin had bought down from Wales when I decided to dip one toe gently into the Mod waters a few months earlier. The on came the band. The Modes or was it the Mods? Rickenhbacker guitars, ampheatimine energy and not a single memorable song. But… I was hooked. I stood at the front loving every minute of it. An Asian kid in a boating blazer next to me was speeding of his head. He just kept shaking me and telling me how fucking great everything was. His knuckles were white from clenching them and I was terrified.

All over and back in the lorry. People were talking now. A few weeks earlier some Rockers had turned up at the club and some Mod from Hounslow had bought a gun down and shot them – funny it wasn't in the Middlesex Chronicle Paper? I was high on life and brut 45 aftershave. It had been brilliant.

The transport rattled along until all of a sudden it stopped. I heard talking outside and Robert who stood next to me said "*I think we have been ambushed by Skinheads. We are all gonna get such a kickin*".

The sliding door at the back of the lorry opened and outside was not 100 Skinheads but a couple of Police Officers. They shone a torch into the back shrugged their shoulders and got back in their car. Is that it?

We arrived back in Sunbury borders about 15 minutes later. I had promised my mum I wouldn't be late and it was a Thursday. I was dropped off bout a mile from my house and the driver refused to take me any further.

One of the older chaps had been following the lorry in case anything happened happened to have a spare helmet. I climbed on the back of his Lambretta. I felt like a God. I got home ran inside and went straight to bed. If I was to re-write history Id tell that I got into my room. Took down the Beatles Posters, took out and compass and some ink and tattooed "MODS" onto my forearm. I didn't. But I did persuade my parents to take me to Kingston the following week and for Christmas bought some hush puppies, a selection of Brutus trim fit button downs and a very bad 2 button velvet suit jacket from the old mans shop there (I thought it looked like the ones the Kinks wore). My mum kindly adjusted it and made it a three button suit with a pair of scissors and some cotton.

I was 15 years old. I looked in the mirror in my parent's bathroom. Hello I'm Paul Hallam and I'm a Mod...
Paul Hallam

48. Finally, legendary inspiration for the character of Quadrophenia's Jimmy character **"Irish Jack" Lyons** recalls his thoughts on Paul Weller, The Jam, The Style Council and after...

I think I first became aware of The Jam when I heard *David Watts* on the radio. It was the line,"*Wish I could be like David Watts, take my exams and pass the lot*" that reminded me of The Who's *Substitute*. A song where the troubled underdog communicates a desire to swap identities with their hero as in "*But I'm a substitute for another guy, I look pretty tall but my heels are high*".

David Watts was a completely different song structure to *Substitute*, but listening to it I remember thinking, Pete Townshend could have written this. Not long after, I discovered that *David Watts* wasn't written by Paul Weller – I'd forgotten that it was actually written by Ray Davies. Yet no other band could have given it the same credence as The Jam, the way they pumped it up with adrenalin and drynamil. It was like a tailor-made suit.

I remember seeing a picture of The Jam in *Melody Maker* and being very wary of their credentials, because to all intents and purposes they looked like a Who tribute band – though the term 'tribute band' was completely unknown at the time. I like to approach my subject matter a bit left of centre, a bit esoteric, where there's only a slightly subtle hint of what the point is all about. But for me, The Jam in their Union Jack jackets and the Who-like design of their name was shooting straight to bull's-eye, like a straight arrow from Sherwood. I remember back in the '60s absolutely cringing at Donovan's stolen 'This machine kills fascists' motif on his guitar from Woody Guthrie. But I forgave him later when I discovered how good a song writer he was. With Weller it was different.

The more I read about him and his interviews the more I discovered that he was genuine. I could see where he was coming from. There was an almost school-boy innocence about him. He was awkward in his interviews and he repeated himself a lot. But I had this feeling that if I had been living in Woking, he was someone I would have made it my business to get to know, because I know that we would have been speaking the same language. I'm quite capable of being narrow-minded to the point that if I like the name of a band then there's a good chance I'll give them a listen. I liked the name The Jam. Like The Who, one syllable. I remember thinking that for any band to blatantly copy Who stage accessories, then they would have to be bloody good to get away with this fucking mullarkey. I found myself smiling at the Marshall cabinets and Weller's Rickenbacker... and I bit on my lip.

I know that a lot of my friends who were Who fans back then were very unsettled about the image of The Jam. Normally I would be the first to shout "copyists" but the more I heard their songs, the more I believed that there was more to be discovered about The Jam, and particularly Paul Weller. Sometime in October 1980 I bought my usual copy of *Melody Maker* and there on the front page were the two snotty-nosed urchins, Townshend and Weller, out-Modding each other outside the revered entrance to the Marquee in Wardour Street —a venue I'd known the insides of very well since 1964. The inside story on the pair was that it had taken the best part of six months to bring them face-to-face. I remember thinking before I opened the pages that this could be Bobby Fischer versus Boris Spassky, or whoever. Despite the massive build-up to the 'interview of the year', it all soon fizzled out when they both discovered that beyond the subject of three-minute pop classics and the fact Townshend had never seen The Jam perform... they tended to disagree on everything after that, especially Townshend's views about the importance of touring America.

I still didn't give up on Weller. In retrospect the idea to get the two of them together for such a well-spun meeting of the minds had been a recipe for disaster. They were both individual composers and fusion-by-interview didn't work. But what did work for me was Paul Weller's revelation that the news of his band being signed to Polydor had been overshadowed by his discovery of a mislaid Who badge at home in the back of a drawer. I loved that. He was a man of the people alright. I liked the fact he owned a Lambretta GP 150. Townshend had never owned a scooter. I stand corrected, but the only serious musicians I remember owning scooters was Peter Quaife of the Kinks and my old mate Ronnie Lane of the Small Faces, who had taken a job of delivering false teeth just to buy the scooter.

I remembered reading in an interview where band associate Steve Carver said that Paul was obsessed with London. According to Carver, it was not unusual for the young Woking Mod to travel up to London with a tape recorder just to record *London*. Something I would have done had I not grown up there because Soho absolutely fascinated me. I spent a lot of my youth fiddling around with an old wide-spool Bush tape recorder, imitating accents and commentating on fictional Oxford-Cambridge boat races.

How ironic then that Paul Weller, who couldn't wait to tell people that he was at long last moving out of sleepy Woking for the bright spots of London, should move to Baker Street. You would have thought that Paul would've been, if anything, really inspired by his historical and cosmopolitan surroundings and influenced by local artisans. But apparently this didn't happen and somehow his isolation in London was reflected in the disappointment of the much-anticipated album *This is The Modern World*. Once Paul moved back to the bosom of his family and friends in Woking, he regained his indigenous confidence and this new breath of life was the making of the outstanding success of *All Mod Cons*. The single, *Down In The Tube Station At Midnight*, held a particular resonance for me. Even it's very title brought me back to myself in 1964, standing every Tuesday night on the platform at Piccadilly, my clothes drenched in sweat after seeing The Who play their Tuesday residency at the Marquee. I'd be dressed like a well-plumed peacock, Mod head-to-toe, and very wary and nervous of half-pissed yobs eyeing me up and down hissing, "*Hello, darling*", as I walked by.

I remember being surprised and disappointed when I read that The Jam had called it a day. Sometimes, a move like that can be the end of an artist. I wondered, what's Weller going to do now? For me, the formation of The Style Council seemed a natural progression for him. Usually, fans and audiences don't have a clue what's going on in an artist's head. And after a while Weller must have truly felt suffocated by The Jam. People forget that a 'band' or 'group' only represents the end result of an artist's song writing creativity. It's in the person inside where the engine room is, that drives that creativity. So for Paul Weller to disband The Jam and seek new horizons, more fresh air, wasn't such a surprise. Only a lot of people didn't see it coming. I liked his adopting French-Mod apparitions with Mick Talbot in *Cafe Bleu*. Weller seemed more at ease with himself with his writing once free of the shackles of The Jam. It was healthy as well to run The Style Council on a random roster of members, with Weller holding the basic trio of himself, Steve White and Talbot. In fact, some of the songs seemed to be more Mod than the hard-driven Punk sound of The Jam.

Another thing that in retrospect brought a smile to my face and satisfaction with the man Weller was remembering photographer Peter Anderson's fly poster image of Paul's shoe with the Eiffel Tower in the background. Years later I found myself in Paris with The Who on their *Quadrophenia* tour and eccentric that I am, armed with a cheap box camera which no self-respecting junk dealer would even accept, I did two things on the day we played the Zenith in Northern Paris. I was desperate to re-live The Who's first photo session in a Parisian sidestreet from 1965. The cobbled stones were still there on Rue Tholozé as I posed in my Henley boating jacket and desert boots on the exact same spot Pete Townshend had stood with the other three outside Le Nazir Cafe in 1965. Then I went to the exact same spot where Weller and Mick Talbot posed for Peter Anderson with the Eiffel Tower in the background. I know no French, so in broken English coming from the mouth of an Irishman (though it wouldn't surprise me if adrenalin driven I was using my cockney accent that day!), I asked a confused French couple if they would take a shot of me with the Eiffel Tower in the background, a la Weller and Talbot. The Eiffel Tower's electric clock said in bright neon: 'Je 963 Avant L'an 2000'. It was May 1997 and we were that many days away from the millennium... and 14 years after Paul and Mick.

Another little coincidence with France and Weller's adopting Franch-Mod lifestyle is that he told an interviewer that on his 18th birthday he took the train to London and travelled out to Pete Townshend's house on the Embankment in Twickenham. Unfortunately his hero was not at home. No, he wasn't. Because on that very day May 25th 1976 Pete was in Lyons with the Who performing *'The Punk And The Godfather'*

When Red Wedge formed I wasn't a bit surprised by Paul Weller's involvement as a leading spokesman. It figured that from his young days in Woking and his no-nonsense upbringing and direct influence of his parents that he would embrace working class and, indeed, left-wing attitudes. Perhaps the great divide itself in his home town of Woking, where council estates bordered the 'posh' houses, entrenched his resolve. Perhaps Paul Weller's love of his working class roots is a knee-jerk reaction to living in a place like Woking, where two distinct social classes live side-by-side. Little wonder that he would eventually write such a memorable album as *Stanley Road*. It seemed so fitting in a way that Billy Bragg would become the appointed spokesman for the Red Wedge collective and that Paul would provide the artistic overtures.

Yet sometimes, for me, there seemed an uncomfortable balance about The Style Council, as if it was some kind of on-going experiment only Paul Weller knew the secret to. Sometimes they seemed quite capable of producing great sounding second-generation soulful Mod songs while on the other hand they seemed content to front the Red Wedge cause, though admittedly doing admirable agitating work for causes like the miners' strike, fox hunting and CND. Weller scored a bulls-eye with *Walls Come Tumbling Down* and his unforgettable quote in a music paper,"*We can actually try changing things..."* must have surely galvanised a lot of people and woken them up to the fact that Margaret Thatcher as Prime Minister was an enemy of the working classes. If anyone ever had any doubts, for me *Walls Come Tumbling Down* proved that popular music was one of the most powerful weapons of enlightenment *and* protest.

After The Style Council had run its course and what must have been a nightmare finale for the many genuine fans of the band to see them arrive on stage in their bizarre Bermuda shorts at the sold-out Royal Albert Hall to perform a dismissive set of songs, some set in a house idiom – less than half of which the audience would have been familiar with. I remember reading somewhere that having taken The Style Council to unexpected heights it was sad to see that the end was sour. It was almost as if this was a way to definitively 'kill off' the band despite what had been achieved. I might be wrong, but it was almost as if Paul was saying, "*Two fingers to you mate. Thanks, but there won't ever be another Style Council!*" No wonder the band was booed. So many true believers must have taken the train home disillusioned and feeling betrayed. Many of them would have taken a fucking bullet for the genius from Woking.

After the demise of The Style Council there came the unavoidable hiatus where Weller sat back from the easel and re-evaluated what was in his head. I'd pick up a music magazine and there'd be a photo of Paul mixing socially at places like Dingwalls and other clubs that were hot spots for the emerging acid jazz scene. More and more people, by now turned off the tired warehouse party culture, were finding their way towards the more intimate and refined acid jazz community. Sounds that resounded of the early and mid '70s Funk, Soul and Jazz. It was hypnotic stuff and a million miles from The Jam, and yet the vibrancy and energy was still there. Weller had even DJ'd at Dingwalls the night before The Style Council's nightmare finale at the Royal Albert Hall. Surely a telling and poignant note of intent. An old Mod mate of mine, Eddie Piller, who ran the credible Mod fanzine *Extraordinary Sensations*, became one of the founding members, along with Gilles Peterson of the Acid Jazz label. And Eddie always had his finger on the right groove at the right time. It may matter not to some, but for me Eddie telling me first time we met that his mum, Fran Piller, had been The Small Faces fan club secretary was enough. This to an old Mod who had befriended and idolised Ronnie Lane. So, Piller was a cool geezer with a cool label.

As time went on I checked for Weller's progress full of admiration and hoping that one day, maybe one day, our paths would cross. Many of my Mod friends were surprised to learn we had never met. He spoke my Mod language. His hang-up with Townshend. He must've heard of me... surely? I befriended Steve Cradock when Ocean Colour Scene came to play in Cork. He and his band were such lovely welcoming people and his dad, Chris. We all had dinner on the day of the gig and I spun some Who stories, as is my wont. Cradock thought I was a fucking God, the way he kept shaking his head saying "*Fucking hell, the original Mod. Quadrophenia. And hand-written letters from Townshend. Jesus!*" I couldn't believe it when he told me that they had brought Mick Talbot along for the show on keyboards. I asked Talbot about Weller. "*Heard of you? What, Paul? 'Course he's heard of you?*"

Sometime later, Paul Weller appeared solo at a venue called Souths in Tramore in Waterford. I was desperate to meet him. I phoned Black Barn Studios and spoke to Kenny Wheeler explaining who I wasn't. He thanked me for the call as I stood in the street telephone box in my Post Office uniform with my mail sack around my neck and a bundle of letters in my left hand. He told me he would see on the night – no promises, though. I drove to Tramore from Cork with two Weller lunatics, Eamonn and P. Cassidy. When we got to the venue, which was absolutely jammed to the rafters, I was gob-smacked to discover that "Irish Jack" was on the guest list. At some stage of the show with Weller sitting on a stool with guitar I was just stunned listening to his playing. I remember thinking, he might as well just do *I'm One* from *Quadrophenia*.

As usual with me, I was nattering into some guy's ear with one eye on Weller. A young Mod who had recognised me earlier tapped me on the shoulder saying, "*He's talking about you.*" I said, "*What?*" I was just in time to hear, "*...So this is for Irish Jack...*" Bang! *That's Entertainment*. "*A police car and a screaming siren...*" I thought the roof was going to cave in. It was like being on drynamil. When the show was over I went in by the dressing room and saw Kenny Wheeler guarding it. Paul had left his apologies. He was out on his feet and wasn't seeing anyone. I was extremely disappointed but was still on a high over the dedication.

A few years went by and Weller was back in Cork playing the Marquee Festival. By now my old mate Steve Cradock was a permanent fixture in the band. I arrived at the hotel after the show with two friends, brothers John and Mick Cronin, who play with the band Aftermath. Weller was in the packed bar having a drink surrounded by a knot of people. Cradock dragged me through the crowd. "*Paul? Irish Jack!*" He nearly broke my hand with the handshake.

I had brought along some pieces from the old days. A handwritten letter from Townshend written to me in 1969; my old 1964 Marquee Club concession card with Townshend on the front in Maximum R&B pose, and my original Goldhawk Club membership card from 1966. I asked Paul if we could find a quiet corner. We moved to a private spot and I showed him the pieces. He was genuinely amazed. I noticed as we spoke he had a habit of saying "*man*". After 20 minutes I stood up and shook his hand. I said, "*You might as well know that I'm shaking hands with a hero of mine*". I was in no way ready for what was to follow. He gripped my hand and said, "*Jack, I've been reading about you since I was what, sixteen?*" I looked at him stunned. He said, "*Y'know, they call me the Modfather... well, you're the fucking Godfather. Yeh, man.*" I looked at my watch and it was five minutes to two. My curfew was two. When you get as old as I am your wife gives you a curfew. A quick photo with Paul and the Cronin brothers and I was heading home in a cab. I was 63, old enough to be his dad, but I was walking around in a dream for the next couple of days. Paul Weller. You can bury him a Mod. Surrey Council should've built an altar to him!

Interview with Jack Lyons - Friday, 24thFebruary 2012 (copyrighted only to Stu Deabill and Ian Snowball)

OUTRO
THE KIDS ARE UNITED

Fast forward now to 2011. I'm polishing my Black leather Brogues and playing a Ruby Andrews album (*Casanova*) in the back ground. In two days I will be heading down to the Pontins camp at Camber Sands for this year's scooter rally that is organised by the Chelmsford Scooter Club.

My intention will be to meet up with some old friends and hopefully make some new ones. There will be many familiar faces that I see at Northern Soul do's or Mod nights or scooter events or at gigs. There will be loads of nods and hand shakes. I will be sharing one of the tired old chalets with a few other mates and in between catching a few Zzzzz's I will be dancing in either the Soul room or the Reggae room. I will probably leave the dance floor around 3am with a very sweaty shirt, sticky pants, talcum powder all over my Brogues and heels of my trousers and my legs and feet will ache. But I will feel satisfied that I have had another top draw evening.

And I know I will not be alone. At least a couple of thousand attend the Camber Sands Scooter Rally year in and year out. And if it is not this rally it will be another rally, or a Soul do somewhere else or a gig some place. Most of the people at these events are in there late thirties, forties and many now in their fifties. They still ride scooters, wear Brogues, dance and make the effort to support events. Nowadays if you wake up on a Saturday morning and you feel like a night of Soul you can log onto the brilliant Soul Source site and access a long list of events happening that night. A few hours later you could find yourself shuffling from side to side on the dance floor at Stoke, Blackpool Tower, Bisley or at the wonderful venue that the kent Soul Club are fortunate to use. Or if you fancy a Mod night you could check the sites from the New Untouchables, Friday Street or if Reggae is your thing check the Set The Tone or Klub Skank web pages.

May be you may prefer the scooter scene and so check the sites from any clubs like the Bar Italia Scooter Club, the Medway Aces Scooter Club or the Sid James Scooter Club, the list for Scooter Clubs within the U.K is enormous. Perhaps there is a hunger to see a band and these days you can go and catch The Chords, Secret Affair or The Purple Hearts, brilliant if you missed the first time around. Or you may just fancy a bit of Aunt Nelly, Modus or The Higher State or The Bresslaws.

If you have time on your hands also check out some of the multitude of pages relating to the tribes on Face book. Examples are 8o's Casuals, Mods, Old Skool Ravers, Skinhead girls, Northern Soul matters, Brand Medway Garage Music to name just a few. Or dip into YouTube and discover an Aladdin's cave of musical treasures. YouTube offers an extensive source of education either through music or original footage of just about any of the tribes. With a click of a button you can watch clips of original Skinheads, Raves, Mods on Brighton beach or Casuals on their terraces. Hours will pass by as you get sucked deeper and deeper into it. But hey, it's better than watching the soaps.

There are also some fantastic 'Zines' and Magazines available these days like Double Breasted, Heavy Soul, Shindig and Soul Up North. They are all great reads and incredibly supportive of 'their' scenes. And even though a few pirate radio stations still exist these days there are hundreds of online radio stations delivering soul, house, ska and scooter sounds.

Return home from another Camber Sands weekender. Especially enjoyed the Northern Soul room where I pretty much camped out for the two days. This year's Northern Soul dance comp has a new judge. Will, who has won the comp before but this year cannot compete due an injury. Matty the Chimp is in and gets through to the last six dancers but bows out gracefully. There are three dancers left. Jay a young lad from Essex who has been honing his skills as one of the dancers in the new film being made on northern soul by Elaine. There is a young female called Sophie who looks the biz demonstrating some nice spins and splits and Aaron a twelve year old boy. All three perform well and the large crowd surrounding them are cheering and supporting their favourite. Young Aaron gets a tap on the shoulder. Never mind lad, come back next year. Keep on keeping on. Then it's head to head with Jay and Sophie. I'm watching on thinking this is like a scene from Pete Mckenna's northern soul novel 'Who the hells Frank Wilson'. The two young people kick, spin and enjoy themselves. This is the future for the soul room. Sophie just pips Jay to the post. He knows he will try again next year and fair play. Well done Sophie, she clearly loves the music and loves to dance.

So, these young examples and just hopefully the original subscribers of the tribes will continue to keep the faith and march on until their dying days. I suspect each one of us will and in the process attract a few young bucks too. After all it is in the blood isn't it?

THE END....OR NOT

Also Available on Heavy Soul Records;
Long Hot Summer
To Be Someone: Mods In Ireland
Every Bank Holiday Weekend (coming 2013)
Heavy Soul fanzine

Also Available from the authors;
Who the Hell's Frank Wilson
Nightshift
In The Blood

www.heavysoul45s.co.uk